Turkish

PHRASEBOOK & DICTIONARY

Acknowledgments

Publisher Mina Patria
Associate Product Director Angela Tinson
Product Editor Briohny Hooper
Series Designer James Hardy
Language Writer Arzu Kürklü
Cover Image Researcher Naomi Parker

Thanks

Elizabeth Jones, Chris Love, Kate Mathews, Wayne Murphy, Yuksel Siva, Samantha Tyson

Published by Lonely Planet Publications Pty Ltd

ABN 36 005 607 983

5th Edition – August 2014
ISBN 978 1 74321 195 3
Text © Lonely Planet 2014
Cover Image Grand Bazaar, İstanbul, Gavin Hellier/Corbis
Printed in China   10 9 8 7 6 5 4 3 2 1

Contact lonelyplanet.com/contact

MIX
Paper from
responsible sources
FSC™ C021741
www.fsc.org

social 103

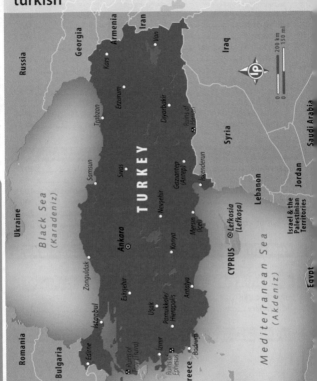

turkish

- official language
- widely understood

For more details, see the **introduction**.

ABOUT TURKISH
sunuş

For a language which traces its roots as far back as 3500BC, has travelled through Central Asia, Persia, North Africa and Europe and been written in both Arabic and Latin script, you'll be surprised that Turkish is a highly regular language with no genders, one irregular noun and only one irregular verb. So how did it transform itself from a nomad's tongue spoken in Mongolia into the language of modern Turkey, with a prestigious interlude as the diplomatic language of the Ottoman Empire?

The first evidence of the Turkish language was found on stone monuments, dating back to the 8th century BC, in what's now Outer Mongolia. When their Mongol neighbours took control of the Turks' pasturage in the 8th century AD, the tribe migrated to the south and west. By the 11th century, most Turks in the Middle East had become Muslims. Among them was the Seljuq clan, which invaded large tracts of Asia Minor (Anatolia) and imposed their language on the peoples they ruled. Over time, Arabic and Persian vocabulary was adopted to express artistic and philosophical concepts and Arabic script began to be used. By the 14th century, another clan – the Ottomans – was Turkey's dominant power, and was busy establishing the empire that was to control Eurasia for centuries. In their wake, they left the Turkish language. There were then two levels of

at a glance ...

language name: Turkish

name in language:
Türkçe, Osmanlı
tewrk·che, os·man·luh

language family: Ural-Altaic

approximate number of speakers: 70 million worldwide

close relatives: Azeri, Gagauz, Qashqay, Turkmen

donations to English:
baklava, bridge (the game), caviar, horde, kaftan, kismet, khan, sequin, shish kebab, yoghurt

introduction

9

Turkish – ornate Ottoman Turkish, with flowery Persian phrases and Arabic honorifics (words showing respect), used for diplomacy, business and art, and the language of the common Turks, which still used 'native' Turkish vocabulary and structures.

The Ottoman Empire fell in 1922; the military hero, amateur linguist and historian Kemal Atatürk came to power and led the new Republic of Turkey. With the backing of a strong language reform movement, he devised a phonetic Latin script that reflected Turkish sounds more accurately than Arabic script. On 1 November 1928, the new writing system was unveiled: within two months, it was illegal to write Turkish in the old script.

In 1932 Atatürk created the Türk Dil Kurumu (Turkish Language Society) and gave it the brief of simplifying the Turkish language to its 'pure' form of centuries before. The vocabulary and structure was completely overhauled. As a consequence, Turkish has changed so drastically that even Atatürk's own speeches (he died in 1938) are barely comprehensible to today's speakers of öztürkçe ('pure Turkish').

Turkish is now the official language of Turkey and the Turkish Republic of Northern Cyprus (an area recognised as a nation only by itself and the Turkish government). Elsewhere, the language is also called Osmanlı, and is spoken by large populations in Bulgaria, Macedonia, Greece, Germany and the '-stans' of Central Asia.

This book gives you the practical phrases you need to get by in Turkish, as well as all the fun, spontaneous phrases that can lead to a better understanding of Turkey and its people. Once you've got the hang of how to pronounce Turkish words, the rest is just a matter of confidence. Local knowledge, new relationships and a sense of satisfaction are on the tip of your tongue. So don't just stand there, say something!

abbreviations used in this book

a	adjective	gen	genitive	nom	nominative
abl	ablative	inf	informal	pl	plural
acc	accusative	lit	literal translation	pol	polite
adv	adverb	loc	locative	sg	singular
dat	dative	m	masculine	v	verb
f	feminine	n	noun		

Pronouncing Turkish is pretty simple for English speakers as it uses sounds which are similar to ones you already use. You'll hear some variation in pronunciation throughout Turkey, but this phrasebook is based on standard pronunciation so you'll be understood wherever you go.

vowel sounds

Most Turkish vowel sounds can be found in English, although in Turkish they're generally shorter and slightly harsher.

symbol	english equivalent	turkish example	transliteration
a	father	*abide*	a·bee·*de*
ai	aisle	*hayvan*	hai·*van*
ay	**say**	*ney*	nay
e	red	*ekmek*	ek·*mek*
ee	bee	*ile*	ee·le
er	her	*özel*	er·*zel*
ew	**ee** with rounded lips, like 'few' or the French *tu*	*üye*	ew·ye
o	go	*oda*	o·*da*
oo	moon	*uçak*	oo·chak
uh	habit	*ıslak*	uhs·*lak*

consonant sounds

Most Turkish consonants sound the same as in English, so they're straightforward to pronounce. The exception is the Turkish r, which is always rolled.

symbol	english equivalent	turkish example	transliteration
b	**big**	*bira*	*bee*·ra
ch	**church**	*çanta*	chan·*ta*
d	**day**	*deniz*	de·*neez*
f	**fun**	*fabrika*	fab·ree·*ka*
g	**g**o	*gar*	gar
h	**house**	*hala*	ha·*la*
j	**jam**	*cadde*	jad·*de*
k	**kilo**	*kadın*	ka·*duhn*
l	**loud**	*lider*	lee·*der*
m	**man**	*maç*	mach
n	**no**	*nefis*	ne·*fees*
p	**pig**	*paket*	pa·*ket*
r	**run** (but rolled)	*rehber*	reh·*ber*
s	**sea**	*saat*	sa·*at*
sh	**ship**	*şarkı*	shar·*kuh*
t	**tin**	*tas*	tas
v	**van** (but softer, between 'v' and 'w')	*vadi*	va·*dee*
y	**you**	*yarım*	ya·*ruhm*
z	**zoo**	*zarf*	zarf
zh	plea**s**ure	*jambon*	zham·*bon*

syllables & word stress

In the coloured pronunciation guides, words are divided into syllables separated by a dot (eg *giriş* gee·*reesh*) to help you pronounce them. Word stress is quite light in Turkish, and generally falls on the last syllable of the word. Most two-syllable placenames, however, are stressed on the first syllable (eg *Kıbrıs* *kuhb*·ruhs), and in three-syllable placenames the stress is usually on the second syllable (eg *İstanbul* ees·*tan*·bool). Another common exception occurs when a verb has a form of the negative marker *me* (*me* me, *ma* ma, *mı* muh, *mi* mee, *mu* moo, or *mü* mew) added to it. In those cases, the stress goes onto the syllable before the negative marker, for example *gelmiyorlar* gel·mee·yor·lar (they're not coming).

vowel harmony

Word endings in Turkish need to 'rhyme' with the final vowel in the word they're attached to. This is called vowel harmony. In the examples below, both the endings -*da* ·da and -*de* ·de mean 'at'. The reason they have different forms is because they need to harmonise with the vowel sounds in the root words (in this case, Ankara and Cevizli).

Does it stop at Ankara?
    Ankara'da durur mu?   an·ka·*ra*·da doo·*roor* moo
    (lit: Ankara-at stop *mu*)

Does it stop at Cevizli?
    Cevizli'de durur mu?   je·veez·*lee*·de doo·*roor* moo
    (lit: Cevizli-at stop *mu*)

The rules of vowel harmony are quite regular, and you'll soon get the hang of them as you practise speaking Turkish. We've put the patterns into the table below.

if the final vowel in the noun is …	*a* or *ı*	*o* or *u*	*e* or *i*	*ö* or *ü*
it can be followed by …	*a* or *ı*	*u* or *a*	*e* or *i*	*ü* or *e*

reading & writing

Turkish has a phonetic alphabet with 29 letters. It's the same as the Latin alphabet, except for 'q', 'w' and 'x', and has additional letters which were invented specially or borrowed from German. For spelling purposes (like when you spell your name to book into a hotel), the pronunciation of each letter is provided. The order shown below has been used in the **menu decoder** and **turkish–english dictionary**.

The letter *c* is pronounced like the English 'j'. The letter *h* is never silent, so always pronounce it as in 'house', eg *sabah* sa·*bah* (morning). The *ğ* is a silent letter which extends the vowel before it – it acts like the 'gh' combination in 'weigh', and is never pronounced. When you see a double vowel, such as *saat* sa·*at* (hour) you need to pronounce both vowels.

Be careful of the symbols *ı* and *i* – *ı* uh is undotted in both lower and upper case (like Isparta uhs·*par*·ta), while *i* ee has dots in both cases (like İzmir eez·meer). It's easy to read both of these as an English 'i', but you can be misunderstood if you don't pronounce the two sounds distinctly – *sık* suhk means 'dense', 'tight' or 'frequent' but *sik* seek means 'fuck'. Take the same care with *o/ö* o/er and *u/ü* oo/ew – *kızları oldu* kuhz·la·*ruh* ol·*doo* means 'they had a baby girl' but *kızları öldü* kuhz·la·*ruh* erl·*dew* means 'their daughter died'.

alphabet							
Aa a	*Bb* be	*Cc* je	*Çç* che	*Dd* de	*Ee* e	*Ff* fe	*Gg* ge
Ğğ yu·*moo*·shak ge		*Hh* he	*Iı* uh	*İi* ee	*Jj* zhe	*Kk* ke	
Ll le	*Mm* me	*Nn* ne	*Oo* o	*Öö* er	*Pp* pe	*Rr* re	*Ss* se
Şş she	*Tt* te	*Uu* oo	*Üü* ew	*Vv* ve	*Yy* ye	*Zz* ze	

contents

The index below grammatical structures you can use to say what you want. Look under each function – in alphabetical order – for information on how to build your own phrases. For example, to tell the taxi driver where your hotel is, look for **giving directions/orders** and you'll be directed to information on **case**, **demonstratives**, **verbs**, etc. A glossary of grammatical terms is included at the end of this chapter to help you. Abbreviations such as **nom** and **acc** in the literal translations for each example refer to the case of the nouns – this is explained in the glossary and in **case**.

adjectives & adverbs

describing things

Adjectives and adverbs only have one form for singular and plural, and come before nouns and verbs respectively. Most adjectives can also be used as adverbs. See also **articles**.

That was a good concert.
İyi bir konserdi.   ee·*yee* beer kon·*ser*·dee
(lit: good a concert-nom-was)

Did you sleep well?
İyi uyudun mu?   ee·*yee* oo·yoo·*doon* moo
(lit: well sleep-you *mu*)

articles

describing things • naming things/people

There is no word in Turkish for 'the', so the word *pazar* pa·*zar* means both 'bazaar' and 'the bazaar'.

Bir beer means both 'a/an' and 'one' and comes before the noun it modifies.

I'd like to hire a car.
Bir araba kiralamak   beer a·ra·*ba* kee·ra·la·*mak*
istiyorum.   ees·*tee*·yo·room
(lit: a car-nom to-hire would-like-I)

There was only one car in the car park.
Otoparkta yalnızca   o·to·park·*ta* yal·nuhz·*ja*
bir araba vardı.   beer a·ra·*ba* var·duh
(lit: car-park-loc-in only one car-nom there-was)

In phrases where the noun is described by an adjective, *bir* usually appears between the noun and the adjective.

I'd like a local speciality.
  Bu yöreye özgü bir   boo yer·re·ye erz·gew beer
  yemek istiyorum.   ye·mek ees·tee·yo·room
  (lit: this region-**dat**-to special a meal-**nom** want-I)

be

The Turkish equivalent of 'be' is a suffix (word ending) added to the noun or adjective. If the final letter in the noun or adjective is a vowel (as for *iyi* in the first example below), you'll need to add the letter *y*, pronounced like the 'y' in 'yes'. The next table gives the suffixes for the present tense.

We're well.
  İyiyiz.   ee·yee·yeez
  (lit: well-are-we)
I'm English.
  İngilizim.   een·gee·lee·zeem
  (lit: English-**nom**-am-I)

For the negative of 'be', the noun or adjective remains unchanged, and the same endings from the table on the next page are added to the separate form *değil* de·*eel*.

I'm not a student.
  Ben öğrenci değilim.   ben er·ren·jee de·ee·leem
  (lit: I student-**nom** am-I-not)

See also **adjectives**, **negatives**, **suffixes**, **verbs**, and the box on **vowel harmony** on page 13.

'be' – present tense

final vowel in noun/adjective	*a* or *ı* (eg *avukat* lawyer)	*e* or *i* (eg *öğrenci* student)
I	-(y)ım *avukatım* a·voo·*ka*·tuhm	-(y)im *öğrenciyim* er·ren·*jee*·yeem
you sg inf	-sın *avukatsın* a·voo·*kat*·suhn	-sin *öğrencisin* er·ren·*jee*·seen
he/she/it	no ending *avukat* a·voo·*kat*	no ending *öğrenci* er·ren·*jee*
we	-(y)ız *avukatız* a·voo·*ka*·tuhz	-(y)iz *öğrenciyiz* er·ren·*jee*·yeez
you sg pol & pl inf/pol	-sınız *avukatsınız* a·voo·*kat*·suh·nuhz	-siniz *öğrencisiniz* er·ren·*jee*·see·neez
they	-lar *avukatlar* a·voo·*kat*·lar	-ler *öğrenciler* er·ren·*jee*·ler
final vowel in noun/adjective	*o* or *u* (eg *doktor* doctor)	*ö* or *ü* (eg *gözlükçü* optometrist)
I	-(y)um *doktorum* dok·*to*·room	-(y)üm *gözlükçüyüm* gerz·lewk·*chew*·yewm
you sg inf	-sun *doktorsun* dok·*tor*·soon	-sün *gözlükçüsün* gerz·lewk·*chew*·sewn
he/she/it	no ending *doktor* dok·*tor*	no ending *gözlükçü* gerz·lewk·*chew*
we	-(y)uz *doktoruz* dok·*to*·rooz	-(y)üz *gözlükçüyüz* gerz·lewk·*chew*·yewz
you sg pol & pl inf/pol	-sunuz *doktorsunuz* dok·*tor*·soo·nooz	-sünüz *gözlükçüsünüz* gerz·lewk·*chew*·sew·newz
they	-lar *doktorlar* dok·*tor*·lar	-ler *gözlükçüler* gerz·lewk·*chew*·ler

case

doing things • giving directions/orders • indicating location • naming things/people • possessing

Turkish is a 'case' language, which means that endings are added to nouns and pronouns to show their relationship to other elements in the sentence.

nominative nom – shows the subject of the sentence

This bag is very heavy.
*Bu **çanta** çok ağır.*
(lit: this bag very heavy)

accusative acc – shows the object of the sentence

Did you see that bag?
*Şu **çantayı** gördün mü?*
(lit: that bag saw-you mü)

genitive gen – shows possession ('of')

The colour of this bag is very nice.
*Bu **çantanın** rengi çok güzel.*
(lit: this bag-of colour very nice)

dative dat – shows the indirect object with verbs like 'happen' ('to')

What happened to your bag?
*Çanta**na** ne oldu?*
(lit: bag-your-to what happened)

locative loc – shows location ('in', 'on', 'at', 'with' etc)

It's in her bag.
*Onun **çantasında**.*
(lit: her bag-in)

ablative abl – shows point of origin in space or time ('from')

He pulled the timetable from the bag.
*Tarifeyi çanta**sından** çıkardı.*
(lit: timetable bag-his-from pulled)

The forms of the six cases are outlined in the following table, and they're all governed by the rules of vowel harmony (see the box on page 13).

case endings for nouns				
	the vowel in the noun's last syllable is ...			
	a or *ı* (eg *kitap* book)	*e* or *i* (eg *ev* house)	*o* or *u* (eg *okul* school)	*ö* or *ü* (eg *göl* lake)
nominative	no ending *kitap* kee·*tap*	no ending *ev* ev	no ending *okul* o·*kool*	no ending *göl* gerl
accusative (ending in a consonant) *	*-ı* *kitabı* kee·ta·*buh*	*-i* *evi* e·*vee*	*-u* *okulu* o·koo·*loo*	*-ü* *gölü* ger·*lew*
	* For a noun ending in a vowel, add *y* y before the ending above.			
genitive (ending in a consonant) *	*-ın* *kitabın* kee·ta·*buhn*	*-in* *evin* e·*veen*	*-un* *okulun* o·koo·*loon*	*-ün* *gölün* ger·*lewn*
	* For a noun ending in a vowel, add *n* n before the ending above.			
dative (ending in a consonant) *	*-a* *kitaba* kee·ta·*ba*	*-e* *eve* e·*ve*	*-a* *okula* o·koo·*la*	*-e* *göle* ger·*le*
	* For a noun ending in a vowel, add *y* y before the ending above.			
locative	*-da/-ta* *kitapta* kee·tap·*ta*	*-de/-te* *evde* ev·*de*	*-da/-ta* *okulda* o·kool·*da*	*-de/-te* *gölde* gerl·*de*
ablative	*-dan/-tan* *kitaptan* kee·tap·*tan*	*-den/-ten* *evden* ev·*den*	*-dan/-tan* *okuldan* o·kool·*dan*	*-den/-ten* *gölden* gerl·*den*

In this **phrasebuilder**, the case of each noun has been given to show you how the system works. The lists in this book and the **dictionary** are in the nominative case. You can use the nominative case in phrases and be understood just fine, even though they aren't completely correct without one of the endings on the previous page.

demonstratives

giving directions/orders • indicating location •
naming things/people • pointing things out

The Turkish words for 'this' and 'that' are listed below.

this (near the speaker)	*bu*	boo	these (near the speaker)	*bunlar*	boon·*lar*
that (just over there)	*şu*	shoo	those (just over there)	*şunlar*	shoon·*lar*
that (far away)	*o*	o	those (far away)	*onlar*	on·*lar*

The concept of *bu* boo and *bunlar* boon·*lar* is more precise than the English idea of 'this' – in Turkish it means only what is directly in front of you. *Şu* shoo and *şunlar* shoon·*lar* are just a bit away from you and *o* o and *onlar* on·*lar* are not between the speakers. To ask a salesperson about their wares, don't ask 'What's that?' – instead, you'd need to say *Bu nedir?* boo *ne·*deer (lit: this what-is). As in this example, these words can stand alone; they always come before the noun.

have

Turkish doesn't use a word for 'have' as English does. To express ownership, see **possession**.

negatives

For all verb forms except the present simple tense, the negative is formed by placing the particle *ma* ma or *me* me directly after the verb stem before any other ending. When this ending begins with a vowel, you need to use the form *mı* muh, *mi* mee, *mu* moo or *mü* mew instead of *ma* ma or *me* me. A *y* y is added to these negative particles to separate the two vowels. Negative endings function according to vowel harmony (see the box on page 13).

| **Come!** | *Gel!* | gel |
| **Don't come!** | *Gelme!* | gel·me |

The bus is coming.
   Otobüs geliyor.   o·to·bews ge·lee·yor
   (lit: bus-**nom** coming)

The bus is not coming.
   Otobüs gelmiyor.   o·to·bews gel·mee·yor
   (lit: bus-**nom** come-not-ing)

The negative in the present simple tense has an irregular form. This is laid out in the table below. See also **be**, **there is/are** and **verbs**.

negative particle in present simple tense			
	I	**we**	**you** sg&inf, **he, she, it, they**
verbs that end in *a, ı, o* or *u*	*ma* ma	*may* ma·y	*maz* maz
verbs that end in *e, i, ö* or *ü*	*me* me	*mey* me·y	*mez* mez

nouns

naming things/people

Turkish nouns have different forms as case endings and suffixes are added to show the noun's role in the sentence. See **case**, **plurals**, **possession**, **suffixes** and the box on **vowel harmony** on page 13.

personal pronouns

doing things • naming things/people • possessing

Pronouns in Turkish change according to their case. This table shows only the nominative case – though not always completely correct, you'll be understood when you use it. The verb form always shows who the subject of the sentence is, so pronouns are only used for emphasis, as in the example below. See also **case** and **nouns**.

I	*ben*	ben	we	*biz*	beez
you sg inf	*sen*	sen	**you** sg pol & pl inf/pol	*siz*	seez
he/she/it	*o*	o	**they**	*onlar*	on·*lar*

We **booked these seats, not you.**
  Bu koltukları **biz**   boo kol·took·la·*ruh* beez
  ayırttık **siz** *değil.*   a·yuhrt·*tuhk* seez de·*eel*
  (lit: this seats we booked you not)

plurals

naming things/people

Show the plural of a noun by adding *-lar* ·lar or *-ler* ·ler, depending on vowel harmony (see page 13). Add *-lar* to words with *a*, *ı*, *o* and *u* and *-ler* to words with *e*, *i*, *ö* and *ü* respectively. The

BASICS

plural suffix is the first suffix added to a noun, and stress moves from the last syllable of the root word to *-lar* or *-ler*. See also **case**.

plane	*uçak*	oo·chak	**meal**	*yemek*	ye·mek
planes	*uçaklar*	oo·chak·*lar*	**meals**	*yemekler*	ye·mek·*ler*

possession

naming things/people • possessing

There are several ways to show possession in Turkish. One of the easiest ways is to use the words *var* var (lit: there is/are) and *yok* yok (lit: there isn't/aren't). See also **there is/are**.

I have a ticket.
  Biletim var.   bee·le·*teem* var
  (lit: I-ticket-**gen** there-is)
I don't have a ticket.
  Biletim yok.   bee·le·*teem* yok
  (lit: I-ticket-**gen** there-isn't)

Another simple way is to use possessive pronouns (the equivalents of 'my', 'your' etc) shown in the next table, plus the noun that's owned. (This isn't strictly correct, but you'll be understood.) These pronouns can also mean 'mine', 'yours' etc.

my/mine	*benim*	be·*neem*	our/ours	*bizim*	bee·*zeem*
your/ yours sg	*senin*	se·*neen*	your/ yours pl	*sizin*	see·*zeen*
his/ her(s)/its/ somebody's	*onun*	o·*noon*	their/ theirs	*onların*	on·la·*ruhn*

pen	*kalem-***nom**	ka·*lem*
your pen	*sizin kaleminiz-***gen**	see·*zeen* ka·le·mee·*neez*
backpack	*sırt çantası-***nom**	suhrt chan·ta·*suh*
her backpack	*onun sırt çantası-***gen**	o·*noon* suhrt chan·ta·*suh*

See also **case** and **personal pronouns**.

postpositions

**doing things • giving directions/orders •
indicating location • pointing things out**

Postpositions are used in Turkish the way prepositions like 'for'
and 'near' are in English, except they come after the noun. For
each postposition, the noun takes a particular case ending – in
the example below, with *için* ee·*cheen* (for), the noun *çocuklar*
cho·jook·*lar* (children) takes the nominative case. Useful postpositions are listed in the **dictionary**. See also **case** and **suffixes**.

for the children
    çocuklar için   cho·jook·*lar* ee·*cheen*
    (lit: the-children-**nom** for)

questions

asking a question

To form a yes/no question, add the word *mi* mee, *mı* muh, *mu*
moo or *mü* mew (depending on vowel harmony, page 13) after
the verb.

The bus is coming.
    Otobüs geliyor.   o·to·*bews* ge·lee·yor
    (lit: bus-**nom** coming)

Is the bus coming?
    Otobüs geliyor mu?   o·to·*bews* ge·lee·yor moo
    (lit: bus-**nom** coming *mu*)

Another way to form questions is to place a question word (in
the next table) before the verb. Note that if the question uses
the verb 'be', the question word usually goes at the end of the
phrase (see also **be**).

Where's the taxi rank?
    Taksi durağı nerede?   tak·*see* doo·ra·*uh* ne·re·de
    (lit: taxi-**nom** rank-**acc** where)

how?	nasıl?	na·suhl
how many?	kaç?	kach
how much?	ne kadar?	ne ka·dar
what?	ne?	ne
what kind?	ne tür?	ne tewr
what size?	kaç beden?	kach be·den
when?	ne zaman?	ne za·man
where?	nerede?	ne·re·de
which?	hangi?	han·gee
who?	kim?	keem
why?	neden?	ne·den

suffixes

**doing things • giving directions/orders • indicating
location • pointing things out**

Turkish uses case endings and suffixes to show how elements
in a sentence are related. It's an agglutinative language, meaning that the endings are added to the root word. *Düşünemedim*
dew·shew·ne·me·deem means 'I was unable to think' – *düşün*
(think) + *e* (able) + *me* (un) + *di* (was) + *m* (I). When several endings are added, the plural comes first, then the case marking,
then possessive and other suffixes. All suffixes change according to vowel harmony (see page 13). In the table below are
some useful suffixes. See also **case**, **postpositions** and **verbs**.

english	turkish	translit	example	translit
by/using	-la, -le	·la, ·le	*trenle* (lit: train-by)	*tren·le*
with	-lı, -li, -lu, -lü	·luh, ·lee, ·loo, ·lew	*buzlu* (lit: ice-with)	booz·loo
without	-sız, -siz, -suz, -süz	·suhz, ·seez, ·sooz, ·sewz	*sütsüz* (lit: milk-without)	sewt·sewz

there is/are

To express 'there is' or 'there are', Turkish uses the word *var* var. To say 'there isn't' or 'there aren't', use the word *yok* yok. These are also the words used to show ownership (see **possession**).

There's a telephone in my room.
Odamda telefon var.   o·dam·*da* te·le·*fon* var
(lit: room-**loc**-my-in telephone-**nom** there-is)

There isn't a telephone in my room.
Odamda telefon yok.   o·dam·*da* te·le·*fon* yok
(lit: room-**loc**-my-in telephone-**nom** there-isn't)

verbs

Turkish verbs have a regular structure. The infinitives of Turkish verbs (the dictionary form) end with -*mak* mak or -*mek* mek, such as *konuşmak* ko·noosh·*mak* (speak) or *gelmek* gel·*mek* (come). Suffixes replace this ending to form different tenses.

She wants to speak.
O konuşmak istiyor.   o ko·noosh·*mak* ees·*tee*·yor
(lit: she to-speak wanting)

She is speaking.
O konuşuyor.   o ko·noo·*shoo*·yor
(lit: she speaking)

She will speak.
O konuşacak.   o ko·noo·sha·*jak*
(lit: she speak-will)

The following table shows the suffixes used to form regular present tense verbs. In cases where the verb stem ends in a vowel, such as *yaşa* in *yaşamak* ya·sha·*mak* (live), drop the first vowel from the ending (marked in brackets in the table below). For example, 'I live' would be *yaşarım* ya·sha·*ruhm*.

present tense verb forms				
	if the final vowel in the stem is ...			
	a or ı (eg *almak* get/buy)	**e or i** (eg *bilmek* know)	**o or u** (eg *oturmak* reside)	**ö or ü** (eg *yüzmek* swim)
I	*-(ı)rım/* *-(a)rım* *alırım* a·*luh*· ruhm	*-(i)rim/* *-(e)rim* *bilirim* bee·*lee*· reem	*-(u)rum/* *-(a)rım* *otururum* o·too·*roo*· room	*-(ü)rüm/* *-(e)rim* *yüzerim* yew·ze· reem
you sg inf	*-(ı)rsın/* *-(a)rsın* *alırsın* a·*luhr*· suhn	*-(i)rsin/* *-(e)rsin* *bilirsin* bee·*leer*· seen	*-(u)rsun/* *-(a)rsın* *oturursun* o·too·*roor*· soon	*-(ü)rsün/* *-(e)rsin* *yüzersin* yew·*zer*· seen
he/ **she/it**	*-(ı)r/-(a)r* *alır* a·*luhr*	*-(i)r/-(e)r* *bilir* bee·*leer*	*-(u)r/-(a)r* *oturur* o·too·*roor*	*-(ü)r/-(e)r* *yüzer* yew·*zer*
we	*-(ı)rız/-(a)rız* *alırız* a·*luh*·ruhz	*-(i)riz/-(e)riz* *biliriz* bee·*lee*·reez	*-(u)ruz/-(a)rız* *otururuz* o·too·roo·rooz	*-(ü)rüz/-(e)riz* *yüzeriz* yew·ze·reez
you sg pol & pl inf/pol	*-(ı)rsınız/* *-(a)rsınız* *alırsınız* a·*luhr*·suh· nuhz	*-(i)rsiniz/* *-(e)rsiniz* *bilirsiniz* bee·*leer*· see·neez	*-(u)rsunuz/* *-(a)rsınız* *oturursunuz* o·too·*roor*· soo·nooz	*-(ü)rsünüz/* *-(e)rsiniz* *yüzersiniz* yew·*zer*· see·neez
they	*-(ı)rlar/* *-(a)rlar* *alırlar* a·*luhr*·lar	*-(e)rler/* *-(e)rler* *bilirler* bee·*leer*·ler	*-(u)rlar/* *-(a)rlar* *otururlar* o·too·*roor*·lar	*-(ü)rler/* *-(e)rler* *yüzerler* yew·*zer*·ler

See also **be**, **suffixes**, and the box on **vowel harmony**, page 13.

word order

asking a question • doing things •
giving directions/orders • negating

Word order in Turkish is very flexible – the case endings and
suffixes mean that you can change the order of words in a sentence and still know how they relate to each other. In speech
it's often changed for emphasis or rhythm so you might hear
words in a different order to the way we have them in this
book. The most important element in a sentence is mentioned
first – the place you're going, the person you're talking to, or
the topic you're talking about. The main verb comes at the
end, adjectives come before nouns and adverbs before verbs.
See also **adjectives & adverbs**, **case**, **questions** and **suffixes**.

formal is as formal does

When speaking in Turkish you need either polite or informal
language. The informal *sen* sen form (meaning 'you' sg inf)
can be used with individual friends or relatives, while the
siz seez form (meaning 'you' sg pol & pl inf/pol) must be
used for strangers, important people, or more than one
friend or relative. As a traveller, it's best to use the *siz* form
with new people you meet. Nouns, verbs and personal pronouns ('you', 'she', 'we' and so on) will change depending
on whether you're being polite or informal.

In this book we've chosen the appropriate form for the
situation that the phrase is used in. For phrases where
either form might be appropriate we have given both.
Look for the symbols **pol** (polite) and **inf** (informal) to find
out what form the phrase is in.

glossary

ablative	type of *case marking* which shows where/when the *subject* is from – 'the man **from the CIA**'
accusative	type of *case marking*, usually used for the *object* of the sentence – 'she searched **the files**'
adjective	a word that describes something – 'the **hidden** agenda'
adverb	a word that explains how an action was done – 'he answered **carefully**'
article	the words 'a', 'an' and 'the'
case (marking)	word ending (suffix) which tells us the role of a thing or person in the sentence
dative	type of *case marking* which shows the indirect *object* – 'I gave the file **to the agent**'
genitive	type of *case marking* which shows ownership or possession – 'the **spy's** notebook'
locative	type of *case marking* which shows where the *subject* is – 'the camera is **in the room**'
nominative	type of *case marking* used for the *subject* of the sentence – 'the **investigation** ended'
noun	a thing, person or idea – 'the **briefcase**'
object	the thing or person in the sentence that has the action directed to it – 'I found the **evidence**'
possessive pronoun	a word that means 'mine', 'yours', etc

postposition	a word like 'for' or 'before' in English; in Turkish these come after the noun or pronoun
present simple tense	the verb tense which tells what is happening now – 'the government **works** to protect the country'
pronoun	a word that means 'I', 'you', etc
subject	the thing or person in the sentence that does the action – 'the **police** entered the building'
suffix	extra syllable(s) added to the end of a word, eg ly is added to 'secret' to make 'secret**ly**'
transliteration	pronunciation guide for words and phrases
verb	the word that tells you what action happened – 'I **broke** the code'
verb stem	the part of a verb which does not change – 'search' in '**search**ing' and '**search**ed'

language difficulties

Do you speak (English)?
(İngilizce) konuşuyor musunuz?
(een·gee·*leez*·je) ko·noo·*shoo*·yor moo·soo·*nooz*

Does anyone speak (English)?
(İngilizce) bilen var mı?
(een·gee·*leez*·je) bee·*len* var muh

Do you understand?
Anlıyor musun?
an·*luh*·yor moo·*soon*

Yes, I understand.
Evet, anlıyorum.
e·*vet* an·*luh*·yo·room

No, I don't understand.
Hayır, anlamıyorum.
ha·yuhr an·*la*·muh·yo·room

I understand.
Anlıyorum.
an·*luh*·yo·room

I don't understand.
Anlamıyorum.
an·*la*·muh·yo·room

I speak (English).
(İngilizce) konuşuyorum.
(een·gee·*leez*·je) ko·noo·*shoo*·yo·room

I don't speak (Turkish).
(Türkçe) bilmiyorum.
(*tewrk*·che) *beel*·mee·yo·room

I speak a little.
Biraz konuşuyorum.
bee·raz ko·noo·*shoo*·yo·room

What does 'kitap' mean?
'Kitap' ne demektir?
kee·*tap* ne de·*mek*·teer

I would like to practise (Turkish).
(Türkçe) pratik yapmak istiyorum.
(*tewrk*·che) pra·*teek* yap·*mak* ees·*tee*·yo·room

Let's speak (Turkish).
(Türkçe) konuşalım.
(*tewrk*·che) ko·noo·*sha*·luhm

Pardon?
Anlamadım?
an·*la*·ma·duhm

33

How do you write 'yabancı'?

'Yabancı' kelimesini
nasıl yazarsınız?

ya·ban·juh ke·lee·me·see·nee
na·suhl ya·zar·suh·nuhz

How do you pronounce this?

Bunu nasıl
telaffuz edersiniz?

boo·noo na·suhl
te·laf·fooz e·der·see·neez

**Could you
please ...?**

Lütfen ...?

lewt·fen ...

repeat that

tekrarlar
mısınız

tek·rar·lar
muh·suh·nuhz

**speak more
slowly**

daha yavaş
konuşur
musunuz

da·ha ya·vash
ko·noo·shoor
moo·soo·nooz

write it down

yazar
mısınız

ya·zar
muh·suh·nuhz

signs

Açık	a·chuhk	Open
Çıkış	chuh·kuhsh	Exit
Danışma	da·nuhsh·ma	Information
Erkek	er·kek	Men
Fotoğraf Çekmek	fo·to·raf chek·mek	No Photography
Yasaktır	ya·sak·tuhr	
Giriş	gee·reesh	Entrance
Kadın	ka·duhn	Women
Kapalı	ka·pa·luh	Closed
Sigara	see·ga·ra	No Smoking
İçilmez	ee·cheel·mez	
Tuvaletler	too·va·let·ler	Toilets/WC
Yasak	ya·sak	Prohibited

BASICS

34

numbers & amounts
sayılar & miktarlar

cardinal numbers

sayılar

You say Turkish numbers in the same order as English ones but you don't need a word for 'and'. The words for the individual numbers are normally joined together when you write them, so 517 is written as *beşyüzonyedi* besh·yewz·on·ye·dee (lit: five-hundred-ten-seven).

When you're counting nouns, the noun always takes the singular form – 'two books' is *iki kitap* ee·kee kee·tap (lit: two book).

0	*sıfır*	suh·*fuhr*
1	*bir*	beer
2	*iki*	ee·*kee*
3	*üç*	ewch
4	*dört*	dert
5	*beş*	besh
6	*altı*	al·*tuh*
7	*yedi*	ye·*dee*
8	*sekiz*	se·*keez*
9	*dokuz*	do·*kooz*
10	*on*	on
11	*onbir*	on·*beer*
12	*oniki*	on·ee·*kee*
13	*onüç*	on·*ewch*
14	*ondört*	on·*dert*
15	*onbeş*	on·*besh*
16	*onaltı*	on·al·*tuh*
17	*onyedi*	on·ye·*dee*
18	*onsekiz*	on·se·*keez*
19	*ondokuz*	on·do·*kooz*
20	*yirmi*	yeer·*mee*
21	*yirmibir*	yeer·*mee*·beer
22	*yirmiiki*	yeer·*mee*·ee·*kee*

30	otuz	o·tooz
40	kırk	kuhrk
50	elli	el·lee
60	altmış	alt·muhsh
70	yetmiş	yet·meesh
80	seksen	sek·sen
90	doksan	dok·san
100	yüz	yewz
200	ikiyüz	ee·kee·yewz
1,000	bin	been
1,000,000	bir milyon	beer meel·yon
1,000,000,000	bir milyar	beer meel·yar

hand gestures

To beckon or say 'follow me', Turks scoop one of their hands downward and toward themselves. Some people, particularly women, hold their hand the same way but flutter their fingers instead of scooping.

ordinal numbers

sıra sayılar

Ordinal numbers are formed by adding the suffix -ıncı ·uhn·juh to the number. This suffix can also be -inci ·een·jee, -uncu ·oon·joo or -üncü ·ewn·jew, depending on the last vowel in the number (see **vowel harmony**, page 13).

In writing, a full stop is put after a number to show that it's an ordinal. So '1st chapter' is written as 1. bölüm bee·reen·jee ber·lewm and '7th month' is 7. ay ye·deen·jee ai.

1st	birinci	bee·reen·jee
2nd	ikinci	ee·keen·jee
3rd	üçüncü	ew·chewn·jew
4th	dördüncü	der·dewn·jew
5th	beşinci	be·sheen·jee

fractions

a quarter	çeyrek	chay·*rek*
a third	üçte bir	ewch·*te* beer
a half	yarım	ya·*ruhm*
three-quarters	üç çeyrek	ewch chay·*rek*
all	hepsi	*hep*·see
none	hiç	heech

decimals

Turkish decimals are easy – use the same word order as in English and say *nokta* nok·*ta* (dot) instead of 'point'.

3.14	üç nokta ondört	ewch nok·*ta* on·dert
4.2	dört nokta iki	dert nok·*ta* ee·*kee*
5.1	beş nokta bir	besh nok·*ta* beer

yes & no

When you look in the English-Turkish dictionary, you'll find that *evet* e·*vet* means 'yes' and *hayır* ha·yuhr means 'no'. But it's not always that straightforward …

When answering questions, Turks sometimes say *var* var (lit: it-exists) instead of *evet* for 'yes'. They show this with body language by nodding their heads once, forward and down.

Wagging your head from side to side doesn't mean 'no' in Turkish, it means 'I don't understand'. To show 'no' Turks nod their heads up and back, lifting their eyebrows at the same time – simply raising the eyebrows means the same thing. They may also say tsk.

numbers & amounts

37

useful amounts

How much?	Ne kadar?	ne ka·dar
How many?	Kaç tane?	kach ta·ne
Please give	Lütfen bana	lewt·fen ba·na
me ...	... verin.	... ve·reen
(100) grams	(yüz) gram	(yewz) gram
half a dozen	yarım	ya·ruhm
	düzine	dew·zee·ne
half a kilo	yarım kilo	ya·ruhm kee·lo
a kilo	bir kilo	beer kee·lo
a bottle	bir şişe	beer shee·she
a jar	bir kavanoz	beer ka·va·noz
a packet	bir paket	beer pa·ket
a slice	bir dilim	beer dee·leem
a tin	bir kutu	beer koo·too
a few	birkaç tane	beer·kach ta·ne
less	daha az	da·ha az
(just) a little	(sadece) biraz	(sa·de·je) bee·raz
a lot/many	çok	chok
more	daha fazla	da·ha faz·la
some	biraz	bee·raz

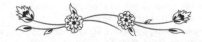

ums & ahs

In those dreaded moments when your Turkish won't flow freely, try not to say 'um' to fill the gap. In Turkish you're actually saying *am* am (a vulgar term for 'vagina') – if your audience has a good sense of humour, they could be hiding a smirk, but you could also be causing serious offence. Use the more neutral 'ah' instead.

time & dates
zaman & tarih

telling the time

Telling the time in Turkish is quite straightforward. For the hour, say *saat* sa·*at* and the number (eg *saat yedi* sa·*at* ye·*dee* is 'it's seven o'clock'), and for half-hours say *saat* plus the hour and the word *buçuk* boo·*chook* (eg *saat yedi buçuk* sa·*at* ye·*dee* boo·*chook* is 'it's half-past seven').

For times 'to' or 'past' the hour, say the hour first, then the minutes plus *geçiyor* ge·*chee*·yor for 'past' or *var* var for 'to'. Use *çeyrek* chay·*rek* for a quarter of an hour. For example, 'it's twenty past six' is *saat yediyi yirmi geçiyor* sa·*at* ye·*dee*·yee yeer·*mee* ge·*chee*·yor, and 'it's a quarter to two' is *saat ikiye çeyrek var* sa·*at* ee·*kee*·ye chay·*rek* var.

What time is it?	*Saat kaç?*	sa·*at* kach
It's (ten) o'clock.	*Saat (on).*	sa·*at* (on)
Five past (ten).	*(Onu) beş geçiyor.*	(o·*noo*) besh ge·*chee*·yor
Quarter past (ten).	*(Onu) çeyrek geçiyor.*	(o·*noo*) chay·*rek* ge·*chee*·yor
Half past (ten).	*(On) buçuk.*	(on) boo·*chook*
Twenty to (eleven).	*(Onbire) yirmi var.*	(on·bee·*re*) yeer·*mee* var
Quarter to (eleven).	*(Onbire) çeyrek var.*	(on·bee·*re*) chay·*rek* var
At what time ...?	*Saat kaçta ...?*	sa·*at* kach·*ta* ...
At (ten).	*Saat (onda).*	sa·*at* (on·*da*)
At 7.57pm.	*Akşam saat yedi elliyedide.*	ak·sham sa·*at* ye·*dee* el·*lee*·ye·dee·*de*
	(lit: evening hour seven fifty-seven-at)	

Saat sa·*at* means 'hour', 'watch', 'clock' or 'o'clock', depending on context. When *saat* comes before a number it means 'o'clock', but when it follows it means 'hour' – *saat beş* sa·*at* besh means 'it's five o'clock', while *beş saat* besh sa·*at* means 'five hours'. *Beş saat* would also be 'five clocks' or 'five watches'.

the calendar

takvim

days

Monday	*Pazartesi*	pa·*zar*·te·see
Tuesday	*Salı*	sa·*luh*
Wednesday	*Çarşamba*	char·sham·*ba*
Thursday	*Perşembe*	per·shem·*be*
Friday	*Cuma*	joo·*ma*
Saturday	*Cumartesi*	joo·*mar*·te·see
Sunday	*Pazar*	pa·*zar*

months

January	*Ocak*	o·*jak*
February	*Şubat*	shoo·*bat*
March	*Mart*	mart
April	*Nisan*	nee·*san*
May	*Mayıs*	ma·*yuhs*
June	*Haziran*	ha·zee·*ran*
July	*Temmuz*	tem·*mooz*
August	*Ağustos*	a·oos·*tos*
September	*Eylül*	ay·*lewl*
October	*Ekim*	e·*keem*
November	*Kasım*	ka·*suhm*
December	*Aralık*	a·ra·*luhk*

dates

What date is it today?
Bugün ayın kaçı? boo·gewn a·*yuhn* ka·chuh

It's (18 October).
(Onsekiz Ekim). (on·se·keez e·keem)
(lit: eighteen October)

---

a hot date

Onsekiz Ekim on·se·*keez* e·keem (18 October) can also be
written as *18 Ekim*, without an equivalent of the English 'th'
on '18th'. Years are said without 'and' in the same way as
other numbers – 2007 is *ikibinyedi* ee·kee·been·ye·dee (lit:
two-thousand-seven).

---

seasons

spring	*ilkbahar*	*eelk*·ba·har
summer	*yaz*	yaz
autumn/fall	*sonbahar*	son·ba·har
winter	*kış*	kuhsh

present

şimdiki zaman

now	*şimdi*	*sheem*·dee
today	*bugün*	boo·gewn
tonight	*bu gece*	boo ge·*je*
this ...	*bu ...*	boo ...
morning	*sabah*	sa·*bah*
afternoon	*öğleden sonra*	er·le·*den* son·ra
week	*hafta*	haf·*ta*
month	*ay*	ai
year	*yıl*	yuhl

past

geçmiş zaman

day before yesterday	*bir önceki gün*	beer ern·je·*kee* gewn
(three days) ago	*(üç gün) önce*	(ewch gewn) *ern*·je
since (May)	*(Mayıs'tan) beri*	(ma·yuhs·*tan*) be·*ree*
last ...	*geçen ...*	ge·*chen* ...
night	*gece*	ge·*je*
week	*hafta*	haf·*ta*
month	*ay*	ai
year	*yıl*	yuhl
yesterday ...	*dün ...*	dewn ...
morning	*sabah*	sa·*bah*
afternoon	*öğleden sonra*	er·le·*den* son·ra
evening	*akşam*	ak·*sham*

---

12 or 24?

In speech, the Turkish use the 12-hour clock, but you'll see the 24-hour clock written in schedules and timetables.

---

future

gelecek zaman

day after tomorrow	*öbür gün*	er·*bewr* gewn
in (six days)	*(altı gün) içinde*	(al·*tuh* gewn) ee·cheen·*de*
until (June)	*(Haziran'a) kadar*	(ha·zee·ra·*na*) ka·*dar*
next ...	*gelecek ...*	ge·le·*jek* ...
week	*hafta*	haf·*ta*
month	*ay*	ai
year	*yıl*	yuhl

tomorrow ...	yarın ...	ya·ruhn ...
morning	sabah	sa·bah
afternoon	öğleden sonra	er·le·den son·ra
evening	akşam	ak·sham

during the day

afternoon	öğleden sonra	er·le·den son·ra
dawn	şafak	sha·fak
day	gün	gewn
evening	akşam	ak·sham
midday	gün ortası	gewn or·ta·suh
midnight	gece yarısı	ge·je ya·ruh·suh
morning	sabah	sa·bah
night	gece	ge·je
sunrise	gün doğumu	gewn do·oo·moo
sunset	gün batımı	gewn ba·tuh·muh

when is it again?

You can say 'morning' or 'am' in two ways in Turkish. To refer to any time between midnight and noon, say *sabah* sa·bah. For times between breakfast and lunch, you can also use *öğleden evvel* er·le·den ev·vel (lit: noon before). After lunch, use *öğleden sonra* er·le·den son·ra (lit: noon after) for 'pm'. Between 6pm and 8pm say *akşam* ak·sham (evening) and from 8pm onwards say *gece* ge·je (night).

time & dates

43

Bayram bai·*ram* means 'religious or national festival'. There are two religious *bayrams* in Turkey, and during both it's customary for young people to visit older family members and friends and kiss their hands.

One is called *Şeker Bayramı* she·*ker* bai·ra·*muh* (the feast of the sweets) or *Ramazan Bayramı* ra·ma·*zan* bai·ra·*muh* (the feast of Ramadan). During the lunar month of Ramadan that precedes *Ramazan Bayramı*, Muslims fast during the day and feast at night for one month. At the end of the month they celebrate this three-day *bayram* and public holiday, making sweets and visiting each other. Children also go from house to house wishing people *Mutlu bayramlar!* moot·*loo* bai·ram·*lar* (Happy *Bayrams!*) and receiving sweets, chocolate or money.

During *Kurban Bayramı* koor·*ban* bai·ra·*muh* (the feast of the sacrifice), the second *bayram*, people make animal sacrifices and give the meat to the poor and needy. This festival lasts for four days and is also a public holiday.

Below are some other *bayrams* held in Turkey.

National Sovereignty and Children's Festival (23 April)
23 Nisan Ulusal Egemenlik ve Çocuk Bayramı
yeer·*mee*·ewch nee·*san* oo·loo·*sal* e·ge·men·*leek* ve cho·*jook* bai·ra·*muh*

Commemoration of Atatürk and Youth & Sports Festival (19 May)
19 Mayıs Atatürk'ü Anma ve Gençlik ve Spor Bayramı
on·do·*kooz* ma·*yuhs* a·ta·tewr·kew an·*ma* ve gench·*leek* ve spor bai·ra·*muh*

Victory Festival (30 August)
30 Ağustos Zafer Bayramı
o·*tooz* a·oos·*tos* za·*fer* bai·ra·*muh*

Republic Festival (29 October)
29 Ekim Cumhuriyet Bayramı
yeer·*mee*·do·*kooz* e·*keem* joom·hoo·ree·*yet* bai·ra·*muh*

How much is it?
Bu ne kadar?   boo ne ka·*dar*

Can you write down the price?
Fiyatı yazabilir   fee·ya·*tuh* ya·za·bee·leer
misiniz?   mee·see·*neez*

Do you accept …?	*… kabul ediyor musunuz?*	… ka·*bool* e·*dee*·yor moo·soo·*nooz*
credit cards	*Kredi kartı*	kre·dee kar·*tuh*
debit cards	*Banka kartı*	ban·ka kar·*tuh*
foreign currency	*Döviz*	der·*veez*
travellers cheques	*Seyahat çeki*	se·ya·*hat* che·kee

I'd like to …	*… istiyorum.*	… ees·*tee*·yo·room
cash a cheque	*Çek*	chek
	bozdurmak	boz·door·*mak*
change money	*Para*	pa·ra
	bozdurmak	boz·door·*mak*
change a	*Seyahat çeki*	se·ya·hat che·kee
travellers cheque	*bozdurmak*	boz·door·*mak*
get a cash advance	*Avans çekmek*	a·vans chek·*mek*
withdraw money	*Para çekmek*	pa·ra chek·*mek*

What's the …?	*… nedir?*	… ne·deer
charge	*Ücreti*	ewj·re·*tee*
exchange rate	*Döviz kuru*	der·veez koo·*roo*

I'd like … please.	*… istiyorum lütfen.*	… ees·*tee*·yo·room *lewt*·fen
my change	*Paramın üstünü*	pa·ra·*muhn* ews·tew·*new*
a receipt	*Makbuz*	mak·*booz*
a refund	*Para iadesi*	pa·ra ee·a·de·*see*
to return this	*Bunu iade etmek*	boo·noo ee·a·de et·*mek*

Where's (a/an) ...?	... nerede var?	... ne·re·de var
automated teller machine	Bankamatik	ban·ka·ma·teek
foreign exchange office	Döviz bürosu	der·veez bew·ro·soo

How much is it per ...?	... ne kadar?	... ne ka·dar
day	Günlüğü	gewn·lew·ew
game	Oyun ücreti	o·yoon ewj·re·tee
hour	Saati	sa·a·tee
(five) minutes	(Beş) dakikası	(besh) da·kee·ka·suh
night	Geceliği	ge·je·lee·ee
page	Sayfası	sai·fa·suh
person	Kişi başına ücreti	kee·shee ba·shuh·na ewj·re·tee
tent	Çadır başına ücreti	cha·duhr ba·shuh·na ewj·re·tee
week	Haftalığı	haf·ta·luh·uh
vehicle	Araç başına ücreti	a·rach ba·shuh·na ewj·re·tee
visit	Giriş	gee·reesh

It's ...		
free	Ücretsiz.	ewj·ret·seez
(12) euros	(Oniki) euro.	(on·ee·kee) yoo·ro
(25) lira	(Yirmibeş) lira.	(yeer·mee·besh) lee·ra

---

on the money

Denizde kum onda para.
de·neez·de koom on·da pa·ra **He/She has money to burn.**
(lit: sea has sand, he/she has money)

para içinde yüzmek
pa·ra ee·cheen·de yewz·mek **to be rich**
(lit: to float in money)

parayı denize atmak
pa·ra·yuh de·nee·ze at·mak **to spend money foolishly**
(lit: to throw money into the sea)

getting around

gezerken

You'll often use a *dolmuş* dol·*moosh* or *midibüs* mee·dee·*bews* while travelling in the cities and busier regions of Turkey. The *dolmuş* was originally a shared taxi (nowadays often minibuses), and a *midibus* is a small bus which operates on routes that aren't busy enough for a bus or coach. To let the driver know you want to get off, say *inecek var* ee·ne·*jek* var (someone wants to get off) or *sağda* sa·*da* ('on the right', meaning 'pull over here').

Which ... goes	*Hangi* ...	*han*·gee ...
to (Sirkeci)?	*(Sirkeci'ye) gider?*	*(seer*·ke·jee·ye) gee·*der*
Is this the ...	*(Sirkeci'ye) giden*	*(seer*·ke·jee·ye) gee·*den*
to (Sirkeci)?	... *bu mu?*	... boo moo
boat	*vapur*	va·*poor*
bus	*otobüs*	o·to·*bews*
dolmuş	*dolmuş*	dol·*moosh*
midibus	*midibüs*	mee·dee·*bews*
minibus	*minibüs*	mee·nee·*bews*
shuttle bus	*servis otobüsü*	ser·*vees* o·to·bew·*sew*
train	*tren*	tren

When's the	... *(otobüs)*	... (o·to·*bews)*
... (bus)?	*ne zaman?*	ne za·*man*
first	*İlk*	eelk
last	*Son*	son
next	*Sonraki*	son·ra·*kee*

Where's the bus terminal?
Otobüs terminali nerede? o·to·*bews* ter·mee·na·*lee* ne·re·de

How do I get to the bus terminal?
Otobüs terminaline o·to·*bews* ter·mee·na·lee·*ne*
nasıl gidebilirim? na·suhl gee·de·bee·lee·reem

What time does it leave?
Ne zaman kalkacak?   ne za·*man* kal·ka·*jak*

What time does it get to (Beşiktaş)?
(Beşiktaş'a) ne zaman varır?   (be·*sheek*·ta·sha) ne za·*man* va·*ruhr*

How long will it be delayed?
Ne kadar gecikecek?   ne ka·*dar* ge·jee·ke·*jek*

Please tell me when we get to (Beşiktaş).
(Beşiktaş'a)   (be·*sheek*·ta·sha)
vardığımızda   var·duh·uh·muhz·*da*
lütfen bana söyleyin.   *lewt*·fen ba·*na* say·*le*·yeen

Please stop here.
Lütfen burada durun.   *lewt*·fen boo·ra·*da* doo·*roon*

How long do we stop here?
Burada ne kadar   boo·ra·*da* ne ka·*dar*
duracağız?   doo·ra·*ja*·uhz

Are you waiting for more people?
Daha fazla yolcu   da·*ha* faz·*la* yol·*joo*
mu bekliyorsunuz?   moo bek·*lee*·yor·soo·nooz

How many people can ride on this?
Buna kaç kişi   boo·*na* kach kee·*shee*
binebilir?   bee·*ne*·bee·leer

Can you take us around the city, please?
Bizi şehirde   bee·*zee* she·heer·*de*
dolaştırabilir   do·lash·tuh·*ra*·bee·leer
misiniz?   mee·see·*neez*

Is this seat available?
Bu koltuk boş mu?   boo kol·*took* bosh moo

That's my seat.
Burası benim yerim.   boo·ra·*suh* be·*neem* ye·*reem*

tickets

bilet

Where do I buy a ticket?
Nereden bilet   ne·re·den bee·*let*
alabilirim?   a·*la*·bee·lee·reem

Where's a ticket kiosk?
Bilet gişesi nerede var?   bee·*let* gee·she·*see* ne·re·de var

Do I need to book (well in advance)?
(Çok önceden) Yer   (chok ern·je·*den*) yer
ayırtmam gerekli mi?   a·yuhrt·*mam* ge·rek·*lee* mee

A ... ticket	*(Bostancı'ya) ...*	(bos·*tan*·juh·ya) ...
to (Bostancı).	*bir bilet lütfen.*	beer bee·*let* lewt·fen
1st-class	*birinci mevki*	bee·reen·*jee* mev·*kee*
2nd-class	*ikinci mevki*	ee·keen·*jee* mev·*kee*
child's	*çocuk için*	cho·*jook* ee·*cheen*
return	*gidiş-dönüş*	gee·deesh·der·*newsh*

A one-way ticket to (Bostancı).
(Bostancı'ya) bir   (bos·*tan*·juh·ya) beer
gidiş bileti lütfen.   gee·*deesh* bee·le·*tee* lewt·fen

A student ticket to (Trabzon).
(Trabzon'a) bir   (trab·zo·na) beer
öğrenci bileti.   er·ren·*jee* bee·le·*tee*

I'd like	... bir yer	... beer yer
a/an ... seat.	istiyorum.	ees·tee·yo·room
aisle	Koridor	ko·ree·dor
	tarafında	ta·ra·fuhn·da
nonsmoking	Sigara	see·ga·ra
	içilmeyen	ee·cheel·me·yen
	kısımda	kuh·suhm·da
smoking	Sigara	see·ga·ra
	içilen kısımda	ee·chee·len kuh·suhm·da
window	Cam kenarı	jam ke·na·ruh
Is there (a) ...?	... var mı?	... var muh
air conditioning	Klima	klee·ma
blanket	Battaniye	bat·ta·nee·ye
sick bag	Kusma torbası	koos·ma tor·ba·suh
toilet	Tuvalet	too·va·let

How much is it?
Şu ne kadar? shoo ne ka·dar

That's too expensive.
Çok pahalı. chok pa·ha·luh

How long does the trip take?
Yolculuk ne kadar sürer? yol·joo·look ne ka·dar sew·rer

Is it a direct route?
Direk güzergah mı? dee·rek gew·zer·gah muh

Can I get a stand-by ticket?
Açık bilet alabilir a·chuhk bee·let a·la·bee·leer
miyim? mee·yeem

Can I get a sleeping berth?
Yataklı bir yer istiyorum. ya·tak·luh beer yer ees·tee·yo·room

What time should I check in?
Ne zaman giriş ne za·man gee·reesh
yapmalıyım? yap·ma·luh·yuhm

I'd like to ... my	Biletimi ...	bee·le·tee·mee ...
ticket, please.	istiyorum.	ees·tee·yo·room
cancel	iptal ettirmek	eep·tal et·teer·mek
change	değiştirmek	de·eesh·teer·mek
confirm	onaylatmak	o·nai·lat·mak

luggage

bagaj

Where can I find a trolley?
Nereden trolli   ne-re-den *trol*-lee
bulabilirim?   boo-*la*-bee-lee-reem

Where's (a/the)...?   ... *nerede?*   ... ne-re-de
  baggage claim   *Bagaj*   ba-*gazh*
     konveyörü   kon-ve-yer-*rew*
  left-luggage   *Emanet*   e-ma-*net*
  office   *bürosu*   bew-ro-*soo*
  luggage locker   *Emanet dolabı*   e-ma-*net* do-la-*buh*

My luggage   *Bagajım ...*   ba-ga-*zhuhm* ...
has been ...
  damaged   *zarar gördü*   za-*rar* ger-*dew*
  lost   *kayboldu*   kai-bol-*doo*
  stolen   *çalındı*   cha-luhn-*duh*

transport

51

That's (not) mine.
Bu benim (değil).   boo be·*neem* (de·*eel*)

Can I have some tokens?
Jeton alabilir miyim?   zhe·*ton* a·la·bee·leer mee·*yeem*

plane

uçak

Where does flight (TK0060) …?	(TK0060) *sefer sayılı uçak …*	(*te*·ka suh·*fuhr* suh·*fuhr* alt·*muhsh*) se·*fer* sa·yuh·*luh* oo·chak …
arrive	*nereye iniyor*	ne·re·ye ee·*nee*·yor
depart	*nereden kalkıyor*	ne·re·den kal·*kuh*·yor
Where's (the) …?	*… nerede?*	… *ne*·re·de
airport shuttle	*Servis otobüsü*	ser·*vees* o·to·bew·*sew*
arrivals hall	*Gelen yolcu bölümü*	ge·*len* yol·*joo* ber·lew·*mew*
departures hall	*Giden yolcu bölümü*	gee·*den* yol·*joo* ber·lew·*mew*
duty-free shop	*Gümrüksüz satış mağazası*	gewm·rewk·*sewz* sa·*tuhsh* ma·a·za·*suh*
gate (7)	*(Yedi) numaralı kapı*	(ye·*dee*) noo·ma·ra·*luh* ka·*puh*

listen for …

aktarma	ak·tar·*ma*	**transfer**
biniş kartı	bee·*neesh* kar·*tuh*	**boarding pass**
pasaport	pa·sa·*port*	**passport**
transit	tran·*seet*	**transit**

bus & coach

How often do buses come?
Otobüs ne kadar zamanda   o·to·*bews* ne ka·*dar* za·man·*da*
bir geliyor?   beer ge·*lee*·yor

What's the next stop?
Sonraki durak hangisi?   son·ra·*kee* doo·rak han·gee·see

Does it stop at (Kadıköy)?
(Kadıköy'de) durur mu?   (ka·*duh*·kay·de) doo·*roor* moo

I'd like to get off at (Kadıköy).
(Kadıköy'de) inmek   (ka·*duh*·kay·de) een·*mek*
istiyorum.   ees·*tee*·yo·room

city n	şehir	she·*heer*
dolmuş	dolmuş	dol·*moosh*
intercity a	şehirlerarası	she·heer·*ler*·a·ra·suh
local a	yerel	ye·*rel*
midibus	midibüs	mee·dee·*bews*
minibus	minibüs	mee·nee·*bews*
municipal bus	belediye otobüsü	be·le·dee·ye o·to·bew·*sew*
private bus	özel otobüs	er·*zel* o·to·*bews*
shuttle bus	servis otobüsü	ser·*vees* o·to·bew·*sew*

For bus numbers, see **numbers & amounts**, page 35.

train

What station is this?
Bu hangi istasyon?   boo *han*·gee ees·tas·*yon*

What's the next station?
Sonraki istasyon   son·ra·*kee* ees·tas·*yon*
hangisi?   *han*·gee·see

Does it stop at (Maltepe)?
(Maltepe'de) durur mu?   (*mal*·te·pe·de) doo·*roor* moo

transport

Do I need to change?	Aktarma yapmam gerekli mi?	ak·tar·ma yap·mam ge·rek·lee mee
Is it ...?	... mi?	... mee
direct	Aktarmasız gider	ak·tar·ma·suhz gee·der
express	Ekspres	eks·pres
Which carriage is (for) ...?	Hangisi ... vagon?	han·gee·see ... va·gon
1st class	birinci mevki	bee·reen·jee mev·kee
dining	yemekli	ye·mek·lee
Pullman (reclining seats)	pulman	pool·man
I'd like a ... compartment.	... kuşet istiyorum.	... koo·shet ees·tee·yo·room
European-style sleeping	Örtülü	er·tew·lew
four-bed couchette	Dört yataklı bir	dert ya·tak·luh beer
six-bed couchette	Altı kişilik bir	al·tuh kee·shee·leek beer

boat

vapur

What's the sea like today?
Bugün deniz nasıl? — boo·gewn de·neez na·suhl

Are there life jackets?
Can yeleği var mı? — jan ye·le·ee var muh

What island/beach is this?
Bu hangi ada/sahil? — boo han·gee a·da/sa·heel

I feel seasick.
Deniz tutuyor. — de·neez too·too·yor

cabin	kamara	ka·*ma*·ra
captain	kaptan	kap·*tan*
car deck	araba güvertesi	a·ra·*ba* gew·ver·te·*see*
car ferry	araba vapuru	a·ra·*ba* va·poo·*roo*
cruise n	gemi gezisi	ge·*mee* ge·zee·*see*
deck	güverte	gew·ver·*te*
ferry	feribot	fe·ree·*bot*
hammock	hamak	ha·*mak*
lifeboat	filika	fee·lee·*ka*
life jacket	can yeleği	jan ye·le·*ee*
yacht	yat	yat

taxi

taksi

I'd like a taxi ...	... bir taksi istiyorum.	... beer tak·*see* ees·tee·yo·room
at 9am	Sabah dokuzda	sa·*bah* do·kooz·*da*
now	Hemen	*he*·men
tomorrow	Yarın	*ya*·ruhn

Where's the taxi rank?
Taksi durağı nerede? — tak·*see* doo·ra·*uh* ne·re·de

Is this taxi available?
Bu taksi boş mu? — boo tak·*see* bosh moo

Please put the meter on.
Lütfen taksimetreyi çalıştırın. — *lewt*·fen tak·*see*·met·re·yee cha·luhsh·*tuh*·ruhn

How much is it (to Şişli)?
(Şişli'ye) Ne kadar? — (*sheesh*·lee·ye) ne ka·*dar*

I agree to pay that amount.
Bu fiyatı ödemeyi kabul ediyorum. — boo fee·ya·*tuh* er·de·me·*yee* ka·*bool* e·*dee*·yo·room

I won't pay a flat fare.
Sabit ücret ödemeyi reddediyorum. — sa·*beet* ewj·*ret* er·de·me·*yee* red·de·*dee*·yo·room

t
r
a
n
s
p
o
r
t

55

I'm going to complain to the police.
Sizi polise şikayet   see·*zee* po·lee·*se* shee·ka·*yet*
edeceğim.   e·de·*je*·eem

Please take me to (this address).
Lütfen beni (bu adrese)   *lewt*·fen be·*nee* (boo ad·re·*se*)
götürün.   ger·*tew*·rewn

Please ...	*Lütfen ...*	*lewt*·fen ...
slow down	*yavaşlayın*	ya·vash·*la*·yuhn
stop here	*burada durun*	boo·ra·*da* doo·roon
wait here	*burada*	boo·ra·*da*
	bekleyin	bek·*le*·yeen

For other useful phrases, see **directions**, page 63.

car & motorbike

car & motorbike hire

I'd like to hire a/an ...	*Bir ... kiralamak istiyorum.*	beer ... kee·ra·la·*mak* ees·*tee*·yo·room
4WD	*dört çeker*	dert che·*ker*
automatic	*otomatik*	o·to·ma·*teek*
	vitesli araba	vee·tes·*lee* a·ra·ba
car	*araba*	a·ra·ba
driver	*şoför*	sho·*fer*
manual	*vitesli araba*	vee·tes·*lee* a·ra·ba
motorbike	*motosiklet*	mo·to·seek·*let*

How much for ... hire?	*... kirası ne kadar?*	... kee·ra·*suh* ne ka·*dar*
daily	*Günlük*	gewn·*lewk*
weekly	*Haftalık*	haf·ta·*luhk*

Does that include insurance/mileage?
Buna sigorta/kilometre   boo·*na* see·*gor*·ta/kee·*lo*·met·re
dahil mi?   da·*heel* mee

Do you have a guide to the road rules (in English)?
  (İngilizce) Yol kuralları   (een·gee·*leez*·je) yol koo·ral·la·*ruh*
  kitabınız var mı?   kee·ta·buh·*nuhz* var muh

Do you have a road map?
  Yol haritanız var mı?   yol ha·ree·ta·*nuhz* var muh

on the road

What's the speed limit?
  Hız sınırı nedir?   huhz suh·nuh·*ruh* ne·deer

Is this the road to (Taksim)?
  (Taksim'e) giden   (tak·see·me) gee·*den*
  yol bu mu?   yol boo moo

Where's a petrol station?
  Benzin istasyonu nerede?   ben·*zeen* ees·tas·yo·*noo* ne·re·de

Please fill it up.
  Lütfen depoyu doldurun.   *lewt*·fen de·po·*yoo* dol·*doo*·roon

I'd like (20) litres.
  (Yirmi) litre istiyorum.   (yeer·*mee*) *leet*·re ees·*tee*·yo·room

diesel	*dizel*	dee·*zel*
leaded	*kurşunlu*	koor·shoon·*loo*
LPG	*LPG*	le·pe·*ge*
regular	*normal*	nor·*mal*
premium	*birinci kalite*	bee·reen·*jee* ka·lee·*te*
unleaded	*kurşunsuz*	koor·shoon·*sooz*
unleaded	*kurşunsuz*	koor·shoon·*sooz*
Can you	*Lütfen ... kontrol*	*lewt*·fen ... kon·*trol*
check the ...?	*eder misiniz?*	e·*der* mee·see·*neez*
oil	*yağını*	ya·uh·*nuh*
tyre pressure	*lastikleri*	las·teek·le·*ree*
water	*suyunu*	soo·yoo·*noo*

ehliyet	eh·lee·*yet*	**drivers licence**
kilometre	kee·*lo*·met·re	**kilometres**
parkmetre	*park*·met·re	**parking meter**
ücretsiz	ewj·ret·*seez*	**free**

How long can I park here?
    Buraya ne kadar süre   boo·ra·*ya* ne ka·*dar* sew·*re*
    park edebilirim?   park e·*de*·bee·lee·reem

Do I have to pay?
    Park ücreti ödemem   park ewj·re·*tee* er·de·*mem*
    gerekli mi?   ge·rek·*lee* mee

problems

I need a mechanic.
    Tamirciye ihtiyacım var.   ta·meer·jee·*ye* eeh·tee·ya·*juhm* var

I've had an accident.
    Kaza yaptım.   ka·*za* yap·*tuhm*

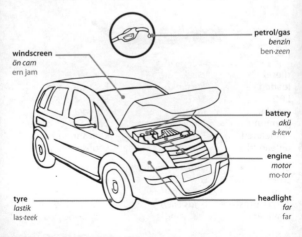

petrol/gas
benzin
ben·*zeen*

windscreen
ön cam
ern jam

battery
akü
a·*kew*

engine
motor
mo·*tor*

tyre
lastik
las·*teek*

headlight
far
far

The car/motorbike has broken down (at Osmanbey).
Arabam/motosikletim   a·ra·*bam*/mo·to·seek·le·*teem*
(Osmanbey'de) bozuldu.   (os·*man*·bay·de) bo·zool·*doo*

The car/motorbike won't start.
Arabam/motosikletim   a·ra·*bam*/mo·to·seek·le·*teem*
çalışmıyor.   cha·*luhsh*·muh·yor

I have a flat tyre.
Lastiğim patladı.   las·tee·*eem* pat·la·*duh*

I've lost my car keys.
Anahtarlarımı kaybettim.   a·nah·tar·la·ruh·*muh* kai·bet·*teem*

I've locked the keys inside.
Anahtarlarımı   a·nah·tar·la·ruh·*muh*
içeride unuttum.   ee·che·ree·*de* oo·noot·*toom*

I've run out of petrol.
Benzinim bitti.   ben·zee·*neem* beet·*tee*

Can you fix it (today)?
(Bugün) Tamir   (*boo*·gewn) ta·*meer*
edebilir misiniz?   e·*de*·bee·leer mee·see·*neez*

How long will it take?
Ne kadar sürer?   ne ka·*dar* sew·*rer*

signs

Dur	door	Stop
Girilmez	gee·*reel*·mez	No Entry
Giriş	gee·*reesh*	Entrance
Otoban	o·to·*ban*	Motorway
Otoban Çıkışı	o·to·*ban* chuh·kuh·*shuh*	Exit Freeway
Otoyol	o·*to*·yol	Expressway
Otoyol Gişeleri	o·*to*·yol gee·she·le·*ree*	Toll Booths
Paralı Yol	pa·ra·*luh* yol	Toll Highway
Park Yeri	park ye·*ree*	Parking Garage
Şehir Merkezi	she·*heer* mer·ke·*zee*	City Centre
Tek Yön	tek yern	One Way
Ücret Ödenir	ewj·*ret* er·de·*neer*	Toll Collection
Yavaş	ya·*vash*	Slow Down
Yol Ver	yol ver	Give Way

transport

bicycle

bisiklet

I'd like ...	... istiyorum.	... ees·tee·yo·room
my bicycle	Bisikletimin	bee·seek·le·tee·meen
repaired	tamir	ta·meer
	edilmesini	e·deel·me·see·nee
to buy a bicycle	Bisiklet almak	bee·seek·let al·mak
to hire a bicycle	Bisiklet	bee·seek·let
	kiralamak	kee·ra·la·mak

I'd like a ... bike.	Bir ... istiyorum.	beer ... ees·tee·yo·room
mountain	dağ bisikleti	da bee·seek·le·tee
racing	yarış	ya·ruhsh
	bisikleti	bee·seek·le·tee
second-hand	ikinci-el	ee·keen·je·el
	bisiklet	bee·seek·let

How much is it per ...?	... ne kadar?	... ne ka·dar
day	Günlüğü	gewn·lew·ew
hour	Saati	sa·a·tee

Do I need a helmet?
Kask takmam gerekli mi?   kask tak·mam ge·rek·lee mee

Are there bicycle paths?
Bisiklet yolu var mı?   bee·seek·let yo·loo var muh

Is there a bicycle-path map?
Bisiklet yolu haritası   bee·seek·let yo·loo ha·ree·ta·suh
var mı?   var muh

I have a puncture.
Lastiğim patladı.   las·tee·eem pat·la·duh

---

traffic monsters

Prominent road signs advise drivers *İçinizdeki trafik canavarını control edin!* ee·chee·neez·de·kee tra·feek ja·na·va·ruh·nuh kon·trol e·deen (Control the Traffic Monster Inside You!).

border crossing

sınırdan geçerken

I'm ...	*Ben ...*	ben ...
in transit	*transit yolcuyum*	tran·*seet* yol·*joo*·yoom
on business	*iş gezisindeyim*	eesh ge·zee·seen·*de*·yeem
on holiday	*tatildeyim*	ta·teel·*de*·yeem

I'm here for ...	*Ben ... buradayım.*	ben ... boo·ra·*da*·yuhm
(10) days	*(on) günlüğüne*	(on) gewn·lew·ew·*ne*
(three) weeks	*(üç) haftalığına*	(ewch) haf·ta·luh·uh·*na*
(two) months	*(iki) aylığına*	(ee·*kee*) ai·luh·uh·*na*

I'm going to (Sarıyer).
(Sarıyer'e) gidiyorum.   (sa·*ruh*·ye·re) gee·dee·*yo*·room

I'm staying at (the Divan).
(Divan'da) kalıyorum.   (*dee*·van·da) ka·luh·*yo*·room

The children are on this passport.
Çocuklar bu pasaportta yazılı.   cho·jook·*lar* boo pa·sa·port·ta ya·zuh·*luh*

listen for ...		
aile	a·ee·*le*	**family**
gurup	goo·*roop*	**group**
pasaport	pa·sa·*port*	**passport**
vize	*vee*·ze	**visa**
yalnız	yal·*nuhz*	**alone**

at customs

I have nothing to declare.
Beyan edecek   be·*yan* e·de·*jek*
hiçbir şeyim yok.   *heech*·beer she·*yeem* yok

I have something to declare.
Beyan edecek bir şeyim var.   be·*yan* e·de·*jek* beer she·*yeem* var

Do I have to declare this?
Bunu beyan   boo·*noo* be·*yan*
etmem gerekli mi?   et·*mem* ge·rek·*lee* mee

That's (not) mine.
Bu benim (değil).   boo be·*neem* (de·*eel*)

I didn't know I had to declare it.
Bunu beyan etmem   boo·*noo* be·*yan* et·*mem*
gerektiğini   ge·rek·tee·ee·*nee*
bilmiyordum.   *beel*·mee·yor·doom

I didn't realise I couldn't take this out of the country.
Bunu ülkeden   boo·*noo* ewl·ke·*den*
çıkaramıyacağımı   chuh·ka·*ra*·muh·ya·ja·uh·muh
bilmiyordum.   *beel*·mee·yor·doom

I have permission to take this out of the country.
Bunu ülkeden   boo·*noo* ewl·ke·*den*
çıkarma iznim var.   chuh·kar·*ma* eez·*neem* var

For phrases on payments and receipts, see **money**, page 45.

signs

Göçmen Bürosu	gerch·*men* bew·ro·*soo*	**Immigration**
Gümrük	gewm·*rewk*	**Customs**
Gümrüksüz	gewm·rewk·*sewz*	**Duty-Free**
Satış	sa·*tuhsh*	
Karantina	ka·ran·tee·*na*	**Quarantine**
Pasaport	pa·sa·*port*	**Passport Control**
Kontrolü	kon·tro·*lew*	

directions
yön bildirme

Where's (the tourist office)?
(Turizm bürosu) nerede?   (too·reezm bew·ro·soo) ne·re·de

What's the address?
Adresi nedir?   ad·re·see ne·deer

How do I get there?
Oraya nasıl   o·ra·ya na·suhl
gidebilirim?   gee·de·bee·lee·reem

How far is it?
Ne kadar uzakta?   ne ka·dar oo·zak·ta

Can you show me (on the map)?
Bana (haritada)   ba·na (ha·ree·ta·da)
gösterebilir misiniz?   gers·te·re·bee·leer mee·seen·neez

It's ...

close	*Yakın.*	ya·kuhn
here	*Burada.*	boo·ra·da
on the corner	*Köşede.*	ker·she·de
straight ahead	*Tam karşıda.*	tam kar·shuh·da
there	*Şurada.*	shoo·ra·da

It's ...

behind ...	*... arkasında.*	... ar·ka·suhn·da
in front of ...	*... önünde.*	... er·newn·de
near ...	*... yakınında.*	... ya·kuh·nuhn·da
next to ...	*... yanında.*	... ya·nuhn·da
opposite ...	*... karşısında.*	... kar·shuh·suhn·da

listen for ...

dakika	da·kee·ka	**minutes**
kilometre	kee·lo·met·re	**kilometres**
metre	met·re	**metres**

directions

north	*kuzey*	koo·*zay*
south	*güney*	gew·*nay*
east	*doğu*	do·*oo*
west	*batı*	ba·*tuh*
Turn ...	*... dön.*	... dern
at the corner	*Köşeden*	ker·she·*den*
at the	*Trafik*	tra·*feek*
traffic lights	*ışıklarından*	uh·shuhk·la·ruhn·*dan*
left	*Sola*	so·*la*
right	*Sağa*	sa·*a*
What ... is this?	*Bu hangi ...?*	boo *han*·gee ...
avenue	*cadde*	jad·*de*
boulevard	*bulvar*	bool·*var*
lane	*ara sokak*	a·*ra* so·*kak*
square	*meydan*	may·*dan*
street	*sokak*	so·*kak*
village	*köy*	kay

For information on Turkish addresses, see the box on page 72.

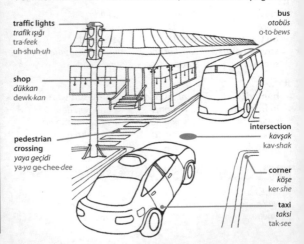

traffic lights
trafik ışığı
tra·*feek*
uh·shuh·*uh*

bus
otobüs
o·to·*bews*

shop
dükkan
dewk·*kan*

intersection
kavşak
kav·*shak*

pedestrian crossing
yaya geçidi
ya·*ya* ge·chee·*dee*

corner
köşe
ker·*she*

taxi
taksi
tak·*see*

finding accommodation

kalacak yer ararken

Where's a ...?	*Buralarda nerede ... var?*	boo·ra·lar·*da* ne·re·de ... var
bed and breakfast	*yatacak yer ve kahvaltı veren bir yer*	ya·ta·*jak* yer ve kah·val·*tuh* ve·*ren* beer yer
camping ground	*kamp yeri*	kamp ye·*ree*
guesthouse	*misafirhane*	mee·*sa*·feer·ha·ne
hotel	*otel*	o·*tel*
(one)-star hotel	*(bir) yıldızlı otel*	(beer) yuhl·duhz·*luh* o·*tel*
pension	*pansiyon*	pan·see·*yon*
room in a private home	*kiralık oda*	kee·ra·*luhk* o·*da*
tree house	*ağaç ev*	a·*ach* ev
youth hostel	*gençlik hosteli*	gench·*leek* hos·te·*lee*

Can you recommend somewhere ...?	*... bir yer tavsiye edebilir misiniz?*	... beer yer tav·see·ye e·*de*·bee·leer mee·see·*neez*
cheap	*Ucuz*	oo·*jooz*
good	*İyi*	ee·*yee*
luxurious	*Lüks*	lewks
nearby	*Yakın*	ya·*kuhn*
romantic	*Romantik*	ro·man·*teek*
safe for women travellers	*Bayanlar için emniyetli*	ba·yan·*lar* ee·*cheen* em·nee·yet·*lee*

What's the address?	*Adresi nedir?*	ad·re·*see* ne·deer

For responses, see **directions**, page 63, and also page 72 of this chapter.

booking ahead & checking in

I'd like to book a room, please.
Bir oda ayırtmak
istiyorum lütfen.
beer o·*da* a·yuhrt·*mak*
ees·*tee*·yo·room *lewt*·fen

I have a reservation.
Rezervasyonum var.
re·zer·vas·yo·*noom* var

My name's ...
Benim ismim ...
be·*neem* ees·*meem* ...

For (three) nights/weeks.
(Üç) geceliğine/
haftalığına.
(ewch) ge·je·lee·ee·*ne*/
haf·ta·luh·uh·*na*

From (2 July) to (6 July).
(2 Temmuz'dan)
(6 Temmuz'a) kadar.
(ee·*kee* tem·mooz·dan)
(al·*tuh* tem·moo·za) ka·*dar*

Do I need to pay upfront?
Ön ödeme yapmam
gerekli mi?
ern er·de·*me* yap·*mam*
ge·rek·*lee* mee

Do you have a ... room?	... *odanız* *var mı?*	... o·da·*nuhz* var muh
single	*Tek kişilik*	tek kee·shee·*leek*
double	*İki kişilik*	ee·*kee* kee·shee·*leek*
twin	*Çift yataklı*	cheeft ya·tak·*luh*

How much is it per ...?	... *ne kadar?*	... ne ka·*dar*
night	*Geceliği*	ge·je·lee·*ee*
person	*Kişi başına*	kee·*shee* ba·shuh·*na*
week	*Haftalığı*	haf·ta·luh·*uh*

signs		
banyo	*ban*·yo	**bathroom**
boş oda	bosh o·*da*	**vacancy**
boş yer yok	bosh yer yok	**no vacancy**

Can I see it?	Görebilir miyim.	ger·re·bee·leer mee·yeem
I'll take it.	Tutuyorum.	too·too·yo·room
Can I pay by ...?	... ile ödeyebilir miyim?	... ee·le er·de·ye·bee·leer mee·yeem
credit card	Kredi kartı	kre·dee kar·tuh
travellers cheque	Seyahat çeki	se·ya·hat che·kee

For other methods of payment, see **money**, page 45, and **banking**, page 89.

For other methods of payment, see money, page 45, and banking, page 89.

---

listen for ...

Kaç gece için?	kach ge·je ee·cheen	How many nights?
anahtar	a·nah·tar	key
dolu	do·loo	full
pasaport	pa·sa·port	passport
resepsiyon	re·sep·see·yon	reception

---

requests & queries

ricalar & sorular

When/Where is breakfast served?
Kahvaltı ne zaman/
nerede veriliyor?
kah·val·tuh ne za·man/
ne·re·de ve·ree·lee·yor

Is breakfast included?
Kahvaltı dahil mi?
kah·val·tuh da·heel mee

Please wake me at (seven).
Lütfen beni
(yedide) kaldırın.
lewt·fen be·nee
(ye·dee·de) kal·duh·ruhn

Can I use the ...?	... kullanabilir miyim?	... kool·la·na·bee·leer mee·yeem
kitchen	Mutfağı	moot·fa·uh
laundry	Çamaşırlığı	cha·ma·shuhr·luh·uh
telephone	Telefonu	te·le·fo·noo

a knock at the door ...

Who is it?	Kim o?	keem o
Just a moment.	Bir dakika.	beer da·kee·ka
Come in.	Girin.	gee·reen
Come back later, please.	Lütfen sonra gelin.	lewt·fen son·ra ge·leen

Do you have a/an ...?	... var mı?	... var muh
elevator	Asansör	a·san·ser
laundry service	Çamaşır yıkama hizmetiniz	cha·ma·shuhr yuh·ka·ma heez·me·tee·neez
message board	İlan panonuz	ee·lan pa·no·nooz
safe	Kasanız	ka·sa·nuhz
swimming pool	Yüzme havuzu	yewz·me ha·voo·zoo

Do you ... here?	Burada ... musunuz?	boo·ra·da ... moo·soo·nooz
arrange tours	tur düzenliyor	toor dew·zen·lee·yor
change money	döviz bozuyor	der·veez bo·zoo·yor

Could I have (a) ..., please?	... alabilir miyim?	... a·la·bee·leer mee·yeem
my key	Anahtarımı	a·nah·ta·ruh·muh
mosquito net	Cibinlik	jee·been·leek
receipt	Makbuz	mak·booz

Is there a message for me?
Bana mesaj var mı?   ba·na me·sazh var muh

Can I leave a message for someone?
Birisi için mesaj bırakabilir miyim?   bee·ree·see ee·cheen me·sazh buh·ra·ka·bee·leer mee·yeem

I'm locked out of my room.
Dışarıda kaldım.   duh·sha·ruh·da kal·duhm

complaints

şikayetler

It's too …	Çok …	chok …
bright	aydınlık	ai·duhn·*luhk*
cold	soğuk	so·*ook*
dark	karanlık	ka·ran·*luhk*
expensive	pahalı	pa·ha·*luh*
noisy	gürültülü	gew·rewl·tew·*lew*
small	küçük	kew·*chewk*

The … doesn't work.	… çalışmıyor.	… cha·*luhsh*·muh·yor
air conditioning	Klima	*klee*·ma
fan	Fan	fan
toilet	Tuvalet	too·va·*let*

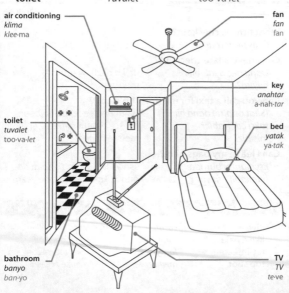

air conditioning
klima
klee·ma

fan
fan
fan

key
anahtar
a·nah·*tar*

toilet
tuvalet
too·va·*let*

bed
yatak
ya·*tak*

bathroom
banyo
ban·yo

TV
TV
te·ve

Can I get another (blanket)?
 Başka bir (battaniye) bash·ka beer (bat·ta·nee·ye)
 alabilir miyim? a·la·bee·leer mee·yeem

This (pillow) isn't clean.
 Bu (yastık) temiz değil. boo (yas·tuhk) te·meez de·eel

There's no hot water.
 Sıcak su yok. suh·jak soo yok

checking out

What time is checkout?
 Çıkış ne zaman? chuh·kuhsh ne za·man

Can I have a late checkout?
 Daha geç ayrılabilir da·ha gech ay·ruh·la·bee·leer
 miyim? mee·yeem

Can you call a taxi for me (for 11 o'clock)?
 (Saat onbire) bana bir (sa·at on·bee·re) ba·na beer
 taksi çağırabilir tak·see cha·uh·ra·bee·leer
 misiniz? mee·seen·neez

Can I leave my bags here?
 Eşyalarımı burada esh·ya·la·ruh·muh boo·ra·da
 bırakabilir miyim? buh·ra·ka·bee·leer mee·yeem

local talk		
dive n	*vasat*	va·sat
like a palace	*saray gibi*	sa·rai gee·bee
rat-infested	*fare yuvası*	fa·re yoo·va·suh
top spot	*merkezi yer*	mer·ke·zee yer

PRACTICAL

70

I'm leaving now.
   Şimdi ayrılıyorum.   *sheem·*dee ai·ruh·*luh·*yo·room

There's a mistake in the bill.
   Hesapta bir yanlışlık var.   he·sap·*ta* beer yan·luhsh·*luhk* var

I had a great stay, thank you.
   Çok rahat ettim,   chok ra·*hat* et·*teem*
   teşekkürler.   te·shek·kewr·*ler*

I'll recommend it to my friends.
   Arkadaşlarıma burayı   ar·ka·dash·la·ruh·*ma* boo·ra·*yuh*
   tavsiye edeceğim.   tav·see·*ye* e·de·je·eem

Could I have	*... alabilir*	*... a·la·*bee·leer
my ... please?	*miyim lütfen?*	mee·*yeem* lewt·fen
deposit	*Depozitomu*	de·po·zee·to·*moo*
passport	*Pasaportumu*	pa·sa·por·too·*moo*
valuables	*Değerli*	de·er·*lee*
	eşyalarımı	esh·ya·la·ruh·*muh*

I'll be back ...	*... geri döneceğim.*	*... ge·*ree der·ne·je·eem
in (three) days	*(Üç) gün*	(ewch) gewn
	içinde	ee·cheen·de
on (Tuesday)	*(Salı) günü*	(sa·luh) gew·new

camping

Do you have	*... var mı?*	*... var muh*
(a) ...?		
electricity	*Elektrik*	e·lek·*treek*
laundry	*Çamaşırhane*	cha·ma·shuhr·ha·ne
shower facilities	*Duş imkanı*	doosh eem·ka·*nuh*
site	*Yer*	yer
tents for hire	*Kiralık çadır*	kee·ra·*luhk* cha·duhr

In Turkish addresses, the street name comes first and is followed by the house or street number. The street and floor numbers are separated by a *taksim* tak·seem (slash), then comes the apartment number, suburb, city and country. *Kat* kat means 'floor' and *daire* da·ee·re (written as *D:* as in the example below) means 'apartment'. A building's *zemin kat* ze·meen kat (ground floor) is always marked 'Z'. So apartment 21 on the 5th floor of 1137 Mithatpaşa Avenue in the suburb of Güzelyalı in İzmir is written as:

Mithatpaşa Cad. No:1137/5 D:21
Güzelyalı 35290
İzmir-Türkiye

How much	… *başına ücreti*	… ba·shuh·na ewj·re·tee
is it per …?	*ne kadar?*	ne ka·dar
caravan	*Karavan*	ka·ra·van
person	*Kişi*	kee·shee
tent	*Çadır*	cha·duhr
vehicle	*Araç*	a·rach

Can I …?	… *miyim?*	… mee·yeem
camp here	*Burada kamp*	boo·ra·da kamp
	yapabilir	ya·pa·bee·leer
park next to	*Çadırımın*	cha·duh·ruh·muhn
my tent	*yanına*	ya·nuh·na
	park edebilir	park e·de·bee·leer

Who do I ask to stay here?
Burada kalmak için   boo·ra·da kal·mak ee·cheen
kimden izin alabilirim?   keem·den ee·zeen a·la·bee·lee·reem

Is it coin-operated?
Madeni parayla   ma·de·nee pa·rai·la
mı çalışıyor?   muh cha·luh·shuh·yor

Is the water drinkable?
Su içilebilir mi?   soo ee·chee·le·bee·leer mee

renting

kalacak yer kiralarken

I'm here about the ... for rent.	Kiralık ... için buradayım.	kee·ra·luhk ... ee·cheen boo·ra·da·yuhm
Do you have a/an ... for rent?	Kiralık ... var mı?	kee·ra·luhk ... var muh
apartment	daireniz	da·ee·re·neez
cabin	kabininiz	ka·bee·nee·neez
house	eviniz	e·vee·neez
room	odanız	o·da·nuhz
villa	villanız	veel·la·nuhz
(partly) furnished	(yarı) mobilyalı	(ya·ruh) mo·beel·ya·luh
unfurnished	mobilyasız	mo·beel·ya·suhz

staying with locals

yöre halkına misafir olurken

Can I stay at your place?
Sizde kalabilir miyim?   seez·de ka·la·bee·leer mee·yeem

Is there anything I can do to help?
Benim yapabileceğim   be·neem ya·pa·bee·le·je·eem
birşey var mı?   beer·shay var muh

I have my own ...	Kendi ... var.	ken·dee ... var
mattress	şiltem	sheel·tem
sleeping bag	uyku tulumum	ooy·koo too·loo·moom

> ### visiting etiquette
>
> When visiting someone, it's polite to offer gifts of fine whisky or liqueurs to your host (if you're sure they drink alcohol), chocolates, a scarf or flowers to your hostess and chocolates or small toys to any children. In business situations items for the office, such as good quality pens with your company's logo, will be appreciated.

accommodation

73

Turks eat three sit-down meals a day, and all family members
generally attend. If you're staying with a family they'll expect
you to eat with them unless you've told them otherwise.

When you sit down to share a meal, say *Kesenize bereket!*
ke·se·nee·ze be·re·ket (May it contribute to your wealth!) or
Elinize sağlık! e·lee·nee·ze sa·luhk (Health to your hand!) to
thank your host or hostess for their generosity.

Can I ...?	... miyim?	... mee·yeem
bring anything	*Yemek için*	ye·mek ee·cheen
for the meal	*birşeyler*	beer·shay·ler
	getirebilir	ge·tee·re·bee·leer
do the dishes	*Bulaşığı*	boo·la·shuh·uh
	yıkayabilir	yuh·ka·ya·bee·leer
set/clear	*Sofrayı*	sof·ra·yuh
the table	*kurabilir/*	koo·ra·bee·leer/
	kaldırabilir	kal·duh·ra·bee·leer
take out	*Çöpleri*	cherp·le·ree
the rubbish	*çıkarabilir*	chuh·ka·ra·bee·leer

Thanks for your hospitality.
  Misafirperverliğiniz   mee·sa·feer·per·ver·lee·ee·neez
  için çok teşekkürler.   ee·cheen chok te·shek·kewr·ler

The food was delicious.
  Yiyecekler nefisti.   yee·ye·jek·ler ne·fees·tee

To compliment your hosts' cooking, see **eating out**, page 155.

PRACTICAL

looking for ...

Where's a (carpet shop)?
Buralarda (halıcı)
nerede var?
boo·ra·lar·*da* (ha·luh·*juh*)
ne·re·de var

Where's the (bazaar)?
(Pazar yeri) nerede?
(pa·*zar* ye·*ree*) *ne·re·de*

Where can I buy (a padlock)?
Nereden (asma kilit)
alabilirim?
ne·re·den (as·*ma* kee·*leet*)
a·*la*·bee·lee·reem

For more items and shopping locations, see the **dictionary**. For
directions, see page 63, and address information on page 72.

making a purchase

I'm just looking.
Sadece bakıyorum.
sa·de·*je* ba·*kuh*·yo·room

I'd like to buy (an adaptor plug).
(Adaptör priz) almak
istiyorum.
(a·dap·*ter* preez) al·*mak*
ees·*tee*·yo·room

How much is it?
Ne kadar?
ne ka·*dar*

Can you write down the price?
Fiyatı yazabilir
misiniz?
fee·ya·*tuh* ya·*za*·bee·leer
mee·see·*neez*

Do you have any others?
Başka var mı?
bash·*ka* var muh

Can I look at it?
Bakabilir miyim?
ba·*ka*·bee·leer mee·*yeem*

bargain n	*pazarlık*	pa·zar·*luhk*
rip off	*kazıklamak*	ka·zuhk·la·*mak*
sale	*indirimli satış*	een·dee·reem·*lee* sa·*tuhsh*
specials	*özel indirim*	er·*zel* een·dee·*reem*

Do you accept ...?	... *kabul ediyor musunuz?*	... ka·*bool* e·*dee*·yor moo·soo·*nooz*
credit cards	*Kredi kartı*	*kre*·dee kar·*tuh*
debit cards	*Banka kartı*	*ban*·ka kar·*tuh*
travellers cheques	*Seyahat çeki*	se·ya·*hat* che·*kee*

Could I have a ..., please?	... *alabilir miyim lütfen?*	... a·*la*·bee·leer mee·*yeem* lewt·fen
bag	*Poşet*	po·*shet*
receipt	*Makbuz*	mak·*booz*

I don't need a bag, thanks.
Teşekkür ederim, poşet istemiyorum.
tesh·shek·*kewr* e·*de*·reem po·*shet* ees·te·*mee*·yo·room

Could I have it wrapped?
Sarabilir misiniz?
sa·*ra*·bee·leer mee·see·*neez*

Does it have a guarantee?
Garantisi var mı?
ga·ran·tee·*see* var muh

Can I have it sent abroad?
Yurt dışına gönderebilir misiniz?
yoort duh·shuh·*na* gern·de·*re*·bee·leer mee·see·*neez*

Can you order it for me?
Benim için sipariş eder misiniz?
be·*neem* ee·*cheen* see·pa·*reesh* e·*der* mee·see·*neez*

Can I pick it up later?
Daha sonra alabilir miyim? da·ha son·ra a·*la*·bee·leer mee·*yeem*

It's faulty. (for clothes)
Defolu.
de·fo·*loo*

It doesn't work. (for electrical/mechanical goods)
Arızalı.
a·ruh·za·*luh*

The quality isn't good.
Kalitesi iyi değil.   ka·lee·te·*see* ee·*yee* de·*eel*

I'd like …,	*… istiyorum*	*… ees·tee·yo·*
please.	*lütfen.*	*lewt·*fen.
my change	*Paramın*	pa·ra·*muhn*
	üstünü	ews·tew·*new*
a refund	*Para iadesi*	pa·*ra* ee·a·de·*see*
to return this	*Bunu iade*	boo·*noo* ee·a·*de*
	etmek	et·*mek*

bargaining

pazarlık ederken

That's too expensive.
Bu çok pahalı.   boo chok pa·ha·*luh*

Is that your lowest price?
Son fiyatınız bu mu?   son fee·ya·tuh·*nuhz* boo moo

Do you have something cheaper?
Daha ucuz birşey var mı?   da·*ha* oo·*jooz* beer·*shay* var muh

I'll give you (30 lira).
(Otuz lira) veririm.   (o·*tooz* lee·*ra*) ve·*ree*·reem

books & reading

kitaplar & okuma

Do you have …?	*… var mı?*	*… var muh*
a book by	*(Yaşar Kemal'in)*	(ya·*shar* ke·mal·*een*)
(Yaşar Kemal)	*kitabı*	kee·ta·*buh*
an entertainment	*Eğlence rehberi*	e·len·je reh·be·*ree*
guide		

Is there an (English)-	*(İngilizce)*	(een·gee·*leez*·je)
language …?	*… var mı?*	*… var muh*
bookshop	*yayın satan*	ya·*yuhn* sa·*tan*
	bir dükkan	beer dewk·*kan*
section	*bölümü*	ber·lew·*mew*

s
h
o
p
p
i
n
g

I'd like a ...	... istiyorum.	... ees·tee·yo·room
dictionary	Sözlük	serz·lewk
newspaper	(İngilizce)	(een·gee·leez·je)
(in English)	bir gazete	beer ga·ze·te
notepad	Not defteri	not def·te·ree

Can you recommend a book for me?
Tavsiye ettiğiniz   tav·see·ye et·tee·ee·neez
bir kitap var mı?   beer kee·tap var muh

Do you have Lonely Planet guidebooks?
Lonely Planet'in rehber   lon·lee pla·ne·teen reh·ber
kitapları var mı?   kee·tap·la·ruh var muh

carpets

halı

Is it 100% wool?
Yüzde yüz yün mü?   yewz·de yewz yewn mew

Is it a silk-wool blend?
İpek ve yün   ee·pek ve yewn
karışımı mı?   ka·ruh·shuh·muh muh

I don't believe this is pure wool.
Bunun has yün   boo·noon has yewn
olduğuna   ol·doo·oo·na
inanmıyorum.   ee·nan·muh·yo·room

I'd like something with a tighter weave.
Daha sık dokunmuş   da·ha suhk do·koon·moosh
birşey istiyorum.   beer·shay ees·tee·yo·room

Are they natural dyes?
Bunlar doğal boya mı?   boon·lar do·al bo·ya muh

How old is this carpet?
Bu halı kaç yaşında?   boo ha·luh kach ya·shuhn·da

This carpet has been patched/repainted.
Bu halı yamalanmış/   boo ha·luh ya·ma·lan·muhsh/
boyanmış.   bo·yan·muhsh

clothes

giyim

My size is ...	... beden giyiyorum.	... be·den gee·yee·yo·room
(40)	(Kırk)	(kuhrk)
small	Küçük	kew·chewk
medium	Orta	or·ta
large	Büyük	bew·yewk

Can I try it on?
Deneyebilir miyim? de·ne·ye·bee·leer mee·yeem

It doesn't fit.
Olmuyor. ol·moo·yor

It's not well made.
Kesimi iyi değil. ke·see·mee ee·yee de·eel

For different types of clothing, see the **dictionary**, and for sizes, see **numbers & amounts**, page 35.

electronic goods

elektronik eşyalar

Will this work on any DVD player?
Her DVD'de çalışır mı? her dee·vee·dee·de cha·luh·shuhr muh

Is this a (PAL/NTSC) system?
Bu (PAL/NTSC) sistem mi? boo (pal/ne·te·se·je) sees·tem mee

Is this the latest model?
Bu en son model mi? boo en son mo·del mee

Is this (240) volts?
Bu (ikiyüzkırk) volt mu? boo (ee·kee·yewz·kuhrk) volt moo

Where can I buy duty-free electronic goods?
Gümrüksüz elektronik eşya nereden alabilirim? gewm·rewk·sewz e·lek·tro·neek esh·ya ne·re·den a·la·bee·lee·reem

shopping

79

Başka birşey var mı?
  bash·*ka* beer·*shay* var muh | **Anything else?**

Hayır, hiç kalmadı.
  ha·yuhr heech *kal*·ma·duh | **No, we don't have any.**

Yardımcı olabilir miyim?
  yar·duhm·*juh* o·*la*·bee·leer
  mee·*yeem* | **Can I help you?**

hairdressing

saç bakımı

I'd like (a) ...	... *istiyorum.*	... ees·*tee*·yo·room
colour	*Saçımı*	sa·chuh·*muh*
	boyatmak	bo·yat·*mak*
haircut	*Saçımı*	sa·chuh·*muh*
	kestirmek	kes·teer·*mek*
my beard	*Sakalımı*	sa·ka·luh·*muh*
trimmed	*düzelttirmek*	dew·zelt·teer·*mek*
shave	*Tıraş olmak*	tuh·*rash* ol·*mak*
trim	*Saçımı biraz*	sa·chuh·*muh* bee·*raz*
	kestirmek	kes·teer·*mek*

Don't cut it too short.
  Çok kısa kesmeyin. chok kuh·*sa* kes·me·yeen

Please use a new blade.
  Lütfen yeni jilet kullanın. lewt·fen ye·*nee* jee·*let* kool·*la*·nuhn

Shave it all off!
  Hepsini kes. hep·see·*nee* kes

If your Turkish friend has just had a shave or a haircut, or just emerged from a bath or a shower, you can wish them *Sıhhatler olsun!* suh·hat·*ler* ol·*soon* (Good health to you!).

music

I'd like a ...	... istiyorum.	... ees·tee·yo·room
blank tape	Boş bir kaset	bosh beer ka·set
CD	CD almak	see·dee al·mak
DVD	DVD almak	dee·vee·dee al·mak

I'm looking for something by (Tarkan).
(Tarkan'ın) albümlerine (tar·ka·nuhn) al·bewm·le·ree·ne
bakmak istiyorum. bak·mak ees·tee·yo·room

What's their best recording?
En iyi albümü hangisi? en ee·yee al·bew·mew han·gee·see

Can I listen to this?
Bunu dinleyebilir boo·noo deen·le·ye·bee·leer
miyim? mee·yeem

photography

Can you ...?	... misiniz?	... mee·see·neez
develop digital photos	Dijital fotoğraf basabilir	dee·zhee·tal fo·to·raf ba·sa·bee·leer
develop this film	Bu filmi basabilir	boo feel·mee ba·sa·bee·leer
load my film	Filmi makineye takabilir	feel·mee ma·kee·ne·ye ta·ka·bee·leer
recharge the battery for my digital camera	Dijital kameram için bu pilleri şarj edebilir	dee·zhee·tal ka·me·ram ee·cheen boo peel·le·ree sharzh e·de·bee·leer
transfer photos from my camera to CD	Kameramdaki fotoğrafları CD'ye aktarabilir	ka·me·ram·da·kee fo·to·raf·la·ruh see·dee·ye ak·ta·ra·bee·leer

I need ... film	*Bu kamera için ...*	boo ka·me·*ra* ee·*cheen* ...
for this camera.	*film istiyorum.*	feelm ees·*tee*·yo·room
APS	*APS*	a·pe·*se*
B&W	*siyah-beyaz*	see·*yah*·be·yaz
colour	*renkli*	renk·*lee*
slide	*slayt*	slayt
(200) speed	*(200) hızlı*	(ee·*kee*·yewz) huhz·*luh*

When will it be ready?
Ne zaman hazır olur? ne za·*man* ha·*zuhr* o·*loor*

I need a passport photo taken.
Vesikalık fotoğraf ve·see·ka·*luhk* fo·to·*raf*
çektirmek istiyorum. chek·teer·*mek* ees·*tee*·yo·room

I'm not happy with these photos.
Bu fotoğrafları boo fo·to·raf·la·*ruh*
beğenmedim. be·*en*·me·deem

I don't want to pay the full price.
Fiyatın tamamını fee·ya·*tuhn* ta·ma·muh·*nuh*
ödemek istemiyorum. er·de·*mek* ees·te·*mee*·yo·room

repairs

tamir

Can I have my ...	*... burada tamir*	... boo·ra·*da* ta·*meer*
repaired here?	*ettirebilir*	et·tee·*re*·bee·leer
	miyim?	mee·*yeem*
When can I	*... ne zaman*	... ne za·*man*
pick my ... up?	*alabilirim?*	a·*la*·bee·lee·reem
backpack	*Çantamı*	chan·ta·*muh*
camera	*Kameramı*	ka·me·ra·*muh*
glasses	*Gözlüğümü*	gerz·lew·ew·*mew*
shoes	*Ayakkabımı*	a·yak·ka·buh·*muh*
sunglasses	*Güneş*	gew·*nesh*
	gözlüğümü	gerz·lew·ew·*mew*

PRACTICAL

the internet

internet

Where's the local Internet café?
En yakın internet kafe nerede?
en ya·*kuhn* een·ter·*net* ka·*fe* ne·re·de

I'd like to ...
... istiyorum.
... ees·*tee*·yo·room

    check my email
    E-postama bakmak
    e·pos·ta·ma bak·*mak*

    get Internet access
    İnternete girmek
    een·ter·ne·*te* geer·*mek*

    use a printer/ scanner
    Yazıcıyı/ Tarayıcıyı kullanmak
    ya·zuh·juh·*yuh*/ ta·ra·yuh·juh·*yuh* kool·lan·*mak*

Do you have (a) ...?
... var mı?
... var muh

    PCs *PC* *pee*·see
    Macs *Mac* mak
    Zip drive *Zip drive* zeep draiv

How much per ...?
... ne kadar?
... ne ka·*dar*

    hour *Saati* sa·a·tee
    (five) minutes *(Beş) dakikası* (besh) da·kee·ka·*suh*
    page *Sayfası* sai·fa·*suh*

Please change it to the (English)-language setting.
Lütfen komutları (İngilizce'ye) çevirir misiniz?
lewt·fen ko·moot·la·*ruh* (een·gee·*leez*·je·ye) che·vee·*reer* mee·see·*neez*

Do you have (English) keyboards?
(İngilizce) klavyeniz var mı?
(een·gee·*leez*·je) klav·ye·*neez* var muh

How do I log on?
Nasıl bağlanabilirim?
na·suhl ba·la·*na*·bee·lee·reem

Damn Internet!	*Allah kahretsin şu İnterneti!*	al·*lah* kah·ret·*seen* shoo een·ter·ne·*tee*
It's crashed.	*Kilitlendi.*	kee·leet·len·*dee*
I've finished.	*Bitirdim.*	bee·teer·*deem*

mobile/cell phone

cep telefonu

I'd like a ...	*... istiyorum.*	*... ees·tee·yo·room*
charger for my phone	*Cep telefonum için şarj aleti*	jep te·le·fo·*noom* ee·*cheen* sharzh a·le·*tee*
mobile/cell phone for hire	*Cep telefonu kiralamak*	jep te·le·fo·*noo* kee·ra·la·*mak*
prepaid mobile/ cell phone	*Kontörlü cep telefonu*	kon·ter·*lew* jep te·le·fo·*noo*
SIM card for your network	*Buradaki şebeke için SİM kart*	boo·ra·da·*kee* she·be·*ke* ee·*cheen* seem kart

PRACTICAL

84

What are the rates?
   Ücret tarifesi nedir?   ewj·*ret* ta·ree·fe·*see* ne·deer

(10) *yeni kuruş* per (1) minute.
   (Bir) dakikası   (beer) da·kee·ka·*suh*
   (on) yeni kuruş.   (on) ye·*nee* koo·*roosh*

phone

What's your phone number?
   Telefon numaranız nedir?   te·le·*fon* noo·ma·ra·*nuhz* ne·deer

Where's the nearest public phone?
   En yakın telefon   en ya·*kuhn* te·le·*fon*
   kulübesi nerede?   koo·lew·be·*see* ne·re·de

Can I look at a phone book?
   Telefon rehberine   te·le·*fon* reh·be·ree·*ne*
   bakabilir miyim?   ba·*ka*·bee·leer mee·*yeem*

I want to ...	*... istiyorum.*	*... ees·tee·yo·*room
buy a (100 unit)	*(Yüz kontörlük)*	(yewz kon·ter·*lewk*)
phonecard	*telefon kartı*	te·le·*fon* kar·*tuh*
call (Singapore)	*(Singapur'u)*	(*seen*·ga·poo·roo)
	aramak	a·ra·*mak*
make a	*(Yerel) Bir*	(ye·*rel*) beer
(local) call	*görüşme*	ger·rewsh·*me*
	yapmak	yap·*mak*
reverse the	*Ödemeli*	er·de·me·*lee*
charges	*görüşme*	ger·rewsh·*me*
	yapmak	yap·*mak*
speak for	*(Üç) dakika*	(ewch) da·kee·*ka*
(three) minutes	*konuşmak*	ko·noosh·*mak*

How much	*... ne kadar eder?*	*... ne ka·*dar e·*der*
does ... cost?		
a (three)-	*(Üç) dakikalık*	(ewch) da·kee·ka·*luhk*
minute call	*konuşma*	ko·noosh·*ma*
each extra	*Her ekstra*	her eks·*tra*
minute	*dakika*	da·kee·*ka*

The number is ...
   Telefon numarası ...   te·le·*fon* noo·ma·ra·*suh* ...

What's the area/country code for (New Zealand)?
   (Yeni Zelanda'nın)   (ye·*nee* ze·*lan*·da·nuhn)
   bölge/ülke kodu nedir?   berl·*ge*/ewl·*ke* ko·*doo* ne·deer

It's engaged.
   Hat meşgul.   hat mesh·*gool*

I've been cut off.
   Hat kesildi.   hat ke·seel·*dee*

The connection's bad.
   Bağlantı kötü.   ba·lan·*tuh* ker·*tew*

Hello.   *Alo.*   a·*lo*
It's ...   *Ben ...*   ben ...
Is (Ayşe) there? *(Ayşe) orada mı?* (ai·*she*) o·ra·*da* muh

Please tell him/her I called.
   Lütfen aradığımı   *lewt*·fen a·ra·duh·uh·*muh*
   söyleyin.   say·*le*·yeen

Can I leave a message?
   Mesaj bırakabilir   me·*sazh* buh·ra·*ka*·bee·leer
   miyim?   mee·*yeem*

I don't have a contact number.
   Telefon numaram yok. te·le·*fon* noo·ma·*ram* yok

I'll call back later.
   Daha sonra ararım.   da·*ha* son·ra a·*ra*·ruhm

post office

I want to send a ...	Bir ... göndermek istiyorum.	beer ... gern·der·mek ees·tee·yo·room
fax	faks	faks
letter	mektup	mek·toop
parcel	paket	pa·ket
postcard	kartpostal	kart·pos·tal
I want to buy a/an ...	... satın almak istiyorum.	... sa·tuhn al·mak ees·tee·yo·room
aerogram	hava mektubu	ha·va mek·too·boo
envelope	zarf	zarf
stamp	pul	pool
customs declaration	gümrük beyanı	gewm·rewk be·ya·nuh
domestic	iç	eech
fragile	kırılabilir eşya	kuh·ruh·la·bee·leer esh·ya
international	uluslararası	oo·loos·lar·a·ra·suh
mail n	posta	pos·ta
mailbox	posta kutusu	pos·ta koo·too·soo
postcode	posta kodu	pos·ta ko·doo

Please send it by air/surface mail to (Australia).

Lütfen hava/deniz yoluyla (Avustralya'ya) gönderin.

lewt·fen ha·va/de·neez yo·looy·la (a·voos·tral·ya·ya) gern·de·reen

snail mail		
air a	hava yoluyla	ha·va yo·looy·la
express a	ekspres	eks·pres
registered	taahhütlü	ta·ah·hewt·lew
sea a	deniz yoluyla	de·neez yo·looy·la
surface a	kara veya deniz yoluyla	ka·ra ve·ya de·neez yo·looy·la

87

It contains (souvenirs).
  İçinde (hediyelik   ee·cheen·*de* (he·dee·ye·*leek*
  eşya) var.   esh·*ya*) var

Where's the poste restante section?
  Güdümlü posta   gew·dewm·*lew pos*·ta
  bölümü nerede?   ber·lew·*mew ne*·re·de

Is there any mail for me?
  Bana posta var mı?   ba·*na pos*·ta var muh

---

get with the idiom

I can't bring myself to say it.
  Dilim varmıyor.   dee·*leem* var·muh·*yor*
  (lit: my tongue isn't arriving)

Well said!
  Ağzına sağlık!   a·zuh·*na* sa·*luhk*
  (lit: health to your mouth)

Clean as a whistle.
  Bal dök de yala.   bal derk de ya·*la*
  (lit: pour honey and lick)

Do I smell or something?
  Benim başım kel mi?   be·*neem* ba·*shuhm* kel mee
  (lit: does my head have a bald spot)

He/She couldn't organise a piss-up in a brewery.
  Denize girse kurutur.   de·nee·*ze* geer·*se* koo·roo·*toor*
  (lit: he/she makes the sea dry up if he/she enters it)

He/She can talk the hind legs off a donkey.
  Şiir gibi konuşuyor.   shee·*eer* gee·*bee* ko·noo·shoo·*yor*
  (lit: he/she speaks like a poem)

He/She lies like a pig in mud.
  Bir ayak üstünde bin   beer a·*yak* ews·town·*de* been
  yalan söyler.   ya·*lan* say·*ler*
  (lit: he/she tells thousands of lies on one foot)

Where can I ...?	Nerede ...	ne·re·de ...
	bozdurabilirim?	boz·doo·ra·bee·lee·reem
cash a cheque	çek	chek
change a travellers cheque	seyahat çeki	se·ya·hat che·kee
change money	döviz	der·veez

Where can I ...?	Nerede ...	ne·re·de ...
	çekebilirim?	che·ke·bee·lee·reem
get a cash advance	avans	a·vans
withdraw money	para	pa·ra

Where's (a/an) ...?	Buralarda ... nerede var?	boo·ra·lar·da ... ne·re·de var
automated teller machine	bankamatik	ban·ka·ma·teek
foreign exchange office	döviz bürosu	der·veez bew·ro·soo
post office	postane	pos·ta·ne

What time does the bank open?
Banka ne zaman açılıyor? ban·ka ne za·man a·chuh·luh·yor

---

turkish currency

The currency of Turkey is the Türk Lirası (₺) tewrk lee·ra·*suh* (Turkish Lira), which replaced the *Yeni Türk Lirası* (YTL; New Turkish Lira) that was used between 2005 and 2008. The lira comes in notes of five, 10, 20, 50, 100 and 200, and coins of one, five, 10, 25 and 50 *kuruş* koo·*roosh* and one lira.

banking

Bir problem var.
   beer prob·*lem* var   **There's a problem.**

Bunu yapamayız.
   boo·*noo* ya·*pa*·ma·yuhz   **We can't do that.**

Burayı imzalayın.
   boo·ra·*yuh* eem·za·*la*·yuhn **Sign here, please.**

Hesabınızda para kalmadı.
   he·sa·buh·nuhz·*da*   **You have no funds left.**
   pa·*ra* kal·ma·duh

kimlik   keem·*leek*   **identification**
pasaport   pa·sa·*port*   **passport**

What's the ...?   ... *nedir?*   ... ne·deer
  charge for that   *Ücreti*   ewj·re·*tee*
  exchange rate   *Döviz kuru*   der·*veez* koo·roo

The automated teller machine took my card.
  Bankamatik kartımı aldı.   ban·ka·ma·*teek* kar·tuh·*muh* al·*duh*

I've forgotten my PIN.
  Şifremi unuttum.   sheef·re·*mee* oo·noot·*toom*

Can I use my credit card to withdraw money?
  Kredi kartımla para   kre·dee *kar*·tuhm·la pa·*ra*
  çekebilir miyim?   che·*ke*·bee·leer mee·*yeem*

Has my money arrived yet?
  Param geldi mi?   pa·*ram* gel·*dee* mee

How long will it take to arrive?
  Gelmesi ne kadar sürer?   gel·me·*see* ne ka·*dar* sew·*rer*

For other useful phrases, see **money**, page 45.

tarihi & turistik yerleri gezip görmek

I'd like a/an ...	... istiyorum.	... ees·tee·yo·room
audio set	Kulaklık	koo·lak·luhk
catalogue	Katalog	ka·ta·log
guide	Rehber	reh·ber
guidebook	(İngilizce)	(een·gee·leez·je)
(in English)	Rehber kitap	reh·ber kee·tap
(local) map	(Yerel) Harita	(ye·rel) ha·ree·ta

Do you have	... yerler	... yer·ler
information on	hakkında	hak·kuhn·da
... sights?	bilgi var mı?	beel·gee var muh
cultural	Kültürel	kewl·tew·rel
Graeco-	Roma Yunan	ro·ma yoo·nan
Roman	tarihine ait	ta·ree·hee·ne a·eet
historical	Tarihi	ta·ree·hee
religious	Dini	dee·nee

I'd like to see ...
... görmek istiyorum.   ... ger·mek ees·tee·yo·room

Who made it?
Onu kim yaptı?   o·noo keem yap·tuh

How old is it?
Kaç yaşında?   kach ya·shuhn·da

Could you take a photograph of me?
Benim bir fotoğrafımı   be·neem beer fo·to·ra·fuh·muh
çeker misiniz?   che·ker mee·see·neez

Can I take a photo (of you)?
(Sizin) Bir fotoğrafınızı   (see·zeen) beer fo·to·ra·fuh·nuh·zuh
çekebilir miyim?   che·ke·bee·leer mee·yeem

I'll send you the photograph.
Size foroğrafı   see·ze fo·to·ra·fuh
göndereceğim.   gern·de·re·je·eem

getting in

What time does it open/close?
Saat kaçta açılır/kapanır? sa·*at* kach·*ta* a·chuh·*luhr*/ka·pa·*nuhr*

What's the admission charge?
Giriş ücreti nedir? gee·*reesh* ewj·re·*tee* ne·deer

Is there a discount for ...?	... *indirimi var mı?*	... een·dee·ree·*mee* var muh
children	*Çocuk*	cho·*jook*
families	*Aile*	a·ee·le
groups	*Gurup*	goo·*roop*
older people	*Yaşlılara özel*	yash·luh·la·*ra* er·zel
pensioners	*Emekli*	e·mek·*lee*
students	*Öğrenci*	er·ren·jee

tours

When's the next ...?	*Sonraki ... ne zaman?*	son·ra·*kee* ... ne za·*man*
boat trip	*vapur gezisi*	va·*poor* ge·zee·*see*
day trip	*gündüz turu*	gewn·*dewz* too·*roo*
tour	*tur*	toor

Is ... included?	... *dahil mi?*	... da·*heel* mee
accommodation	*Kalacak yer*	ka·la·*jak* yer
food	*Yemek*	ye·*mek*
transport	*Ulaşım*	oo·la·*shuhm*

The guide will pay.
Tur rehberi ödeyecek. toor reh·be·*ree* er·de·ye·*jek*

How long is the tour?
Tur ne kadar sürer? toor ne ka·*dar* sew·*rer*

What time should we be back?
Saat kaçta dönmeliyiz? sa·*at* kach·*ta* dern·me·*lee*·yeez

doing business

ticaret yaparken

I'm attending a ...	*Bir ...*	beer ...
	katılıyorum.	ka·tuh·*luh*·yo·room
conference	*konferansa*	kon·fe·ran·*sa*
course	*kursa*	koor·*sa*
meeting	*toplantıya*	top·lan·tuh·*ya*
trade fair	*ticaret fuarına*	tee·ja·*ret* foo·a·ruh·*na*

I'm with ...	*... birlikteyim.*	... beer·leek·*te*·yeem
my	*İş*	eesh
colleague(s)	*arkadaşlarımla*	ar·ka·dash·la·*ruhm*·la
(two) others	*Diğer (iki)*	dee·*er* (ee·*kee*)
	kişiyle	kee·*sheey*·le

I'm with (Migros).
(Migros'ta) çalışıyorum.   (meeg·ros·*ta*) cha·luh·*shuh*·yo·room

I'm alone.
Yalnızım.   yal·*nuh*·zuhm

I have an appointment with (Derya).
(Derya Hanım) ile   (der·*ya* ha·*nuhm*) ee·*le*
randevum var.   ran·de·*voom* var

I'm staying at (the Ramada Hotel), room (19).
(Ramada'da), (ondokuz)   (ra·ma·da·*da*) (on·do·*kooz*)
numaralı odada   noo·ma·ra·*luh* o·da·*da*
kalıyorum.   ka·*luh*·yo·room

I'm here for (two) days/weeks.
(İki) günlüğüne/   (ee·*kee*) gewn·lew·ew·*ne*/
haftalığına buradayım.   haf·ta·luh·uh·*na* boo·ra·da·*yuhm*

Can I have your business card?
Bir kartvizitinizi   beer kart·vee·zee·tee·nee·*zee*
alabilir miyim?   a·*la*·bee·leer mee·*yeem*

Where's the ...?	... nerede?	... ne·re·de
business centre	İş merkezi	eesh mer·ke·zee
conference	Konferans	kon·fe·rans
meeting	Toplantı	top·lan·tuh

I need (a/an) ...	... ihtiyacım var.	... eeh·tee·ya·juhm var
computer	Bir bilgisayara	beer beel·gee·sa·ya·ra
Internet	İnternet	een·ter·net
connection	bağlantısına	ba·lan·tuh·suh·na
interpreter	Tercümana	ter·jew·ma·na
more	Daha fazla	da·ha faz·la
business cards	kartvizite	kart·vee·zee·te
some space	Hazırlık yapmak	ha·zuhr·luhk yap·mak
to set up	için daha	ee·cheen da·ha
	geniş yere	ge·neesh ye·re
to send a fax	Faks göndermeye	faks gern·der·me·ye

Here's my ...	Buyurun	boo·yoo·roon
	benim ...	be·neem ...
address	adresim	ad·re·seem
business card	kartvizitim	kart·vee·zee·teem
email address	e-posta adresim	e·pos·ta ad·re·seem
fax number	faks numaram	faks noo·ma·ram
mobile number	cep numaram	jep noo·ma·ram
pager number	çağrı numaram	cha·ruh noo·ma·ram
work number	iş numaram	eesh noo·ma·ram

What's your ...?	Sizin ... nedir?	see·zeen ... ne·deer
address	adresiniz	ad·re·see·neez
email	e-posta	e·pos·ta
address	adresiniz	ad·re·see·neez
fax number	faks numaranız	faks noo·ma·ra·nuhz
mobile number	cep numaranız	jep noo·ma·ra·nuhz
pager	çağrı	cha·ruh
number	numaranız	noo·ma·ra·nuhz
work number	iş numaranız	eesh noo·ma·ra·nuhz

Thank you for your time.
Zaman ayırdığınız   za·man a·yuhr·duh·uh·nuhz
için teşekkürler.   ee·cheen te·shek·kewr·ler

That went very well.
 Çok güzel geçti. chok gew·*zel* gech·*tee*

Shall we go for a drink?
 Birşeyler içelim mi? beer·shay·*ler* ee·che·*leem* mee

Shall we go for a meal?
 Birlikte yemeğe beer·leek·*te* ye·me·*e*
 gidelim mi? gee·de·*leem* mee

It's on me.
 Hesap benden. he·*sap* ben·*den*

looking for a job

Where are jobs advertised?
 Münhal pozisyonlar mewn·*hal* po·zees·yon·*lar*
 nerede ilan ediliyor? ne·re·de ee·*lan* e·dee·*lee*·yor

I'm enquiring about the position advertised.
 İş ilanı ile ilgili eesh ee·la·*nuh* ee·*le* eel·gee·*lee*
 görüşmek istiyorum. ger·rewsh·*mek* ees·*tee*·yo·room

I'm looking for *... arıyorum.* ... a·*ruh*·yo·room
... work.

bar	*Bar işi*	bar ee·*shee*
casual	*Geçici iş*	ge·chee·*jee* eesh
English-	*İngilizce*	een·gee·*leez*·je
teaching	*öğretme işi*	er·ret·me ee·*shee*
fruit-picking	*Meyve*	may·ve
	toplama işi	top·la·ma ee·*shee*
full-time	*Tam mesai iş*	tam me·sa·ee eesh
labouring	*Vasıfsız iş*	va·suhf·*suhz* eesh
nannying	*Dadılık işi*	da·duh·*luhk* ee·*shee*
office	*Ofis işi*	o·fees ee·*shee*
part-time	*Yarım gün*	ya·*ruhm* gewn
volunteer	*Gönüllü*	ger·newl·*lew*
	çalışabileceğim	cha·luh·sha·bee·le·*je*·eem
	bir iş	beer eesh
waitering	*Garsonluk işi*	gar·son·*look* ee·*shee*

I've had experience.
Deneyimim var. — de·ne·yee·*meem* var

What's the wage?
Maaş nedir? — ma·*ash* ne·deer

Do I need (a/an) …?	*… gerekli mi?*	*… ge·rek·lee mee*
contract	*Kontrat yapmam*	kon·*trat* yap·*mam*
experience	*Deneyim*	de·ne·*yeem*
insurance	*Sigorta*	see·gor·ta
my own transport	*Kendi arabam*	ken·*dee* a·ra·*bam*
paperwork	*Kağıt işlemleri*	ka·*uht* eesh·lem·le·ree
uniform	*Üniforma*	ew·nee·for·ma
work permit	*Çalışma izni*	cha·luhsh·ma eez·nee

Here's my …	*Buyurun benim …*	boo·*yoo*·roon be·*neem* …
bank account	*banka hesap*	ban·ka he·sap
CV/résumé	*bilgilerim*	beel·gee·le·reem
visa	*özgeçmişim*	erz·gech·mee·sheem
work permit	*vizem*	vee·zem
	çalışma iznim	cha·luhsh·ma eez·neem

I can start …	*… başlayabilirim.*	*… bash·la·ya·bee·lee·reem*
Can you start …?	*… başlayabilir misin?*	*… bash·la·ya·bee·leer mee·seen*
at (eight) o'clock	*Saat (sekizde)*	sa·at (se·keez·de)
next week	*Gelecek hafta*	ge·le·jek haf·ta
today	*Bugün*	boo·gewn
tomorrow	*Yarın*	ya·ruhn

What time do I …?	*Saat kaçta …?*	sa·at kach·ta …
start	*işe başlarım*	ee·she bash·la·ruhm
finish	*bitiririm*	bee·tee·ree·reem
have a break	*mola verilir*	mo·la ve·ree·leer

I have a disability.
Özürlüyüm.   er·zewr·*lew*·yewm

I need assistance.
Yardıma ihtiyacım var.   yar·duh·*ma* eeh·tee·ya·*juhm* var

What services do you have for people with a disability?
Özürlü kişiler için   er·zewr·*lew* kee·shee·*ler* ee·*cheen*
hangi hizmetleriniz var?   han·gee heez·met·le·ree·*neez* var

Are there disabled toilets?
Özürlü tuvaleti var mı?   er·zewr·*lew* too·va·le·*tee* var muh

Are there disabled parking spaces?
Özürlüler için park   er·zewr·*lew*·ler ee·*cheen* park
yeri var mı?   ye·*ree* var muh

Is there wheelchair access?
Tekerlekli sandalye   te·ker·lek·*lee* san·*dal*·ye
girişi var mı?   gee·ree·*shee* var muh

How wide is the entrance?
Girişin genişliği   gee·ree·*sheen* ge·neesh·lee·*ee*
nedir?   ne·deer

I'm deaf.
Sağırım.   sa·*uh*·ruhm

I have a hearing aid.
İşitme cihazı   ee·sheet·*me* jee·ha·*zuh*
kullanıyorum.   kool·la·*nuh*·yo·room

I'm blind.
Ben körüm.   ben *ker*·rewm

I'm visually impaired.
Görme özürlüyüm.   ger·*me* er·zewr·*lew*·yewm

Are guide dogs permitted?
Rehber köpekler   reh·*ber* ker·pek·*ler*
girebilir mi?   gee·re·bee·leer mee

For extra politeness, add the word *acaba* a·ja·ba (I wonder) to the end of your questions. You could phrase your hunt for the post office as *Postane nerede, acaba?* pos·ta·ne ne·re·de a·ja·ba (lit: post-office where I-wonder).

How many steps are there?
Kaç basamak var?   kach ba·sa·mak var

Is there a lift/elevator?
Asansör var mı?   a·san·ser var muh

Are there rails in the bathroom?
Banyoda tutamak var mı?   ban·yo·da too·ta·mak var muh

Could you call me a disabled taxi?
Bana özürlülere özel   ba·na er·zewr·lew·le·re er·zel
bir taksi çağırabilir   beer tak·see cha·uh·ra·bee·leer
misiniz?   mee·see·neez

Could you help me cross the street safely?
Karşıya geçmeme   kar·shuh·ya gech·me·me
yardım eder misiniz?   yar·duhm e·der mee·see·neez

Is there somewhere I can sit down?
Oturabileceğim   o·too·ra·bee·le·je·eem
bir yer var mı?   beer yer var muh

guide dog	*rehber köpek*	reh·ber ker·pek
older person	*yaşlı kişi*	yash·luh kee·shee
person with a disability	*özürlü kişi*	er·zewr·lew kee·shee
ramp	*rampa*	ram·pa
walking frame	*yürüteç*	yew·rew·tech
walking stick	*baston*	bas·ton
wheelchair	*tekerlekli sandalye*	te·ker·lek·lee san·dal·ye

travelling with children

çocuklarla seyahat

Is there a ...?	*... var mı?*	... var muh
baby change room	*Alt değiştirme odası*	alt de·eesh·teer·me o·da·suh
child discount	*Çocuk indirimi*	cho·jook een·dee·ree·mee
child-minding service	*Çocuk bakım hizmeti*	cho·jook ba·kuhm heez·me·tee
child's portion	*Çocuk porsiyonu*	cho·jook por·see·yo·noo
children's menu	*Çocuk menüsü*	cho·jook me·new·sew
crèche	*Kreş*	kresh
family ticket	*Aile bileti*	a·ee·le bee·le·tee
I need a/an ...	*... ihtiyacım var.*	... eeh·tee·ya·juhm var
baby seat (English-speaking)	*Bebek koltuğuna (İngilizce konuşan)*	be·bek kol·too·oo·na (een·gee·leez·je ko·noo·shan)
babysitter	*dadıya*	da·duh·ya
booster seat	*Yükseltici koltuğa*	yewk·sel·tee·jee kol·too·a
cot	*Çocuk yatağına*	cho·jook ya·ta·uh·na
highchair	*Mama sandalyesine*	ma·ma san·dal·ye·see·ne
plastic sheet	*Plastik yazgıya*	plas·teek yaz·guh·ya
plastic bag	*Naylon torbaya*	nai·lon tor·ba·ya
potty	*Oturağa*	o·too·ra·a
pram	*Çocuk arabasına*	cho·jook a·ra·ba·suh·na
pushchair/stroller	*Pusete*	poo·se·te
sick bag	*Kusma torbasına*	koos·ma tor·ba·suh·na

Where's the nearest ...?	En yakın ... nerede?	en ya·*kuhn* ... *ne*·re·de
drinking fountain	çeşme	chesh·me
park	park	park
playground	oyun alanı	o·*yoon* a·la·*nuh*
swimming pool	yüzme havuzu	yewz·me ha·voo·zoo
tap	musluk	moos·*look*
theme park	eğlence parkı	e·len·je par·*kuh*
toy shop	oyuncakçı	o·yoon·jak·*chuh*

Do you sell ...?	Bebekler için ... satıyor musunuz?	be·bek·*ler* ee·*cheen* ... sa·*tuh*·yor moo·soo·*nooz*
baby wipes	ıslak mendil	uhs·*lak* men·*deel*
disposable diapers/nappies	bez	bez
infant painkillers	ağrı kesici	a·*ruh* ke·see·*jee*
tissues	kutu mendil	koo·*too* men·*deel*

Are there any good places to take children around here?

Burada çocukları götürecek iyi yerler var mı?	boo·ra·*da* cho·jook·la·*ruh* ger·tew·re·*jek* ee·*yee* yer·*ler* var muh

Is there space for a pram?

Çocuk arabası için yer var mı?	cho·*jook* a·ra·ba·*suh* ee·*cheen* yer var muh

Are children allowed?

Çocuklar girebilir mi?	cho·jook·*lar* gee·re·bee·leer mee

Where can I change a nappy/diaper?

Bebeğin bezini nerede değiştirebilirim?	be·be·*een* be·zee·*nee* ne·re·de de·eesh·tee·re·bee·lee·reem

Do you mind if I breast-feed here?

Burada çocuk emzirmemin bir sakıncası var mı?	boo·ra·*da* cho·*jook* em·zeer·me·meen beer sa·kuhn·ja·*suh* var muh

Is this suitable for (three)-year-old children?

Bu (üç) yaşındaki çocuklar için uygun mu?	boo ewch ya·shuhn·da·*kee* cho·jook·*lar* ee·*cheen* ooy·*goon* moo

Do you know a dentist/doctor who is good with children?
> Çocuklar için iyi bir
> dişçi/doktor biliyor
> musunuz?

cho·jook·lar ee·cheen ee·yee beer
deesh·chee/dok·tor bee·lee·yor
moo·soo·nooz

If your child is sick, see **health**, page 191.

talking with children

What's your name?
> Adın ne?

a·duhn ne

How old are you?
> Kaç yaşındasın?

kach ya·shuhn·da·suhn

When's your birthday?
> Doğum günün ne zaman?

do·oom gew·newn ne za·man

Do you go to school/kindergarten?
> Okula/anaokuluna
> gidiyor musun?

o·koo·la/a·na·o·koo·loo·na
gee·dee·yor moo·soon

What grade are you in?
> Kaçıncı sınıftasın?

ka·chuhn·juh suh·nuhf·ta·suhn

Do you like (sport)?
> (Okulu) seviyor musun?

(o·koo·loo) se·vee·yor moo·soon

What do you do after school?
> Okuldan sonra
> neler yapıyorsun?

o·kool·dan son·ra
ne·ler ya·puh·yor·soon

Do you learn (English)?
> (İngilizce) öğreniyor
> musun?

(een·gee·leez·je) er·re·nee·yor
moo·soon

grandma & grandpa

In chitchat with Turkish kids, you could ask them about their *dede* de·de (grandpa) or *nine* nee·ne (grandma).

talking about children

When's the baby due?
Doğum ne zaman?   do·*oom* ne za·*man*

What are you going to call the baby?
Bebeğe ne isim   be·be·*e* ne ee·*seem*
vereceksiniz?   ve·re·*jek*·see·neez

Is this your first child?
İlk çocuğunuz mu?   eelk cho·joo·oo·*nooz* moo

Is it a boy or a girl?
Erkek mi kız mı?   er·*kek* mee kuhz muh

How many children do you have?
Kaç çocuğunuz var?   kach cho·joo·oo·*nooz* var

What a beautiful child!
Ne şirin şey!   ne shee·*reen* shay

What's his/her name?
Adı ne?   a·*duh* ne

How old is he/she?
Kaç yaşında?   kach ya·shuhn·*da*

Does he/she go to school?
Okula gidiyor mu?   o·koo·*la* gee·*dee*·yor moo

He ...	*Oğlunuz ...*	oo·loo·*nooz* ...
She ...	*Kızınız ...*	kuh·zuh·*nuhz* ...
has your eyes	*gözlerini*	gerz·le·ree·*nee*
	sizden almış	seez·*den* al·*muhsh*
looks like you	*size benziyor*	see·*ze* ben·*zee*·yor

---

tempting fate

Turkish parents don't want evil spirits paying attention to their kids, so to praise a child to its parents say *Maşallah!* ma·*shal*·lah (May God preserve him/her from evil!) before or after your compliment to ward the spirits off.

In this chapter, phrases are in the formal *siz* seez (you) form
unless otherwise marked. If you're not sure what this means,
see the box on page 30.

basics

temel sözcükler & cümleler

Yes.	*Evet.*	e·*vet*
No.	*Hayır.*	ha·yuhr
Please.	*Lütfen.*	lewt·fen
Thank you	*(Çok) Teşekkür*	(chok) te·shek·*kewr*
(very much). pol	*ederim.*	e·*de*·reem
Thanks. inf	*Teşekkürler.*	te·shek·kewr·*ler*
You're welcome.	*Birşey değil.*	beer·*shay* de·*eel*
Excuse me.	*Bakar mısınız?*	ba·*kar* muh·suh·*nuhz*
(to get attention)		
Excuse me.	*Affedersiniz.*	a·fe·der·see·neez
(to get past)		
Sorry.	*Özür dilerim.*	er·*zewr* dee·*le*·reem
Be my guest.	*Benim*	be·*neem*
	misafirim olun.	mee·sa·fee·*reem* o·loon
Let's go!	*Gidelim!*	gee·de·*leem*
Of course.	*Tabi.*	ta·*bee*

---

sex, religion & politics

Avoid asking questions about someone's age, religion or
sexual preference, as the Turkish prefer not to discuss these
topics openly. They love talking about politics, but exercise
a little caution when expressing your opinion – some Turks
verge on the fanatical when it comes to the 'p' word.

selamlaşma & ayrılma

Hello.	*Merhaba.*	mer·ha·ba
Hi.	*Selam.*	se·*lam*

Good ...
afternoon	*Tünaydın*	tew·nai·*duhn*
day	*İyi günler*	ee·*yee* gewn·*ler*
morning	*İyi sabahlar*	ee·*yee* sa·bah·*lar*
evening	*İyi akşamlar*	ee·*yee* ak·sham·*lar*

How are you?
Nasılsın/Nasılsınız? inf/pol   na·suhl·suhn/na·suhl·suh·nuhz

Fine. And you?
İyiyim. Ya sen/siz? inf/pol   ee·yee·yeem ya sen/seez

What's your name?
Adınız ne? inf	a·duh·*nuhz* ne
Adınız nedir? pol	a·duh·*nuhz* ne·deer

My name is ...
Benim adım ...   be·*neem* a·*duhm* ...

I'd like to introduce you to ...
Sizi ... ile tanıştırmak   see·*zee* ... ee·*le* ta·nuhsh·tuhr·*mak*
istiyorum.   ees·*tee*·yo·room

This is my ...	*Bu benim ...*	boo be·*neem* ...
colleague	*iş arkadaşım*	eesh ar·ka·da·*shuhm*
daughter	*kızım*	kuh·*zuhm*
friend	*arkadaşım*	ar·ka·da·*shuhm*
husband	*kocam*	ko·*jam*
partner (intimate)	*partnerim*	part·ne·*reem*
son	*oğlum*	o·*loom*
spouse	*eşim*	e·*sheem*
wife	*karım*	ka·*ruhm*

I'm pleased to meet you.
Tanıştığımıza   ta·nuhsh·tuh·uh·muh·*za*
memnun oldum.   mem·*noon* ol·*doom*

When Turks are introduced to each other, they shake hands and/or kiss on both cheeks. At other meetings women kiss women and men kiss men, but kissing the opposite sex is only common between close friends. When you meet someone of the opposite sex who has strong religious beliefs, avoid shaking their hands or kissing them. Instead, greet them with the Arabic words *selamın aleyküm* se·*la*·muhn a·*lay*·kewm (lit: may peace be upon you).

See you later.
Sonra görüşürüz.   son·ra ger·rew·*shew*·rewz

Goodbye. (by person leaving)
Hoşçakal. inf   hosh·*cha*·kal
Hoşçakalın. pol   hosh·*cha*·ka·luhn

Goodbye. (by person staying)
Güle güle.   gew·*le* gew·*le*

Bye.
Bay bay.   bai bai

Good night.
İyi geceler.   ee·*yee* ge·je·*ler*

Bon voyage!
İyi yolculuklar!   ee·*yee* yol·joo·look·*lar*

addressing people

hitap

Polite forms of address are used to show courtesy and acknowledge status, so use the polite *siz* seez (you) form with anyone you don't know well. In informal situations and with friends, use people's first names and address them in the *sen* sen (you) form. For more details see the box on page 30.

Mr/Sir	*Bay*	bai
Ms/Mrs/Miss/Madam	*Bayan*	ba·*yan*

Titles are also used to show respect. Address men as *bey* bay (sir) and women as *hanım* ha·*nuhm* (madam), preceded by their profession if appropriate – the taxi driver is *Şoför Bey* sho·*fer* bay (lit: driver sir) and a female doctor is *Doktor Hanım* dok·*tor* ha·*nuhm* (lit: doctor madam). Here are some titles for people with other occupations:

conductor m	*Kondaktör Bey*	kon·dak·*ter* bay
director f	*Müdire Hanım*	mew·dee·*re* ha·*nuhm*
official m	*Memur Bey*	me·*moor* bay
(police or civil)		
principal m	*Müdür Bey*	mew·*dewr* bay
waiter m	*Garson Bey*	gar·*son* bay

making conversation

What a beautiful day!
Ne güzel bir gün!   ne gew·*zel* beer gewn

Nice/Awful weather, isn't it?
Çok güzel/berbat bir hava,   chok gew·*zel*/ber·*bat* beer ha·*va*
değil mi?   de·*eel* mee

That's (beautiful), isn't it?
Şu çok (güzel), değil mi?   shoo chok (gew·*zel*) de·*eel* mee

What's this called?
Buna ne deniyor?   boo·*na* ne de·*nee*·yor

Can I help you?
Size yardım edebilir   see·*ze* yar·*duhm* e·de·bee·leer
miyim?   mee·*yeem*

What are you doing?
Ne yapıyorsunuz?   ne ya·*puh*·yor·soo·nooz

Where are you going?
Nereye gidiyorsunuz?   ne·re·ye gee·*dee*·yor·soo·nooz

Thanks, I don't smoke.
Teşekkürler,   te·shek·kewr·*ler*
kullanmıyorum.   kool·*lan*·muh·yo·room

How do you like Turkey?
Türkiye'yi nasıl   tewr·kee·ye·yee *na*·suhl
buldunuz?   bool·*doo*·nooz

Do you like it here?
Burayı seviyor   boo·ra·*yuh* se·*vee*·yor
musunuz?   moo·soo·*nooz*

I love it here.
Ben burayı seviyorum.   ben boo·ra·*yuh* se·*vee*·yo·room

Do you live here?
Burada mı   boo·ra·*da* muh
oturuyorsunuz?   o·too·*roo*·yor·soo·nooz

Are you here on holiday?
Buraya tatile mi   boo·ra·*ya* ta·tee·le mee
geldiniz?   gel·*dee*·neez

local talk

Hey!	*Selam!*	se·*lam*
How's it going?	*Naber?*	*na*·ber
Great!	*Harika!*	ha·ree·*ka*
Sure.	*Tabi.*	ta·*bee*
Maybe.	*Belki.*	bel·*kee*
No way!	*İmkansız!*	eem·kan·*suhz*
Just joking.	*Şaka yapıyorum.*	sha·*ka* ya·*puh*·yo·room
Just a minute.	*Bir dakika.*	beer da·kee·*ka*
It's OK.	*Tamam.*	ta·*mam*
No problem.	*Sorun değil.*	so·*roon* de·*eel*

How long are you here for?

Ne kadar süre için buradasınız?	ne ka·*dar* sew·*re* ee·*cheen* boo·ra·*da*·suh·nuhz

I'm here for (four) weeks/days.

(Dört) hafatlığına/ günlüğüne buradayım.	(dert) haf·ta·luh·uh·*na*/ gewn·lew·ew·*ne* boo·ra·*da*·yuhm

I'm here ...

	... *buradayım.*	... boo·ra·*da*·yuhm
for a holiday	*Tatil için*	*ta*·teel ee·*cheen*
on business	*İş için*	eesh ee·*cheen*
to study	*Öğrenim görmek için*	er·re·*neem* ger·*mek* ee·*cheen*

nationalities

To say where you're from, add *-lıyım* ·luh·yuhm, *-liyim* ·l
-luyum ·loo·yoom or *-lüyüm* ·lew·yewm to your country'
This choice depends on vowel harmony (see page 13).

| Where are you from? | *Nerelisiniz?* pol | ne·re·lee·see·neez |
| | *Nerelisin?* inf | ne·re·lee·seen |

I'm from ...	*Ben ...*	ben ...
Australia	*Avustralya'lıyım*	a·voos·tral·ya·luh·yuhm
China	*Çin'liyim*	cheen·lee·yeem
Jordan	*Ürdün'lüyüm*	ewr·dewn·lew·yewm
Singapore	*Singapur'luyum*	seen·ga·poor·loo·yoom

For more countries, see the **dictionary**.

age

yaş

How old ...?	*Kaç ...?*	kach ...
are you	*yaşındasınız* pol	ya·shuhn·da·suh·nuhz
	yaşındasın inf	ya·shuhn·da·suhn
is your son	*yaşında oğlunuz*	ya·shuhn·da o·loo·nooz
is your	*yaşında*	ya·shuhn·da
daughter	*kızınız*	kuh·zuh·nuhz

I'm ... years old.
Ben ... yaşındayım. ben ... ya·shuhn·da·yuhm

He/She is ... years old.
O ... yaşında. o ... ya·shuhn·da

Too old!
Çok yaşlı! chok yash·luh

I'm younger than I look.
Göründüğümden ger·rewn·dew·ewm·den
daha gencim. da·ha gen·jeem

For your age, see **numbers & amounts**, page 35.

meslekler & eğitim

What's your occupation?
Mesleğiniz nedir? pol		mes·le·ee·*neez* ne·deer
Mesleğin nedir? inf		mes·le·*een* ne·deer

I'm a/an ...	Ben ...	ben ...
chef	ahçıyım	ah·*chuh*·yuhm
engineer	mühendisim	mew·hen·*dee*·seem
hairdresser	kuaförüm	koo·a·*fer*·rewm
janitor	kapıcıyım	ka·puh·*juh*·yuhm
journalist	gazeteciyim	ga·ze·te·*jee*·yeem
labourer	işçiyim	eesh·*chee*·yeem
nurse	hemşireyim	hem·shee·*re*·yeem
official	memurum	me·*moo*·room
taxi driver	taksi şoförüyüm	tak·*see* sho·fer·*rew*·yewm
teacher	öğretmenim	er·ret·*me*·neem
tea seller	çaycıyım	chai·*juh*·yuhm

I work in ...	... işinde	... ee·sheen·de
	çalışıyorum.	cha·luh·*shuh*·yo·room
an office	Ofis	o·*fees*
health	Sağlık	sa·*luhk*
sales and	Satış ve	sa·*tuhsh* ve
marketing	pazarlama	pa·zar·la·*ma*

---

well-wishing

In your honour!	Şerefinize!	she·re·fee·nee·*ze*
To your health!	Sağlığınıza!	sa·luh·uh·nuh·*za*
Congratulations!	Tebrikler!	teb·reek·*ler*
Good luck!	İyi şanslar!	ee·yee shans·*lar*
Happy Birthday!	Doğum günün	do·*oom* gew·*newn*
	kutlu olsun!	koot·*loo* ol·*soon*
Merry Christmas!	Yeni yılınız	ye·*nee* yuh·luh·*nuhz*
	kutlu olsun!	koot·*loo* ol·*soon*

I'm ...	Ben ...	ben ...
retired	emekliyim	e·mek·lee·yeem
self-employed	kendi işimin	ken·dee ee·shee·meen
	sahibiyim	sa·hee·bee·yeem
unemployed	işsizim	eesh·see·zeem
What are you studying?	Ne üzerine öğrenim görüyorsunuz?	ne ew·ze·ree·ne er·re·neem ger·rew·yor·soo·nooz
I'm studying ...	... öğreniyorum.	... er·re·nee·yo·room
humanities	Uygarlık tarihi	ooy·gar·luhk ta·ree·hee
science	Fen	fen
Turkish	Türkçe	tewrk·che

family

Do you have (a) ...?	... var mı?	... var muh
brother	Kardeşiniz	kar·de·shee·neez
children	Çocuklarınız	cho·jook·la·ruh·nuhz
daughter	Kızınız	kuh·zuh·nuhz
family	Aileniz	a·ee·le·neez
granddaughter	Kız torununuz	kuhz to·roo·noo·nooz
grandson	Erkek torununuz	er·kek to·roo·noo·nooz
partner (intimate)	Partneriniz	part·ne·ree·neez
sister	Kız kardeşiniz	kuhz kar·de·shee·neez
son	Oğlunuz	o·loo·nooz
spouse	Eşiniz	e·shee·neez

For more kinship terms, see the **dictionary**.

I have (a) ...	... var.	... var
I don't have (a) ...	... yok.	... yok
brother	Kardeşim	kar·de·sheem
children	Çocuğum	cho·joo·oom
daughter	Kızım	kuh·zuhm
family	Ailem	a·ee·lem
granddaughter	Kız torunum	kuhz to·roo·noom
grandson	Erkek torunum	er·kek to·roo·noom
partner (intimate)	Partnerim	part·ne·reem
sister	Kız kardeşim	kuhz kar·de·sheem
son	Oğlum	o·loom
spouse	Eşim	e·sheem

| Are you married? | Evli misiniz? | ev·lee mee·see·neez |

| I live with someone. | Birisiyle yaşıyorum. | bee·ree·seey·le ya·shuh·yo·room |

I'm ...	Ben ...	ben ...
divorced	boşandım	bo·shan·duhm
married	evliyim	ev·lee·yeem
separated	ayrıldım	ay·ruhl·duhm
single	bekarım	be·ka·ruhm

farewells

Tomorrow is my last day here.
Yarın benim burada son günüm.
ya·ruhn be·neem boo·ra·da son gew·newm

If you come to (Scotland) you can stay with me.
Eğer (İskoçya'ya) yolunuz düşerse bende kalabilirsiniz.
e·er (ees·koch·ya·ya) yo·loo·nooz dew·sher·se ben·de ka·la·bee·leer·see·neez

why oh why

Every time you see a y in the pronunciation guide, pronounce it like the 'y' in 'yes'.

SOCIAL

112

Keep in touch!
> *Haberleşelim.*   ha·ber·le·she·*leem*

It's been great meeting you.
> *Tanıştığımıza çok*   ta·nuhsh·tuh·uh·muh·*za* chok
> *memnun oldum.*   mem·*noon* ol·*doom*

Here's my ...	*İşte benim ...*	eesh·te be·*neem* ...
address	*adresim*	ad·re·*seem*
email address	*e-posta adresim*	e·pos·ta ad·re·*seem*
phone number	*telefon*	te·le·*fon*
	numaram	noo·ma·*ram*

What's your ...?	*Sizin ... nedir?*	see·*zeen* ... ne·deer
address	*adresiniz*	ad·re·see·*neez*
email address	*e-posta adresiniz*	e·pos·ta ad·re·see·*neez*
phone number	*telefon*	te·le·*fon*
	numaranız	noo·ma·ra·*nuhz*

meeting people

113

Tongue twisters are called *tekerlemeler* te·ker·le·me·*ler* in Turkish, meaning 'roll round' or 'repeat the same thing over and over again'. Give your tongue a workout with this pair:

Karaağaç, karaağaç,
kabuğu kara karaağaç,
kabuğu kurumuş kara kuru karaağaç.
   ka·*ra*·a·ach ka·*ra*·a·ach
   ka·boo·*oo* ka·*ra* ka·*ra*·a·ach
   ka·boo·*oo* koo·roo·*moosh* ka·*ra* koo·*roo* ka·*ra*·a·ach
   Elm tree, elm tree;
   its bark, black tree;
   its bark dried-up, black withered elm tree.

Hakkı Hakkı'nın hakkını yemiş.
Hakkı Hakkı'dan hakkını istemiş.
Hakkı Hakkı'ya hakkını vermeyince,
Hakkı da haklı olarak Hakkı'nın hakkından gelmiş.
   hak·*kuh* hak·kuh·*nuh* hak·kuh·*nuh* ye·*meesh*
   hak·*kuh* hak·kuh·*dan* hak·kuh·*nuh* ees·te·*meesh*
   hak·*kuh* hak·kuh·*ya* hak·kuh·*nuh* ver·me·yeen·je
   hak·*kuh* da hak·*luh* o·la·*rak* hak·kuh·*nuhn*
   hak·kuhn·*dan* gel·*meesh*
   Hakkı cheated Hakkı of his rights.
   Hakkı asked Hakkı for his rights.
   As Hakkı didn't give Hakkı his due,
   Hakkı rightfully paid Hakkı back.

In this chapter, phrases are in the informal *sen* sen (you) form unless otherwise marked. For more detail, see the box on page 30.

common interests

ortak noktalar

What do you do in your spare time?

Boş zamanlarında		bosh za·man·la·ruhn·*da*
neler yaparsın?		*ne*·ler ya·*par*·suhn

Do you like ...?	... *sever misin?*	... se·*ver* mee·*seen*
I like ...	... *seviyorum.*	... se·*vee*·yo·room
I don't like ...	... *sevmiyorum.*	... *sev*·mee·yo·room
calligraphy	*Hat sanatını*	hat sa·na·tuh·*nuh*
cooking	*Yemek pişirmeyi*	ye·*mek* pee·sheer·me·*yee*
films	*Sinemaya*	see·ne·ma·*ya*
	gitmeyi	geet·me·*yee*
gardening	*Bahçe işlerini*	bah·che eesh·le·ree·*nee*
hiking	*Yürüyüş*	yew·rew·*yewsh*
	yapmayı	yap·ma·*yuh*
marbling paper	*Ebru sanatını*	eb·*roo* sa·na·tuh·*nuh*
photography	*Fotoğrafçılığı*	fo·to·raf·chuh·luh·*uh*
reading	*Okumayı*	o·koo·ma·*yuh*
shopping	*Alış-veriş*	a·luhsh·ve·*reesh*
	yapmayı	yap·ma·*yuh*
sport	*Sporu*	spo·*roo*
travelling	*Seyahat etmeyi*	se·ya·*hat* et·me·*yee*
watching TV	*Televizyon*	te·le·veez·*yon*
	seyretmeyi	say·ret·me·*yee*

For types of sports, see **sport**, page 141, and the **dictionary**.

music

Do you ...?	... misin? inf	... mee·seen
	... misiniz? pol	... mee·see·neez
dance	Dans eder	dans e·der
go to concerts	Konserlere gider	kon·ser·le·re gee·der
listen to music	Müzik dinler	mew·zeek deen·ler
play an	Müzik aleti	mew·zeek a·le·tee
instrument	çalmayı bilir	chal·ma·yuh bee·leer
sing	Şarkı söyler	shar·kuh say·ler

What ...	Hangi ...	han·gee ...
do you like?	seversin? inf	se·ver·seen
	Hangi ...	han·gee ...
	seversiniz? pol	se·ver·see·neez
bands	gurupları	goo·roop·la·ruh
music	müziği	mew·zee·ee
singers	şarkıcıları	shar·kuh·juh·la·ruh

blues	blues	blooz
classical music	klasik müzik	kla·seek mew·zeek
electronic music	elektronik müzik	e·lek·tro·neek mew·zeek
jazz	caz	jaz
Ottoman	klasik Türk	kla·seek tewrk
classical music	musikisi	moo·see·kee·see
pop	pop	pop
rock	rok	rok

... music	... müziği	... mew·zee·ee
Ottoman	tasavvuf	ta·sav·voof
religious		
traditional	geleneksel Türk	ge·le·nek·sel tewrk
Turkish		
Turkish folk	Türk halk	tewrk halk
world	dünya	dewn·ya

Planning to go to a concert? See **tickets**, page 49, and **going out**, page 125.

cinema & theatre

sinema & tiyatro

I feel like going to a ...	*Canım ... izlemeye gitmek istiyor.*	ja·*nuhm* ... eez·le·me·*ye* geet·*mek* ees·*tee*·yor
The ... was good, wasn't it?	*... güzeldi, değil mi?*	... gew·*zel*·dee de·*eel* mee
ballet	*bale*	ba·*le*
film	*film*	feelm
play	*oyun*	o·*yoon*
I thought it was ...	*Bence ...*	ben·*je* ...
excellent	*mükemmeldi*	mew·kem·*mel*·dee
long	*çok uzundu*	chok oo·*zoon*·doo
OK	*fena değildi*	fe·*na* de·*eel*·dee

What's showing at the cinema/theatre tonight?
Bu akşam sinemada/ tiyatroda ne oynuyor?
boo ak·*sham* see·ne·ma·*da*/ tee·yat·ro·*da* ne oy·*noo*·yor

Is it in (English)?
(İngilizce) mi?
(een·gee·*leez*·je) mee

Does it have (English) subtitles?
(İngilizce) Alt yazısı var mı?
(een·gee·*leez*·je) alt ya·zuh·*suh* var muh

Have you seen (Firuze)?
(Firuze'yi) izlediniz mi?
(fee·*roo*·ze·yee) eez·le·dee·*neez* mee

Who's in it?
Kim oynuyor?
keem oy·*noo*·yor

It stars (Demet Akbağ).
(Demet Akbağ) oynuyor.
(de·*met* ak·*ba*) oy·*noo*·yor

Is this seat taken?
Bu koltuk boş mu?
boo kol·*took* bosh moo

I like ...	... seviyorum.	... se·*vee*·yo·room
I don't like ...	... sevmiyorum.	... sev·mee·yo·room
action movies	*Macera filmlerini*	ma·je·*ra* feelm·le·ree·*nee*
animated films (Turkish)	*Animasyonları (Türk)*	a·nee·mas·yon·la·*ruh* (tewrk)
cinema	*sinemasını*	see·ne·ma·suh·*nuh*
comedies	*Komedi filmlerini*	ko·me·*dee* feelm·le·ree·*nee*
documentaries	*Belgeselleri*	bel·ge·sel·le·*ree*
drama	*Dramları*	dram·la·*ruh*
horror movies	*Korku filmlerini*	kor·*koo* feelm·le·ree·*nee*
sci-fi	*Bilim-kurguları*	bee·*leem*·koor·goo·la·ruh
short films	*Kısa filmleri*	kuh·*sa* fee·leem·le·*ree*
thrillers	*Heyecan filmlerini*	he·ye·*jan* feelm·le·ree·*nee*
war movies	*Savaş filmlerini*	sa·*vash* feelm·le·ree·*nee*

french, italian & german

As you start to learn Turkish, you'll notice that there are many words adopted from both French and Italian (and one from German). Francophones will pick up on *garson* gar·*son* (waiter), *plaj* plazh (beach) and *jeton* zhe·*ton* (token), among many others. Italian speakers will spot *banka* ban·ka (bank), *bavul* ba·*vool* (suitcase) and *numara* noo·*ma*·ra (number). German speakers will notice *otoban* o·to·*ban* for 'motorway'. The pronunciation of these words may have changed slightly from the original, but if you pronounce them with a French, Italian or German accent you'll be understood.

In this chapter, phrases are in the informal *sen* sen (you) form only. If you're not sure what this means, see the box on page 30.

feelings

duygular

Are you ...?

cold	*Üşüdün mü?*	ew·shew·*dewn* mew
happy	*Mutlu musun?*	moot·*loo* moo·*soon*
hot	*Sıcakladın mı?*	suh·jak·la·*duhn* muh
hungry	*Aç mısın?*	ach muh·*suhn*
thirsty	*Susadın mı?*	soo·sa·*duhn* muh
tired	*Yorgun musun?*	yor·*goon* moo·*soon*
worried	*Bir endişen mi var?*	beer en·dee·*shen* mee var

I'm ...

cold	*Üşüdüm.*	ew·shew·*dewm*
happy	*Mutluyum.*	moot·*loo*·yoom
hot	*Sıcakladım.*	suh·jak·la·*duhm*
hungry	*Açım.*	a·chuhm
thirsty	*Susadım.*	soo·sa·*duhm*
tired	*Yorgunum.*	yor·*goo*·noom
worried	*Biraz endişeliyim.*	*bee*·raz en·dee·she·*lee*·yeem

I'm not ...

cold	*Üşümedim.*	ew·*shew*·me·deem
happy	*Mutlu değilim.*	moot·*loo* de·*ee*·leem
hot	*Sıcaklamadım.*	suh·jak·*la*·ma·duhm
hungry	*Aç değilim.*	ach de·*ee*·leem
thirsty	*Susamadım.*	soo·sa·ma·duhm
tired	*Yorgun değilim.*	yor·*goon* de·*ee*·leem
worried	*Endişeli değilim.*	en·dee·she·*lee* de·*ee*·leem

showing your feelings		
a little	*biraz*	*bee·raz*
I'm a little sad.	*Biraz üzgünüm.*	*bee·raz ewz·gew·newm*
very/extremely	*çok*	chok
I feel very lucky.	*Kendimi*	ken·dee·mee
	çok şanslı	chok shans·luh
	hissediyorum.	hees·se·dee·yo·room

What happened?
   Ne oldu?   ne ol·*doo*

What's wrong with you?
   Neyin var?   ne·*yeen* var

If you're not feeling well, see **health**, page 191.

opinions

fikirler

Did you like it?
   Beğendin mi?   be·en·*deen* mee

What do you think of it?
   Bunun için ne   boo·*noon* ee·*cheen* ne
   düşünüyorsun?   dew·shew·*new*·yor·soon

It's …	*O …*	o …
I thought it was …	*… olduğunu*	*… ol·doo·oo·noo*
	düşünüyorum.	dew·shew·*new*·yo·room
awful	*korkunç*	kor·*koonch*
beautiful	*güzel*	gew·*zel*
boring	*sıkıcı*	suh·kuh·*juh*
great	*harika*	ha·ree·*ka*
interesting	*ilginç*	eel·*geench*
OK	*idare eder*	ee·da·*re* e·*der*
strange	*acayip*	a·ja·*yeep*
too expensive	*çok pahalı*	chok pa·ha·*luh*

politics & social issues

Who do you vote for?
    Oyunu kime verirsin?   o·yoo·*noo* kee·me ve·*reer*·seen

I support	*... partisini*	*... par·tee·see·nee*
the ... party.	*destekliyorum.*	des·tek·*lee*·yo·room
I'm a member	*... parti üyesiyim.*	*... par·tee* ew·ye·see·yeem
of the ... party.		
communist	*Komünist*	ko·mew·*neest*
conservative	*Muhafazakarların*	moo·ha·fa·za·kar·la·*ruhn*
democratic	*Demokratların*	de·mok·rat·la·*ruhn*
green	*Yeşiller*	ye·sheel·*ler*
liberal	*Liberallerin*	lee·be·ral·le·*reen*
social	*Sosyal*	sos·*yal*
democratic	*demokratların*	de·mok·rat·la·*ruhn*
socialist	*Sosyalistlerin*	sos·ya·leest·le·*reen*

Do you agree with it?
    Katılıyor musun?   ka·tuh·*luh*·yor moo·*soon*

I agree with ...
    ... ile aynı fikirdeyim.   ... ee·*le* ai·*nuh* fee·keer·de·yeem

I don't agree with ...
    ... ile aynı fikirde   ... ee·*le* ai·*nuh* fee·keer·de
    değilim.   de·*ee*·leem

How do people feel about ...?
    Herkes ... hakkında   *her*·kes ... hak·kuhn·*da*
    ne düşünüyor?   ne dew·shew·*new*·yor

How can we support ...?
    ... konusuna nasıl   ... ko·noo·soo·*na na*·suhl
    destek verebiliriz?   des·*tek* ve·re·bee·lee·reez

abortion	*çocuk aldırma*	cho·*jook* al·duhr·*ma*
animal rights	*hayvan hakları*	hai·*van* hak·la·*ruh*
corruption	*yolsuzluk*	yol·sooz·*look*
crime	*suç*	sooch
discrimination	*ayrım*	ai·*ruhm*
drugs	*uyuşturucular*	oo·yoosh·too·roo·joo·*lar*
the economy	*ekonomi*	e·ko·no·*mee*
education	*eğitim*	e·ee·*teem*
the environment	*çevre*	chev·*re*
equal opportunity	*fırsat eşitliği*	fuhr·*sat* e·sheet·lee·*ee*
the European Union	*Avrupa Birliği*	av·roo·pa beer·lee·*ee*
euthanasia	*ötenazi*	er·te·na·*zee*
globalisation	*globalleşme*	glo·bal·lesh·*me*
human rights	*insan hakları*	een·*san* hak·la·*ruh*
immigration	*göç*	gerch
inequality	*eşitsizlik*	e·sheet·seez·*leek*
Kurdish separatism	*kürt ayrımı*	kewrt ai·ruh·*muh*
military intervention in government	*askeri darbe*	as·ke·*ree* dar·*be*
party politics	*parti politikası*	par·*tee* po·lee·tee·ka·*suh*
poverty	*yoksulluk*	yok·sool·*look*
privatisation	*özelleştirme*	er·zel·lesh·teer·*me*
racism	*ırkçılık*	uhrk·chuh·*luhk*
religious fundamentalism	*din fanatizmi*	deen fa·na·teez·*mee*
sexism	*cins ayrımı*	jeens ai·ruh·*muh*
social welfare	*toplum refahı*	top·*loom* re·fa·*huh*
terrorism	*terörizm*	te·rer·*reezm*
unemployment	*işsizlik*	eesh·seez·*leek*
the wearing of headscarves	*başörtüsü takmak*	bash·er·tew·*sew* tak·*mak*

the environment

Is there a … problem here?
Burada bir …   boo·ra·*da* beer …
problemi mi var?   prob·le·*mee* mee var

What should be done about …?
… ile ilgili ne   … ee·*le* eel·gee·*lee* ne
yapılmalı?   ya·puhl·ma·*luh*

Is this a protected (forest)?
Bu koruma altına   boo ko·roo·*ma* al·tuh·*na*
alınmış bir (orman mı)?   a·luhn·*muhsh* beer (or·*man* muh)

air pollution	*hava kirliliği*	ha·*va* keer·lee·lee·*ee*
conservation	*koruma*	ko·roo·*ma*
construction of	*petrol boru*	pet·*rol* bo·*roo*
oil pipelines	*hatlarının*	hat·la·ruh·*nuhn*
	yapımı	ya·puh·*muh*
dam-building	*baraj inşa*	ba·*razh* een·*sha*
projects	*projesi*	pro·zhe·*see*
drought	*kuraklık*	koo·rak·*luhk*
ecosystem	*ekosistem*	e·ko·sees·*tem*
endangered	*nesli tükenmekte*	nes·*lee* tew·ken·mek·*te*
species	*olan türler*	o·*lan* tewr·*ler*
GAP (South-East	*Güney Doğu*	gew·*nay* do·*oo*
Anatolia dam-	*Anadolu Projesi*	a·*na*·do·loo pro·zhe·*see*
building project)		
genetically	*genetiği*	ge·ne·tee·*ee*
modified	*değiştirilmiş*	de·eesh·tee·reel·*meesh*
food	*gıdalar*	guh·da·*lar*
hunting	*avlanma*	av·lan·*ma*
hydroelectricity	*hidro-elektrik*	heed·*ro*·e·lek·treek

immigration	*göç*	gerch
irrigation	*sulama*	soo·la·*ma*
nuclear energy	*nükleer enerji*	newk·le·*er* e·ner·*zhee*
nuclear testing	*nükleer denemeler*	newk·le·*er* de·ne·me·*ler*
overfishing	*aşırı avlanma*	a·shuh·*ruh* av·lan·*ma*
ozone layer	*ozon tabakası*	o·*zon* ta·ba·ka·*suh*
pesticides	*zirai ilaçlar*	zee·ra·*ee* ee·lach·*lar*
petroleum	*Boğaz'da petrol*	bo·az·*da* pet·*rol*
transportation	*taşımacılığı*	ta·shuh·ma·juh·luh·*uh*
through the		
Bosphorus		
pollution	*kirlilik*	keer·lee·*leek*
recycling	*yeniden kazanım*	ye·nee·*den* ka·za·*nuhm*
solar power	*güneş enerjisi*	gew·*nesh* e·ner·zhee·*see*
toxic waste	*zehirli atıklar*	ze·heer·*lee* a·tuhk·*lar*
water supply	*su kaynakları*	soo kai·nak·la·*ruh*

In this chapter, phrases are in the informal *sen* sen (you) form unless otherwise marked. For more details, see the box on page 30.

where to go

nereye gitmeli

What's there to do in the evenings?
Akşamları buralarda   ak·sham·la·ruh boo·ra·lar·*da*
neler yapılabilir?   *ne*·ler ya·puh·*la*·bee·leer

What's on ...?	... *görülecek*	... ger·rew·le·*jek*
	neler var?	*ne*·ler var
locally	*Yerel olarak*	ye·*rel* o·la·*rak*
today	*Bugün*	boo·gewn
tonight	*Bu gece*	boo ge·*je*
this weekend	*Bu hafta sonu*	boo haf·*ta* so·*noo*

Where are the ...?	*Buranın ... nerede?*	boo·ra·*nuhn* ... *ne*·re·de
clubs	*kulüpleri*	koo·lewp·le·*ree*
gay venues	*gey kulüpleri*	gay koo·lewp·le·*ree*
places to eat	*yemek*	ye·*mek*
	yenilebilecek	ye·nee·*le*·bee·le·jek
	yerleri	yer·le·*ree*
pubs	*birahaneleri*	bee·ra·ha·ne·le·*ree*

Is there a	*Buranın yerel ...*	boo·ra·*nuhn* ye·*rel* ...
local ... guide?	*rehberi var mı?*	reh·be·*ree* var muh
entertainment	*eğlence*	e·len·*je*
film	*film*	feelm
music	*müzik*	mew·*zeek*

I feel like going to a/the …	Canım … gitmek istiyor.	ja·nuhm … geet·mek ees·tee·yor
bar	bara	ba·ra
café	kafeye	ka·fe·ye
concert	konsere	kon·se·re
film	sinemaya	see·ne·ma·ya
folk dance display	halk dansları gösterisine	halk dans·la·ruh gers·te·ree·see·ne
folk music concert	halk müziği konserine	halk mew·zee·ee kon·se·ree·ne
hamam (Turkish bath)	hamama	ha·ma·ma
nightclub	gece kulübüne	ge·je koo·lew·bew·ne
party	partiye	par·tee·ye
performance	temsile	tem·see·le
play	oyuna	o·yoo·na
restaurant	restorana	res·to·ra·na
seaside	deniz kenarına	de·neez ke·na·ruh·na
tea house	çay bahçesine	chai bah·che·see·ne

invitations

davetler

What are you doing …?	… ne yapıyorsun?	… ne ya·puh·yor·soon
now	Şimdi	sheem·dee
tonight	Bu akşam	boo ak·sham
this weekend	Bu haftasonu	boo haf·ta·so·noo

We're having a party.
Parti yapıyoruz.   par·tee ya·puh·yo·rooz

You should come.
Gelmelisin.   gel·me·lee·seen

spinning out of control

For some classic Turkish entertainment, check out a *sema ayini* se·ma a·yee·nee, which is the traditional Mevlevi worship ceremony with *dervişler* der·veesh·ler (whirling dervishes). A *hafız* ha·fuhz (person who knows the Koran by heart) will intone a prayer to Mevlana (founder of the Mevlevi order), the *ney* nay (reed flute) will be played to release its soul, and the *şeyh* shayh (sheik/master) will bow his head and lead the dervishes into their whirling ritual.

The music you'll hear during the ceremony is the slightly lugubrious *mevlevi müziği* mev·le·vee mew·zee·ee (*mevlevi* music) which uses a system of tones called *makamlar* ma·kam·lar, similar to Western scales. In other situations, you could find yourself listening to *türkü* tewr·kew (folk music) or *arabesk* a·ra·besk, folk music with an Arabic twist which is slowly gaining kitsch status.

Would you like to go (for a) ...?	... *gitmek ister misin?*	... geet·mek ees·ter mee·seen
I feel like going (for a) ...	*Canım ... gitmek istiyor.*	ja·nuhm ... geet·mek ees·tee·yor
coffee	*kahve içmeye*	kah·ve eech·me·ye
dancing	*dansa*	dan·sa
drink	*birşeyler içmeye*	beer·shay·ler eech·me·ye
meal	*yemeğe*	ye·me·e
out	*bir yere*	beer ye·re
tea	*çay içmeye*	chai eech·me·ye
walk	*yürüyüşe*	yew·rew·yew·she

Do you know a good restaurant?
Bildiğin iyi bir restoran var mı?
beel·dee·een ee·yee beer res·to·ran var muh

Do you want to come to the concert with me?
Benimle konsere gelmek ister misin?
be·neem·le kon·se·re gel·mek ees·ter mee·seen

For more on bars, drinks and partying, see **romance**, page 131, and **eating out**, page 155.

responding to invitations

Sure!
Elbette!   el·bet·te

Yes, I'd love to.
Evet, çok sevinirim.   e·vet chok se·vee·nee·reem

That's very kind of you.
Çok naziksin.   chok na·zeek·seen

Where shall we go?
Nereye gideceğiz?   ne·re·ye gee·de·je·eez

What about tomorrow?
Yarına ne dersin?   ya·ruh·na ne der·seen

No, I'm afraid I can't.
Üzgünüm ama gelemem.   ewz·gew·newm a·ma ge·le·mem

Sorry, I can't ...	*Üzgünüm ama*	ewz·gew·newm a·ma
	ben ... pek	ben ... pek
	bilmiyorum.	beel·mee·yo·room
dance	*dans etmeyi*	dans et·me·yee
sing	*şarkı söylemeyi*	shar·kuh say·le·me·yee

arranging to meet

What time will we meet?
Saat kaçta buluşacağız?   sa·at kach·ta boo·loo·sha·ja·uhz

Where will we meet?
Nerede buluşacağız?   ne·re·de boo·loo·sha·ja·uhz

I'll pick you up.
Seni alırım.   se·nee a·luh·ruhm

Let's meet at ...	*... buluşalım.*	... boo·loo·sha·luhm
(eight) o'clock	*Saat (sekizde)*	sa·at (se·keez·de)
the entrance	*Girişte*	gee·reesh·te

Are you ready?
Hazır mısın?   ha-*zuhr* muh-*suhn*

I'm ready.
Hazırım.   ha-*zuh*-ruhm

I'll be coming later.
Ben daha geç   ben da-*ha* gech
orada olacağım.   o-ra-*da* o-la-*ja*-uhm

Where will you be?
Siz nerede olacaksınız?   seez ne-re-de o-la-*jak*-suh-nuhz

If I'm not there by (nine), don't wait for me.
Eğer (dokuza) kadar   e-*er* (do-koo-*za*) ka-*dar*
orada olmazsam   o-ra-*da* ol-*maz*-sam
beni beklemeyin.   be-*nee* bek-*le*-me-yeen

I'll see you then.
O zaman görüşürüz.   o za-*man* ger-rew-*shew*-rewz

See you later/tomorrow.
Sonra/yarın görüşürüz.   son-ra/ya-ruhn ger-rew-*shew*-rewz

I'm looking forward to it.
Dört gözle bekliyorum.   dert gerz-*le* bek-*lee*-yo-room

Sorry I'm late.
Özür dilerim, geciktim.   er-*zewr* dee-*le*-reem ge-jeek-*teem*

Never mind.
Sağlık olsun.   sa-*luhk* ol-*soon*

drugs

Do you want to have a smoke?
Bir fırt çekmek ister   beer fuhrt chek-*mek* ees-*ter*
misin?   mee-*seen*

Do you have a light?
Ateşin var mı?   a-te-*sheen* var muh

I take ... occasionally.
Ara sıra ... alıyorum.   a-ra suh-ra ... a-*luh*-yo-room

going out

129

I don't take drugs.
Uyuşturucu   oo·yoosh·too·roo·*joo*
kullanmıyorum.   kool·*lan*·muh·yo·room

If the police are talking to you about drugs, see **essentials**, page 190, for useful phrases.

(see essentials, page 190)

---

sex rules

Gender boundaries in Turkey are more strictly observed in some venues than others. For women travellers who'd like to have a drink or two, the best option is the Western-style *barlar* bar·*lar* (bars) which can be found in most tourist destinations. Traditional Turkish watering holes, like the *meyhane* may·*ha*·ne (wine-house) and *birahane* bee·ra·*ha*·ne (beer-house), are all-male preserves and women generally aren't welcome. As a general rule, Turkish women don't drink because they're Muslims, and foreign women overindulging in public isn't well regarded.

The sexes are segregated when bathing at *hamamlar* ha·mam·*lar* (hamams). Sometimes baths will be designated for *erkekler* er·kek·*ler* (men) and *kadınlar* ka·duhn·*lar* (women), or separate bathing times may be posted. Both men and women are offered a *peştemal* pesh·te·*mal* (short, thin sarong), *takunya* ta·*koon*·ya (wooden clogs) and, after the bath, a *havlu* hav·*loo* (towel). Etiquette says that men keep their *peştemal* on at all times, while women could keep their underwear on beneath their *peştemal* until they've assessed the acceptable way to behave in that particular *hamam*.

When visiting mosques or temples, both men and women should wear modest clothing – no t-shirts, singlets or tatty travelling rags. Women should cover their head, arms and shoulders, and wear modest knee-length dresses. A *türban* tewr·*ban* or *eşarp* e·*sharp* (headscarf) can be borrowed (or 'rented' with a donation) at most temples if needed. Kick off your shoes as you go in.

In this chapter, phrases are in the informal *sen* sen (you) form only. If you're not sure what this means, see the box on page 30.

asking someone out

birisine çıkma teklif ederken

Where would you like to go (tonight)?
(Bu akşam) Nereye   (boo ak·*sham*) ne·re·ye
gitmek istersin?   geet·*mek* ees·*ter*·seen

Would you like to do something (tomorrow)?
(Yarın) Birşeyler   (*ya*·ruhn) beer·shay·*ler*
yapmak ister misin?   yap·*mak* ees·*ter* mee·*seen*

Yes, I'd love to.
Evet, çok sevinirim.   e·*vet* chok se·vee·*nee*·reem

Sorry, I can't.
Üzgünüm, bir   ewz·*gew*·newm beer
yere gidemem.   ye·*re* gee·*de*·mem

pick-up lines

tanışma sözleri

Would you like a drink?
Bir içki ister misiniz?   beer eech·*kee* ees·*ter* mee·see·*neez*

You have beautiful eyes.
Ne kadar güzel   ne ka·*dar* gew·*zel*
gözleriniz var.   gerz·le·ree·*neez* var

You look like someone I know.
Tanıdığım birisine   ta·nuh·duh·*uhm* bee·ree·see·*ne*
benziyorsunuz.   ben·*zee*·yor·soo·nooz

You're a fantastic dancer.
   Harika dans ediyorsunuz.   ha·ree·*ka* dans e·*dee*·yor·soo·nooz

Do you have a light?
   Ateşiniz var mı?   a·te·shee·*neez* var muh

Can I …?	… *miyim?*	… mee·*yeem*
dance with you	*Sizinle dans edebilir*	see·*zeen*·le dans e·*de*·bee·leer
sit here	*Buraya oturabilir*	boo·ra·*ya* o·too·*ra*·bee·leer
give you a lift home	*Sizi eve bırakabilir*	see·*zee* e·*ve* buh·ra·*ka*·bee·leer

rejections

No, thank you.
   Hayır, teşekkürler.   ha·yuhr te·shek·kewr·*ler*

I'd rather not.
   Hayır istemiyorum.   ha·*yuhr* ees·*te*·mee·yo·room

I'm here with my girlfriend/boyfriend.
   Kız/Erkek arkadaşımla buradayım.   kuhz/er·*kek* ar·ka·da·*shuhm*·la boo·ra·*da*·yuhm

Excuse me, I have to go now.
   Üzgünüm ama hemen gitmem gerekli.   ewz·*gew*·newm a·*ma* he·*men* geet·*mem* ge·rek·*lee*

local talk		
Leave me alone!	*Git başımdan!*	geet ba·shuhm·*dan*
Piss off!	*Defol!*	de·fol

SOCIAL

132

getting closer

I like you very much.
  Seni çok beğeniyorum.   se·*nee* chok be·e·*nee*·yo·room

You're great.
  Harikasın.   ha·ree·*ka*·suhn

Can I kiss you?
  Seni öpebilir miyim?   se·*nee* er·*pe*·bee·leer mee·*yeem*

Do you want to come inside for a while?
  Biraz içeri gelmek   *bee*·raz ee·che·ree gel·*mek*
  ister misin?   ees·*ter* mee·*seen*

Do you want a massage?
  Sana masaj yapmamı   sa·*na* ma·*sazh* yap·ma·*muh*
  ister misin?   ees·*ter* mee·*seen*

Can I stay over?
  Bu gece burada   boo ge·*je* boo·ra·*da*
  kalabilir miyim?   ka·*la*·bee·leer mee·*yeem*

---

local talk

He/She is …

a babe	*Bebek gibi.*	be·*bek* gee·*bee*
hot	*Çok seksi.*	chok sek·*see*
an idiot	*Aptalın teki o.*	ap·ta·*luhn* te·*kee* o
very attractive	*Çok çekici.*	chok che·kee·*jee*
full of himself/	*Kendini*	ken·dee·*nee*
herself	*beğenmiş.*	be·en·*meesh*

He/She gets around.
  İnsanı kandırmayı   een·sa·*nuh* kan·duhr·ma·*yuh*
  iyi biliyor.   ee·*yee* bee·*lee*·yor

sex

Kiss me.
Öp beni. — erp be·*nee*

I want you.
Seni istiyorum. — se·*nee* ees·*tee*·yo·room

Let's go to bed.
Hadi yatalım. — *ha*·dee ya·ta·*luhm*

Touch me here.
Dokun bana. — do·*koon* ba·*na*

Do you like this?
Hoşuna gidiyor mu? — ho·shoo·*na* gee·*dee*·yor moo

I like that.
Çok hoşuma gidiyor. — chok ho·shoo·*ma* gee·*dee*·yor

I don't like that.
Bundan hiç hoşlanmadım. — boon·*dan* heech hosh·*lan*·ma·duhm

I think we should stop now.
Daha ileri gitmeyelim. — da·*ha* e·le·*ree* geet·me·ye·leem

Do you have a (condom)?
(Prezervatifin) var mı? — (pre·zer·va·tee·*feen*) var muh

Let's use a (condom).
(Prezervatif) kullanalım. — (pre·zer·va·*teef*) kool·la·na·*luhm*

I won't do it without protection.
Korunmasız yapmam. — ko·roon·ma·*suhz yap*·mam

---

sweet nothings

My beauty.	*Güzelim.*	gew·ze·*leem*
My darling.	*Sevgilim.*	sev·gee·*leem*
My dear.	*Canım.*	ja·*nuhm*
My only one.	*Bir tanem.*	beer ta·*nem*
My sweetie.	*Tatlım.*	tat·*luhm*

It's my first time.
Bu benim ilk defam.   boo be·*neem* eelk de·*fam*

Oh my god!	*Aman tanrım!*	a·*man* tan·*ruhm*
That's great.	*Harika!*	ha·ree·*ka*
Easy tiger!	*Yavaş ol!*	ya·*vash* ol

That was …		
amazing	*Harikaydı.*	ha·ree·*kai*·duh
romantic	*Romantikti.*	ro·man·*teek*·tee
wild	*Çılgınlıktı.*	chuhl·guhn·*luhk*·tuh

love

aşk

I think we're good together.
Birbirimizi   beer·bee·ree·mee·*zee*
tamamlıyoruz.   ta·mam·*luh*·yo·rooz

I love you.
Seni seviyorum.   se·*nee* se·*vee*·yo·room

Will you …?	*… misin?*	… mee·*seen*
go out	*Benimle*	be·*neem*·le
with me	*çıkmak ister*	chuhk·*mak* ees·*ter*
meet my	*Anne ve babamla*	an·ne ve ba·bam·*la*
parents	*tanışmak ister*	ta·nuhsh·*mak* ees·*ter*
marry me	*Benimle evlenir*	be·*neem*·le ev·le·*neer*

problems

Are you seeing someone else?
Yoksa bir başkasıyla   yok·sa beer bash·ka·suhy·la
mı çıkıyorsun?   muh chuh·kuh·yor·soon

He/She is just a friend.
O sadece bir arkadaş.   o sa·de·je beer ar·ka·dash

You're just using me for sex.
Beni sadece seks   be·nee sa·de·je seks
için kullanıyorsun.   ee·cheen kool·la·nuh·yor·soon

I never want to see you again.
Seni bir daha asla   se·nee beer da·ha as·la
görmek istemiyorum.   ger·mek ees·te·mee·yo·room

I don't think it's working out.
Bence bu ilişki   ben·je boo ee·leesh·kee
yürümüyor.   yew·rew·mew·yor

We'll work it out.
Bir çözüm bulacağımıza   beer cher·zewm boo·la·ja·uh·muh·za
inanıyorum.   ee·na·nuh·yo·room

leaving

I have to leave (tomorrow).
(Yarın) Gitmem gerekli.   (ya·ruhn) geet·mem ge·rek·lee

I'll …	*Seni …*	se·nee …
keep in touch	*arayacağım*	a·ra·ya·ja·uhm
miss you	*özleyeceğim*	erz·le·ye·je·eem
visit you	*görmeye*	ger·me·ye
	geleceğim	ge·le·je·eem

beliefs & cultural differences
inançlar & kültürel farklılıklar

religion

What's your religion?
Dininiz nedir? pol   dee·nee·*neez* ne·deer
Dinin nedir? inf   dee·*neen* ne·deer

I'm not religious.
Dindar değilim.   deen·*dar* de·*ee*·leem

I'm (a/an) …	*Ben …*	ben …
agnostic	*agnostiğim*	ag·nos·*tee*·eem
Alevi	*Aleviyim*	a·le·*vee*·yeem
Buddhist	*Budistim*	boo·*dees*·teem
Catholic	*Katoliğim*	ka·to·*lee*·eem
Christian	*Hıristiyanım*	huh·rees·tee·*ya*·nuhm
Hindu	*Hinduyum*	heen·*doo*·yoom
Jehovah's	*Yehova*	ye·*ho*·va
Witness	*Şahidiyim*	sha·hee·*dee*·yeem
Jewish	*Yahudiyim*	ya·hoo·*dee*·yeem
Muslim	*Müslümanım*	mews·lew·*ma*·nuhm
Shiite	*Şiiyim*	shee·*ee*·yeem
Sunni	*Sünniyim*	sewn·*nee*·yeem

I believe in …	*Ben …*	ben …
	inanıyorum.	ee·na·*nuh*·yo·room
I don't believe	*Ben …*	ben …
in …	*inanmıyorum.*	ee·*nan*·muh·yo·room
astrology	*astrolojiye*	as·tro·lo·zhee·*ye*
fate	*kadere*	ka·de·*re*
God	*Tanrıya*	tan·ruh·*ya*

137

Where can I ...?	*Nerede ...?*	*ne·re·de*
attend mass	*ayin yapabilirim*	a·*yeen* ya·*pa*·bee·lee·reem
attend a	*ibadet*	ee·*ba*·det
service	*edebilirim*	e·*de*·bee·lee·reem
pray	*dua edebilirim*	doo·*a* e·*de*·bee·lee·reem
worship	*ibadet*	ee·*ba*·det
	yapabilirim	ya·*pa*·bee·lee·reem

cultural differences

Is this a local or national custom?
Bu yerel mi yoksa   boo ye·*rel* mee *yok*·sa
ulusal bir gelenek mi?   oo·loo·*sal* beer ge·le·*nek* mee

I don't want to offend you.
Sizi kırmak istemem.   see·*zee* kuhr·*mak* ees·*te*·mem

I'll try it.
Deneyeceğim.   de·ne·ye·*je*·eem

I'd rather not join in.
Ben size katılmasam   ben see·*ze* ka·*tuhl*·ma·sam
daha iyi.   da·*ha* ee·*yee*

I'm sorry. I didn't mean to do/say anything wrong.
Özür dilerim.   er·*zewr* dee·*le*·reem
Yanlış birşey yapmak/   yan·*luhsh* beer·*shay* yap·*mak*/
söylemek istemedim.   say·le·*mek* ees·*te*·me·deem

I'm sorry, it's	*Üzgünüm ama*	ewz·*gew*·newm a·*ma*
against my ...	*bu benim ...*	boo be·*neem* ...
	aykırı.	ai·kuh·*ruh*
beliefs	*inançlarıma*	ee·nanch·la·ruh·*ma*
religion	*dinime*	dee·nee·*me*

This is ...	*Bu çok ...*	boo chok ...
different	*farklı*	fark·*luh*
fun	*eğlenceli*	e·len·je·*lee*
interesting	*ilginç*	eel·*geench*

In this chapter, phrases are in the informal *sen* sen (you) form only. If you're not sure what this means, see the box on page 30.

When's the gallery/museum open?

Galeri/Müze	ga·le·*ree*/mew·ze
ne zaman açılıyor?	ne za·*man* a·chuh·*luh*·yor

What kind of art are you interested in?

Ne tür sanattan	ne tewr sa·nat·*tan*
hoşlanırsın?	hosh·la·*nuhr*·suhn

What's in the collection?

Koleksiyonda neler var?	ko·lek·see·yon·*da ne*·ler var

What do you think of …?

… hakkında ne	… hak·kuhn·*da* ne
düşünüyorsun?	dew·shew·*new*·yor·soon

It's an exhibition of …

Bu bir … sergisi.	boo beer … ser·gee·*see*

I'm interested in …

Ben … ile	ben … ee·*lee*
ilgileniyorum.	eel·gee·le·*nee*·yo·room

I like the works of …

… eserlerini beğeniyorum.	… e·ser·le·ree·*nee* be·e·*nee*·yo·room

It reminds me of …

Bana … hatırlatıyor.	ba·*na* … ha·tuhr·la·*tuh*·yor

graphic	*grafik*	gra·*feek*
impressionist	*izlenimci*	eez·le·neem·*jee*
Islamic	*İslamcı*	ees·lam·*juh*
modern	*modern*	mo·*dern*
nomadic	*göçebeliğe ait*	ger·che·be·lee·*e* a·*eet*
performance	*eser*	e·*ser*
Renaissance	*Rönesans*	rer·ne·*sans*
Turkish	*geleneksel Türk*	ge·le·nek·*sel* tewrk
traditional art	*sanatı*	sa·na·*tuh*

architecture	*mimari*	mee·ma·*ree*
art	*sanat*	sa·*nat*
artwork	*sanat eseri*	sa·*nat* e·se·*ree*
calligraphy	*güzel yazı sanatı*	gew·*zel* ya·*zuh* sa·na·*tuh*
carpet	*halı*	ha·*luh*
weaving	*dokumacılığı*	do·koo·ma·juh·luh·*uh*
curator	*müze müdürü*	mew·*ze* mew·dew·*rew*
design n	*desen*	de·*sen*
embroidery	*nakış*	na·*kuhsh*
etching	*resim hakketme*	re·*seem* hak·ket·*me*
	sanatı	sa·na·*tuh*
exhibit n	*sergi*	ser·*gee*
exhibition hall	*sergi salonu*	ser·*gee* sa·lo·*noo*
installation	*yerleştirme*	yer·lesh·teer·*me*
Islamic	*İslam mimarisi*	ees·*lam* mee·ma·ree·*see*
architecture		
lace-making	*dantel işleme*	dan·*tel* eesh·le·*me*
metalwork	*metal işçiliği*	me·*tal* eesh·chee·lee·*ee*
opening	*açılış*	a·chuh·*luhsh*
painter	*ressam*	res·*sam*
painting (artwork)	*tablo*	*tab*·lo
painting	*boyama tekniği*	bo·ya·*ma* tek·nee·*ee*
(technique)		
paper marbling	*ebru sanatı*	eb·*roo* sa·na·*tuh*
period	*dönem*	der·*nem*
permanent	*daimi*	da·ee·*mee*
collection	*kolleksiyon*	ko·lek·see·*yon*
porcelain	*porselen*	por·se·*len*
pottery	*çömlekçilik*	cherm·lek·chee·*leek*
print n	*baskı*	bas·*kuh*
sculptor	*heykeltıraş*	hay·kel·tuh·*rash*
sculpture	*heykeltıraşlık*	hay·kel·tuh·rash·*luhk*
statue	*heykel*	hay·*kel*
studio	*stüdyo*	*stewd*·yo
style n	*tarz*	tarz
technique	*teknik*	tek·*neek*
woodworking	*ahşap*	ah·*shap*
	işlemeciliği	eesh·le·me·jee·lee·*ee*

In this chapter, phrases are in the informal *sen* sen (you) form only. If you're not sure what this means, see the box on page 30.

sporting interests

spor merakı

What sport do you follow/play?

Hangi sporu takip		han·gee spo·*roo* ta·keep
ediyorsunuz/		e·*dee*·yor·soo·nooz/
oynuyorsunuz?		oy·*noo*·yor·soo·nooz

I follow ...	*Ben ... oyunlarını*	ben ... o·yoon·la·ruh·*nuh*
	takip ederim.	ta·*keep* e·*de*·reem
I play ...	*Ben ... oynarım.*	ben ... oy·*na*·ruhm
football	*futbol*	*foot*·bol
(soccer)		
tennis	*tenis*	te·*nees*

I do ...	*Ben ... yaparım.*	ben ... ya·*pa*·ruhm
martial arts	*savunma sporları*	sa·voon·*ma* spor·la·*ruh*
scuba diving	*aletli dalış*	a·let·*lee* da·*luhsh*
wrestling	*güreş*	gew·*resh*

I ...	*Ben ...*	ben ...
cycle	*bisiklete*	bee·seek·le·*te*
	binerim	bee·*ne*·reem
run	*koşarım*	ko·*sha*·ruhm

calling the game

The names and terminology of most sports have been translated into Turkish, but you'll also hear English words used. Use the English terms and you'll be clearly understood.

Do you like (cricket)?
(Kriket) sever misin?   (kree-*ket*) se-*ver* mee-*seen*

Yes, very much.
Evet, çok.   e-*vet* chok

Not really.
Pek değil.   pek de-*eel*

I like watching it.
İzlemeyi severim.   eez-le-me-*yee* se-*ve*-reem

Who's your favourite …?	*En sevdiğin …?*	en sev-dee-*een* …
sportsperson	*sporcu kim*	spor-*joo* keem
team	*takım hangisi*	ta-*kuhm* han-gee-see

going to a game

Would you like to go to a game?
Maça gitmek ister misin?   ma-*cha* geet-mek ees-*ter* mee-*seen*

Who are you supporting?
Kimi tutuyorsun?   kee-mee too-too-yor-soon

Who's playing/winning?
Kim oynuyor/kazanıyor?   keem oy-*noo*-yor/ka-za-*nuh*-yor

That was a …	*… bir oyundu!*	… beer o-*yoon*-doo
game!		
bad	*Berbat*	ber-*bat*
boring	*Sıkıcı*	suh-kuh-*juh*
great	*Harika*	ha-ree-*ka*

scoring		
What's the score?	*Skor nedir?*	skor *ne*-deer
draw/even	*berabere*	be-*ra*-be-re
love (tennis)	*sıfır sıfır*	suh-*fuhr* suh-*fuhr*
match-point	*maç sayısı*	mach sa-yuh-*suh*
nil	*sıfır*	suh-*fuhr*

playing sport

Do you want to play?
Oynamak ister misin? oy·na·*mak* ees·*ter* mee·*seen*

Can I join in?
Ben de oynayabilir ben de oy·na·*ya*·bee·leer
miyim? mee·*yeem*

That would be great.
Çok iyi olur. chok ee·*yee* o·*loor*

I can't.
Yapamam. ya·*pa*·mam

I have an injury.
Sakatlığım var. sa·kat·luh·*uhm* var

Your/My point.
Senin/Benim sayım. se·*neen*/be·*neem* sa·*yuhm*

Kick/Pass it to me!
Bana pas ver! ba·*na* pas ver

You're a good player.
İyi bir oyuncusun. ee·*yee* beer o·yoon·*joo*·soon

Thanks for the game.
Oyun için teşekkürler. o·*yoon* ee·*cheen* te·shek·kewr·*ler*

Where's a good place to …?	*… için neresi iyi?*	*… ee·cheen ne·re·see ee·yee*
fish	*Balık avlamak*	ba·*luhk* av·la·*mak*
go horse riding	*Ata binmek*	a·*ta* been·*mek*
run	*Koşmak*	kosh·*mak*
ski	*Kayak yapmak*	ka·*yak* yap·*mak*
snorkel	*Şnorkel*	shnor·*kel*
surf	*Sörf yapmak*	serf yap·*mak*

What a ...!	Ne ...!	ne ...
goal	goldü	gol-dew
hit/kick	vuruştu	voo-roosh-too
pass	pastı	pas-tuh
performance	oyundu	o-yoon-doo

Where's the nearest ...?	En yakın ... nerede?	en ya-kuhn ... ne-re-de
golf course	golf alanı	golf a-la-nuh
gym	jimnastik salonu	zheem-nas-teek sa-lo-noo
swimming pool	yüzme havuzu	yewz-me ha-voo-zoo
tennis court	tenis kortu	te-nees kor-too

What's the charge per ...?	... ne kadar?	... ne ka-dar
day	Günlüğü	gewn-lew-ew
game	Oyun başına ücreti	o-yoon ba-shuh-na ewj-re-tee
hour	Saati	sa-a-tee
visit	Giriş	gee-reesh

Can I hire a ...?	... kiralayabilir miyim?	... kee-ra-la-ya-bee-leer mee-yeem
ball	Top	top
bicycle	Bisiklet	bee-seek-let
court	Kort	kort
racquet	Raket	ra-ket

Do I have to be a member to attend?

Oynamak için üye olmam gerekli mi?	oy-na-mak ee-cheen ew-ye ol-mam ge-rek-lee mee

Is there a women-only session?

Sadece bayanlara özel programınız var mı?	sa-de-je ba-yan-la-ra er-zel prog-ra-muh-nuhz var muh

Where are the changing rooms?

Soyunma odaları nerede?	so-yoon-ma o-da-la-ruh ne-re-de

diving

dalarken

Where's a good diving site?
Dalmak için neresi iyi?   dal·*mak* ee·*cheen* ne·re·see ee·*yee*

I'd like to ...	... *istiyorum.*	... ees·*tee*·yo·room
explore caves/	*Mağaraları/*	ma·a·ra·la·*ruh*/
wrecks	*Batıkları*	ba·tuhk·la·*ruh*
	incelemek	een·je·le·*mek*
go night diving	*Gece dalışına*	ge·*je* da·luh·shuh·*na*
	çıkmak	chuhk·*mak*
go scuba diving	*Aletli dalışa*	a·let·*lee* da·luh·*sha*
	çıkmak	chuhk·*mak*
go snorkelling	*Şnorkelle dalmak*	shnor·*kel*·le dal·*mak*
join a diving	*Dalış turuna*	da·*luhsh* too·roo·*na*
tour	*katılmak*	ka·tuhl·*mak*
learn to dive	*Dalmayı*	dal·ma·*yuh*
	öğrenmek	er·ren·*mek*

Are there ...?	... *var mı?*	... var muh
currents	*Akıntı*	a·kuhn·*tuh*
sharks	*Köpek balıkları*	ker·*pek* ba·luhk·la·*ruh*
whales	*Balinalar*	ba·lee·na·*lar*

Is the visibility good?
Görüş iyi mi?   ger·*rewsh* ee·*yee* mee

How deep is the dive?
Dalış derinliği nedir?   da·*luhsh* de·reen·lee·*ee* ne·deer

Is it a boat/shore dive?
Tekne/Kıyı dalışı mı?   tek·*ne*/kuh·*yuh* da·luh·*shuh* muh

I need an air fill.
Hava doldurmaya   ha·*va* dol·door·ma·*ya*
ihtiyacım var.   eeh·tee·*ya*·juhm var

I want to	… *kiralamak*	… kee·ra·la·*mak*
hire (a) …	*istiyorum.*	ees·*tee*·yo·room
buoyancy vest	*Can yeleği*	jan ye·le·*ee*
diving equipment	*Dalış*	da·*luhsh*
	malzemeleri	mal·ze·me·le·*ree*
flippers	*Palet*	pa·*let*
mask	*Maske*	mas·*ke*
regulator	*Regülatör*	re·gew·la·*ter*
snorkel	*Şnorkel*	shnor·*kel*
tank	*Hava tüpü*	ha·*va* tew·*pew*
weight belt	*Ağırlık kemeri*	a·uhr·*luhk* ke·me·*ree*
wetsuit	*Dalış elbisesi*	da·*luhsh* el·bee·se·*see*

extreme sports

tehlikeli sporlar

I'd like to go …	… *yapmak*	… yap·*mak*
	istiyorum.	ees·*tee*·yo·room
abseiling	*Kaya inişi*	ka·*ya* ee·nee·*shee*
caving	*Mağaracılık*	ma·a·ra·juh·*luhk*
canyoning	*Kanyon*	kan·*yon*
	yürüyüşü	yew·rew·yew·*shew*
game fishing	*Balık tutma*	ba·*luhk* toot·*ma*
	yarışı	ya·ruh·*shuh*
hang-gliding	*Yelkenkanat*	yel·*ken*·ka·nat
	uçuşu	oo·choo·*shoo*
hot-air ballooning	*Balon sporu*	ba·*lon* spo·*roo*
mountain biking	*Dağ bisikleti*	da bee·seek·le·*tee*
paragliding	*Yamaç*	ya·*mach*
	paraşütü	pa·ra·shew·*tew*
	uçuşu	oo·choo·*shoo*
rock climbing	*Kaya*	ka·*ya*
	tırmanışı	tuhr·ma·nuh·*shuh*
skydiving	*Serbest paraşüt*	ser·*best* pa·ra·*shewt*
	uçuşu	oo·choo·*shoo*
snowboarding	*Board kayağı*	bord ka·ya·*uh*
white-water	*Rafting*	raf·*teeng*
rafting		

Is the equipment secure?
Teçhizat emniyetli mi?   tech·hee·*zat* em·nee·yet·*lee* mee

Is this safe?
Bu emniyetli mi?   boo em·nee·yet·*lee* mee

This is insane.
Delilik bu.   de·lee·*leek* boo

For words or phrases you might need while hiking or trekking,
see **outdoors**, page 151, and **camping**, page 71.

fishing

balık avlarken

Where are the good spots?
Balık avlamak için   ba·*luhk* av·la·*mak* ee·*cheen*
neresi iyi?   ne·re·see ee·*yee*

Do I need a fishing permit?
Balık avlama iznine   ba·*luhk* av·la·*ma* eez·nee·*ne*
ihtiyacım var mı?   eeh·tee·ya·*juhm* var muh

Do you do fishing tours?
Balık avlama turları   ba·*luhk* av·la·*ma* toor·la·*ruh*
düzenliyor musunuz?   dew·zen·*lee*·yor moo·soo·*nooz*

What's the best bait?
En iyi yem hangisi?   en ee·*yee* yem *han*·gee·see

Are they biting?
Isırırlar mı?   uh·suh·*ruhr*·lar muh

What kind of fish are you landing?
Ne tür balık   ne tewr ba·*luhk*
çıkarıyorsunuz?   chuh·ka·*ruh*·yor·soo·nooz

How much does it weigh?
Ağırlığı nedir?   a·uhr·luh·*uh* ne·deer

football/soccer

Who plays for (Galatasaray)?
(Galatasaray'da)   (ga·la·*ta*·sa·rai·da)
kimler oynuyor?   *keem*·ler oy·*noo*·yor

He's a great (player).
O çok iyi bir (oyuncu).   o chok ee·*yee* beer (o·yoon·*joo*)

He played brilliantly in the match against (Italy).
(İtalya) maçında   (ee·*tal*·ya) ma·chuhn·*da*
muhteşem oynadı.   mooh·te·*shem* oy·na·*duh*

Which team is at the top of the league?
Hangi takım lig   *han*·gee ta·*kuhm* leeg
birincisi?   bee·reen·jee·*see*

Off to see a match? Check out **going to a game**, page 142.

skiing

kayak

How much is a pass?
Giriş ne kadar?   gee-*reesh* ne ka-*dar*

Can I take lessons?
Ders alabilir miyim?   ders a-*la*-bee-leer mee-*yeem*

I'd like to hire ...	*... kiralamak istiyorum.*	*... kee-ra-la-mak* ees-*tee*-yo-room
boots	*Kayak ayakkabısı*	ka-*yak* a-yak-ka-buh-*suh*
gloves	*Kayak eldiveni*	ka-*yak* el-dee-ve-*nee*
goggles	*Kayak gözlüğü*	ka-*yak* gerz-lew-*ew*
poles	*Baton*	ba-*ton*
skis	*Kayak takımı*	ka-*yak* ta-kuh-*muh*
a ski suit	*Kayak elbisesi*	ka-*yak* el-bee-se-*see*

Is it possible to go ...?	*... yapmak mümkün mü?*	*... yap-mak* mewm-*kewn* mew
Alpine skiing	*Alp kayağı*	alp ka-ya-*uh*
cross-country skiing	*Kayaklı koşu*	ka-yak-*luh* ko-*shoo*
snowboarding	*Board kayağı*	bord ka-ya-*uh*
tobogganing	*Kar kızağı ile kayak*	kar kuh-za-*uh* ee-*le* ka-*yak*

What are the conditions like ...?	*... kayak koşulları nelerdir?*	*... ka-yak* ko-shool-la-*ruh* ne-ler-*deer*
at Palandöken	*Palandöken'de*	pa-*lan*-der-ken-de
higher up	*Yukarı kısımlarda*	yoo-ka-*ruh* kuh-suhm-lar-*da*
on that run	*Bu inişin*	boo ee-*nee*-sheen

Which are the ... slopes?	Hangi kayak pisti ... kayakçılar için?	han·gee ka·yak pees·tee ... ka·yak·chuh·lar ee·cheen
beginner	amatör	a·ma·ter
intermediate	az deneyimli	az de·ne·yeem·lee
advanced	deneyimli	de·ne·yeem·lee

What level is that slope?

| Yamaç yüksekliği nedir? | ya·mach yewk·sek·lee·ee ne·deer |

For more skiing vocabulary, see the **dictionary**.

water sports

Can I book a lesson?

| Ders için randevu alabilir miyim? | ders ee·cheen ran·de·voo a·la·bee·leer mee·yeem |

Can I hire (a) ...?	... kiralayabilir miyim?	... kee·ra·la·ya·bee·leer mee·yeem
boat	Tekne	tek·ne
canoe	Kano	ka·no
kayak	Kayak	ka·yak
life jacket	Can yeleği	jan ye·le·ee
scuba gear	Dalış malzemeleri	da·luhsh mal·ze·me·le·ree
snorkelling gear	Şnorkel	shnor·kel
water-skis	Su kayağı	soo ka·ya·uh
wetsuit	Dalış elbisesi	da·luhsh el·bee·se·see

Are there any ...?	... var mı?	... var muh
reefs	Kayalıklar	ka·ya·luhk·lar
rips	Anafor	a·na·for
water hazards	Herhangi bir su tehlikesi	her·han·gee beer soo teh·lee·ke·see

For the names of water sports, see the **dictionary**.

SOCIAL

hiking

kır gezisi

Where can I ...?	Nereden ...?	ne·re·den ...
buy supplies	erzak alabilirim	er·zak a·la·bee·lee·reem
find someone who knows this area	bu bölgeyi bilen birisini bulabilirim	boo berl·ge·yee bee·len bee·ree·see·nee boo·la·bee·lee·reem
get a map	harita alabilirim	ha·ree·ta a·la·bee·lee·reem
hire hiking gear	yürüyüş malzemeleri kiralayabilirim	yew·rew·yewsh mal·ze·me·le·ree kee·ra·la·ya·bee·lee·reem

How ...?	... nedir?	... ne·deer
high is the climb	Tırmanış yüksekliği	tuhr·ma·nuhsh yewk·sek·lee·ee
long is the trail	Patikanın uzunluğu	pa·tee·ka·nuhn oo·zoon·loo·oo

Is it safe?
Emniyetli mi? — em·nee·yet·lee mee

Do we need a guide?
Rehbere ihtiyacımız var mı? — reh·be·re eeh·tee·ya·juh·muhz var muh

Are there guided treks?
Rehberli yürüyüşleriniz var mı? — reh·ber·lee yew·rew·yewsh·le·ree·neez var muh

Is there a hut?
Orada kulübe var mı? — o·ra·da koo·lew·be var muh

When does it get dark?
Hava ne zaman kararıyor? — ha·va ne za·man ka·ra·ruh·yor

Do we need to take ...?	... almamıza gerek var mı?	... al·ma·muh·za ge·rek var muh
bedding	Uyku tulumu	ooy·koo too·loo·moo
food	Yiyecek	yee·ye·jek
water	Su	soo

Is the track ...?	Patika ...?	pa·tee·ka ...
(well) marked	(iyice) işaretli mi	(ee·yee·je) ee·sha·ret·lee mee
open	açık mı	a·chuhk muh
scenic	manzarası güzel mi	man·za·ra·suh gew·zel mee

Which is the ... route?	En ... yol hangisi?	en ... yol han·gee·see
easiest	kolay	ko·lai
most interesting	ilginç	eel·geench
shortest	kısa	kuh·sa

Where can I find the ...?	... nerede?	... ne·re·de
camping ground	Kamp alanı	kamp a·la·nuh
nearest village	En yakın köy	en ya·kuhn kay
showers	Duşlar	doosh·lar
toilets	Tuvaletler	too·va·let·ler

Where have you come from?
Nereden geliyorsunuz? ne·re·den ge·lee·yor·soo·nooz

How long did it take?
Yol ne kadar sürdü? yol ne ka·dar sewr·dew

Does this path go to (Alandız)?
Bu patika (Alandız'a) gider mi? boo pa·tee·ka (a·lan·duh·za) gee·der mee

Can I go through here?
Buradan geçebilir miyim? boo·ra·dan ge·che·bee·leer mee·yeem

Is the water OK to drink?
Su içilebilir mi? soo ee·chee·le·bee·leer mee

I'm lost.
Kayboldum. kai·bol·doom

beach

Where's the ... beach?	... *nerede?*	... ne·re·de
best	*En iyi plaj*	en ee·*yee* plazh
nearest	*En yakın plaj*	en ya·*kuhn* plazh
nudist	*Çıplaklar plajı*	chuhp·lak·*lar* pla·*zhuh*
public	*Halk plajı*	halk pla·*zhuh*

Is it safe to dive/swim here?
Burada dalmak/yüzmek   boo·ra·*da* dal·*mak*/yewz·*mek*
emniyetli mi?   em·nee·yet·*lee* mee

Is the water polluted?
Su kirli mi?   soo keer·*lee* mee

Are there dangerous currents?
Tehlikeli akıntılar var mı?   teh·lee·ke·*lee* a·kuhn·tuh·*lar* var muh

What time is high/low tide?
Deniz ne zaman   de·*neez* ne za·*man*
kabarıyor/alçalıyor?   ka·ba·*ruh*·yor/al·cha·*luh*·yor

Do we have to pay?
Ödeme yapmamız   er·de·*me* yap·ma·*muhz*
gerekli mi?   ge·rek·*lee* mee

How much for a/an ...?	... *ne kadar?*	... ne ka·*dar*
chair	*Şezlong*	shez·*long*
hut	*Kalif*	ka·*leef*
umbrella	*Şemsiye*	shem·see·*ye*

---

listen for ...

Dalmak yasaktır!	dal·*mak* ya·*sak*·tuhr	**No diving!**
Tehlikeli!	teh·lee·ke·*lee*	**It's dangerous!**
Ters akıntılara	ters a·kuhn·tuh·la·*ra*	**Be careful of**
dikkat edin!	deek·*kat* e·*deen*	**the undertow!**
Yüzmek yasaktır!	yewz·*mek* ya·*sak*·tuhr	**No swimming!**

outdoors

153

weather

What's the weather like?
Hava nasıl? ha·*va* na·suhl

It's ...	*Hava ...*	ha·*va* ...
cloudy	*bulutlu*	boo·loot·*loo*
cold	*soğuk*	so·*ook*
freezing	*buz gibi*	booz gee·*bee*
hot	*sıcak*	suh·*jak*
raining	*yağmurlu*	ya·moor·*loo*
snowing	*kar yağışlı*	kar ya·uhsh·*luh*
sunny	*güneşli*	gew·nesh·*lee*
windy	*rüzgarlı*	rewz·gar·*luh*

flora & fauna

bitki & hayvanlar

What ... is that?	*Bu hangi ...?*	boo *han*·gee ...
animal	*hayvan*	hai·*van*
flower	*çiçek*	chee·*chek*
plant	*bitki*	beet·*kee*
tree	*ağaç*	a·*ach*

For geographical and agricultural terms, and names of animals and plants, see the **dictionary**.

local animals & plants		
Ankara cat	*Ankara kedisi*	an·ka·ra ke·dee·*see*
bald ibis	*kelaynak*	kel·ai·nak
Caretta turtle	*Caretta Caretta*	ka·ret·ta ka·ret·ta
Kangal dog	*Kangal köpeği*	kan·gal ker·pe·ee
partridge	*keklik*	kek·leek
poppy	*gelincik*	ge·leen·jeek
Van cat	*Van kedisi*	van ke·dee·see

basics

temel sözcükler & cümleler

breakfast	*kahvaltı*	kah·val·*tuh*
lunch	*öğle yemeği*	er·*le* ye·me·*ee*
dinner	*akşam yemeği*	ak·*sham* ye·me·*ee*
snack n	*hafif yemek*	ha·*feef* ye·*mek*
eat v	*yemek*	ye·*mek*
drink v	*içmek*	eech·*mek*
I'd like ...	*... istiyorum.*	... ees·*tee*·yo·room
I'm starving!	*Açlıktan*	ach·luhk·*tan*
	ölüyorum!	er·*lew*·yo·room

finding a place to eat

nerede yemeli

Can you	*İyi bir ...*	ee·*yee* beer ...
recommend a ...?	*tavsiye edebilir*	tav·see·ye e·de·bee·leer
	misiniz?	mee·see·*neez*
bar	*bar*	bar
café	*kafe*	ka·*fe*
fireside kebab restaurant	*ocakbaşı*	o·*jak*·ba·shuh
	kebabçısı	ke·bab·chuh·*suh*
kebab restaurant	*kebabçı*	ke·bab·*chuh*
ready-food restaurant	*lokanta*	lo·*kan*·ta
restaurant	*restoran*	res·to·*ran*

listen for ...

Bir dakika.	beer da·kee·*ka*	**One moment.**
Doluyuz.	do·*loo*·yooz	**We're full.**
Kapalıyız.	ka·pa·*luh*·yuhz	**We're closed.**

Where would you go for (a) ...?	... için nereye gidilebilir?	... ee·*cheen* ne·re·ye gee·dee·*le*·bee·leer
celebration	Kutlama yapmak	koot·la·*ma* yap·*mak*
cheap meal	Ucuz bir yemek yemek	oo·*jooz* beer ye·*mek* ye·*mek*
local specialities	Bu yöreye özgü birşeyler yemek	boo yer·re·ye erz·*gew* beer·shay·ler ye·*mek*

I'd like to reserve a table for ...	... bir masa ayırtmak istiyorum.	... beer ma·*sa* a·yuhrt·*mak* ees·*tee*·yo·room
(two) people	(İki) kişilik	(ee·*kee*) kee·shee·*leek*
(eight) o'clock	Saat (sekiz) için	sa·*at* (se·*keez*) ee·*cheer*

Are you still serving food?
Yemek servisi halen devam ediyor mu?
ye·*mek* ser·vee·*see* ha·len de·*vam* e·*dee*·yor moo

How long is the wait?
Ne kadar bekleriz?
ne ka·*dar* bek·*le*·reez

FOOD

156

restaurant

I'd like (a/the)…	… istiyorum.	… ees·tee·yo·room
children's	Çocuk	cho·jook
menu	menüsünü	me·new·sew·new
drink list	İçecek	ee·che·jek
	listesini	lees·te·see·nee
half portion	Yarım porsiyon	ya·ruhm por·see·yon
menu (in	(İngilizce)	(een·gee·leez·je)
English)	menüyü	me·new·yew
nonsmoking	Sigara	see·ga·ra
	içilmeyen	ee·cheel·me·yen
	bir yer	beer yer
smoking	Sigara	see·ga·ra
	içilen bir yer	ee·chee·len beer yer
table for (five)	(Beş) kişilik	(besh) kee·shee·leek
	bir masa	beer ma·sa

What would you recommend?
Ne tavsiye edersiniz?   ne tav·see·ye e·der·see·neez

What's in that dish?
Bu yemekte neler var?   boo ye·mek·te ne·ler var

What's that called?
Şuna ne deniliyor?   shoo·na ne de·nee·lee·yor

I'll have that.
Şunu alayım.   shoo·noo a·la·yuhm

Does it take long to prepare?
Hazırlanması uzun   ha·zuhr·lan·ma·suh oo·zoon
sürer mi?   sew·rer mee

Is it self-serve?
Self servis mi?   self ser·vees mee

Is there a cover charge?
Fiks menü fiyatınız   feeks me·new fee·ya·tuh·nuhz
var mı?   var muh

Is service included in the bill?
Hesaba servis dahil mi?   he·sa·ba ser·vees da·heel mee

Are these complimentary?
Bunlar müessesenin   boon·*lar* mew·es·se·se·*neen*
ikramı mı?   eek·ra·*muh* muh

How much is that dish?
Şu yemek ne kadar?   shoo ye·*mek* ne ka·*dar*

Can you recommend a good local wine?
Güzel bir yöre şarabı   gew·*zel* beer yer·*re* sha·ra·*buh*
tavsiye eder misiniz?   tav·see·*ye* e·der mee·see·*neez*

I'd like (a/the)…	… *istiyorum.*	… ees·*tee*·yo·room
local	*Bu yöreye özgü*	boo yer·re·*ye* erz·*gew*
speciality	*bir yemek*	beer ye·*mek*
meal fit for	*Krallara layık*	kral·la·*ra* la·*yuhk*
a king	*bir yemek*	beer ye·*mek*
that dish	*Şu yemeği*	shoo ye·me·*ee*

I'd like it with/	*Yemeğimi*	ye·me·ee·*mee*
without …	… *istiyorum.*	… ees·*tee*·yo·room
black pepper	*kara biberli/*	ka·*ra* bee·ber·*lee/*
	kara bibersiz	ka·*ra* bee·ber·*seez*
cheese	*peynirli/*	pay·neer·*lee/*
	peynirsiz	pay·neer·*seez*
chilli	*acılı/acısız*	a·juh·*luh*/a·juh·*suhz*
chilli sauce	*acı soslu/*	a·*juh* sos·*loo/*
	acı sossuz	a·*juh* sos·*sooz*
garlic	*sarımsaklı/*	sa·ruhm·sak·*luh/*
	sarımsaksız	sa·ruhm·sak·*suhz*
ketchup	*ketçaplı/*	ket·chap·*luh/*
	ketçapsız	ket·chap·*suhz*
nuts	*fıstıklı/*	fuhs·tuhk·*luh/*
	fıstıksız	fuhs·tuhk·*suhz*
oil	*yağlı/yağsız*	ya·*luh*/ya·*suhz*
salt	*tuzlu/tuzsuz*	tooz·*loo*/tooz·*sooz*
tomato sauce	*domates soslu/*	do·ma·tes sos·*loo/*
	domates sossuz	do·ma·tes sos·*sooz*
vinegar	*sirkeli/sirkesiz*	seer·ke·*lee*/seer·ke·*seez*

For other specific meal requests, see **vegetarian & special meals**, page 173.

FOOD

at the table

masada

Please bring	Lütfen ...	lewt·fen ...
(a/the) ...	getirir misiniz?	ge·tee·reer mee·see·neez
bill	hesabı	he·sa·buh
glass	bir bardak	beer bar·dak
serviette	peçete	pe·che·te
cloth	bir masa silme	beer ma·sa seel·me
	bezi	be·zee
wineglass	bir şarap bardağı	beer sha·rap bar·da·uh

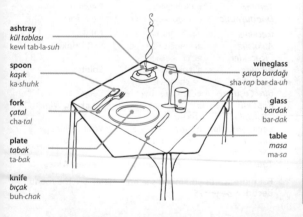

ashtray
kül tablası
kewl tab·la·suh

spoon
kaşık
ka·shuhk

fork
çatal
cha·tal

plate
tabak
ta·bak

knife
bıçak
buh·chak

wineglass
şarap bardağı
sha·rap bar·da·uh

glass
bardak
bar·dak

table
masa
ma·sa

eating out

159

talking food

I love this dish.
Bu yemeğe bayılıyorum.   boo ye·me·*e* ba·yuh·*luh*·yo·room

I love the local cuisine.
Buranın yemeklerine   boo·ra·*nuhn* ye·mek·le·ree·*ne*
bayılıyorum.   ba·yuh·*luh*·yo·room

That was delicious!
Nefisti!   ne·*fees*·tee

I'm full.
Doydum.   doy·*doom*

look for ...

Mezeler	me·ze·*ler*	Appetisers
Çorbalar	chor·ba·*lar*	Soups
Ordövler	or·derv·*ler*	Entrées
Salatalar	sa·la·ta·*lar*	Salads
Ana Yemekler	a·*na* ye·mek·*ler*	Main Courses
Yan Yemekler	yan ye·mek·*ler*	Side Dishes
Tatlılar	tat·luh·*lar*	Desserts
Dondurmalar	don·door·ma·*lar*	Ice Cream
İçecekler	ee·che·jek·*ler*	Drinks
Alkolsüz	al·kol·*sewz*	Soft Drinks
İçecekler	ee·che·jek·*ler*	
Alkollü	al·kol·*lew*	Spirits
İçecekler	ee·che·jek·*ler*	
Bira Çeşitleri	bee·ra che·sheet·le·*ree*	Beers
Köpüklü	ker·pewk·*lew*	Sparkling Wines
Şaraplar	sha·rap·*lar*	
Beyaz Şaraplar	be·*yaz* sha·rap·*lar*	White Wines
Kırmızı	kuhr·muh·*zuh*	Red Wines
Şaraplar	sha·rap·*lar*	
Tatlı Şaraplar	tat·*luh* sha·rap·*lar*	Dessert Wines

For more words you might see on a menu, see the **menu decoder**, page 175.

This is ...	Bu ...	boo ...
burnt	yanık	ya·nuhk
(too) cold	(çok) soğuk	(chok) so·ook
(too) spicy	(çok) acı	(chok) a·juh
spoiled	bozulmuş	bo·zool·moosh
stale	bayat	ba·yat
superb	enfes	en·fes
undercooked	az pişmiş	az peesh·meesh

methods of preparation

yemek pişirme teknikleri

I'd like it ...	... istiyorum.	... ees·tee·yo·room
I don't want it ...	... istemiyorum.	... ees·te·mee·yo·room
boiled	Haşlanmış	hash·lan·muhsh
broiled	Izgara	uhz·ga·ra
fried	Kızarmış	kuh·zar·muhsh
grilled	Izgara	uhz·ga·ra
mashed	Püre	pew·re
medium	Orta karar	or·ta ka·rar
	pişmiş	peesh·meesh
rare	Az pişmiş	az peesh·meesh
reheated	Isıtılmış	uh·suh·tuhl·muhsh
steamed	Buharda	boo·har·da
	pişmiş	peesh·meesh
well-done	İyi pişmiş	ee·yee peesh·meesh
with the dressing	Sosunu	so·soo·noo
on the side	yanında	ya·nuhn·da

nonalcoholic drinks

tea

Contrary to popular belief, the must-have drink in Turkey is *çay* chai (tea), not *kahve* kah·ve (coffee). You may be offered lemon, but don't expect any milk. Order your tea either *açık* a·chuhk (light) or *koyu* ko·yoo (dark) according to taste. Fruit, flower and herb teas are drunk for their health properties and are usually unsweetened.

cup of tea	*bir fincan çay*	beer feen·*jan* chai
glass of tea	*bir bardak çay*	beer bar·*dak* chai
tall glass of tea	*büyük bardak çay*	bew·*yewk* bar·*dak* chai
apple tea	*elma çayı*	el·*ma* cha·*yuh*
chamomile tea	*papatya çayı*	pa·*pat*·ya cha·*yuh*
cinnamon tea	*tarçın çayı*	tar·*chuhn* cha·*yuh*
fruit tea	*meyve çayı*	may·ve cha·*yuh*
island tea (sage)	*ada çayı*	a·*da* cha·*yuh*
lemon tea	*limon çayı*	lee·*mon* cha·*yuh*
linden-flower tea	*ıhlamur çayı*	uh·la·*moor* cha·*yuh*
orange tea	*portakal çayı*	por·ta·*kal* cha·*yuh*
peppermint tea	*nane çayı*	na·ne cha·*yuh*
thyme tea	*kekik çayı*	ke·*keek* cha·*yuh*

coffee

To get a classic 'melt your teaspoon' Turkish coffee, ask for a *Türk kahvesi* tewrk kah·ve·*see*. Each brew is made with different amounts of sugar – you don't put it in yourself – so order using the phrases on the next page. In the eastern parts of Turkey you can also order *mırra* muhr·*ra*, 'old-fashioned coffee' flavoured with *kakule* ka·*koo*·le (cardamom).

(cup of) coffee ...	... bir (fincan) kahve	... beer (feen·jan) kah·ve
with milk	sütlü	sewt·lew
with a little sugar	az şekerli	az she·ker·lee
with some sugar	orta şekerli	or·ta she·ker·lee
with a lot of sugar	çok şekerli	chok she·ker·lee
without sugar	şekersiz/sade	she·ker·seez/sa·de

If European coffee is your poison, try the words below:

... coffee	... bir kahve	... beer kah·ve
black	sütsüz	sewt·sewz
decaffeinated	kafeinsiz	ka·fe·een·seez
iced	buzlu	booz·loo
strong	sert	sert
white	sütlü	sewt·lew

local brews

ayran   ai·ran
A refreshing cold drink made of yogurt, water (or soda water) and salt, usually drunk at mealtimes.

boza   bo·za
A hot, creamy drink made of grain (such as chickpea, bulgur, millet) mixed with cinnamon. It's not drunk with meals and is sold by *bozacı* bo·za·juh (*boza* vendors) who walk the streets at night-time selling their brew.

gül şerbeti   gewl sher·be·tee
A summer drink made with rose-water, water and sugar – a specialty of Sivas.

sahlep   sah·lep
A hot drink of milk and crushed tapioca root extract, usually available in winter. It has a mild, nutty flavour and is drunk mostly for its health and aphrodisiac properties.

şalgam suyu   shal·gam soo·yoo
Juice of dark turnips, served cold and often with a piece of turnip in the glass – a specialty of the Adana region.

Turks call 'breakfast' *kahvaltı* kah·val·*tuh*, which literally means 'under coffee' or 'before coffee'.

cold drinks

orange juice	*portakal suyu*	por·ta·*kal* soo·yoo
soft drink	*alkolsüz içecek*	al·kol·*sewz* ee·che·*jek*
(hot) water	*(sıcak) su*	(suh·*jak*) soo
... mineral water	*maden ...*	ma·*den* ...
sparkling	*sodası*	so·da·*suh*
still	*suyu*	soo·*yoo*

alcoholic drinks

alkollü içecekler

brandy	*brendi*	*bren*·dee
champagne	*şampanya*	sham·*pan*·ya
cocktail	*kokteyl*	kok·*tayl*
local/imported ...	*... yerli/ithal*	... yer·*lee*/eet·*hal*
vermouth	*vermut*	ver·*moot*
vodka	*votka*	*vot*·ka
whisky	*viski*	*vees*·kee
a shot/glass of ...	*bir tek/bardak ...*	beer tek/bar·*dak* ...
(five-star)	*(beş yıldızlı)*	(besh yuhl·duhz·*luh*)
cognac	*konyak*	kon·*yak*
fruit brandy	*meyveli brendi*	may·ve·*lee bren*·dee
gin	*cin*	jeen
rum	*rom*	rom
a ... of beer	*bir ... bira*	beer ... *bee*·ra
can	*kutu*	koo·*too*
glass	*bardak*	bar·*dak*
jug	*sürahi*	sew·ra·*hee*
small bottle	*küçük şişe*	kew·*chewk* shee·*she*
large bottle	*büyük şişe*	bew·*yewk* shee·*she*

a bottle/glass	bir şişe/bardak	beer shee·*she*/bar·*dak*
of ... wine	... şarap	... sha·*rap*
dessert	tatlı	tat·*luh*
red	kırmızı	kuhr·muh·*zuh*
rosé	pembe	pem·*be*
sparkling	köpüklü	ker·pewk·*lew*
white	beyaz	be·*yaz*

in the bar

Excuse me!
Affedersiniz!   a·fe·*der*·see·neez

I'm next.
Benim sıram.   be·*neem* suh·*ram*

I'll have ...
... alayım.   ... a·la·*yuhm*

Rakı ra·*kuh* is the Turkish national drink, made from fermented grapes flavoured with anise. Naturally a strong, clear alcohol, it becomes cloudy white once you mix it. The traditional *meze* me·*ze* (snack) served with *rakı* is *beyaz peynir* be·*yaz* pay·*neer* (white cheese). It's nicknamed *aslan sütü* as·*lan* sew·*tew*, which means 'lion's milk' and it's apparently considered as mere 'milk to strong, powerful lions like Turkish men'. (Think of the lion-god Aslan in the *Chronicles of Narnia* by C.S. Lewis.)

As befits such a prestigious drink, certain rituals must be followed. *Rakı* should be cooled to 8–10°C before being served, and sipped from a tall cylindrical glass. On no account should you knock it back from a shot glass, and mixing *rakı* with other alcohol is done only at your own peril. Never put ice in the glass before you add the *rakı*, as this changes the taste. It's permitted to mix it with water or soda water, or alternate sips of *rakı* with sips of your mixer of choice. True *rakı* drinkers establish their preferred blend, as personal and ingrained as a signature.

To make toasts with *rakı*, wait until everyone has been served and try not to raise your glass higher than anyone else's. Join in the toast of *Şerefe!* she·re·*fe* (Cheers!) and have fun!

Same again, please.
   Aynısından lütfen.   ai·nuh·suhn·*dan* lewt·fen

No ice, thanks.
   Buz koymayın lütfen.   booz *koy*·ma·yuhn *lewt*·fen

I'll buy you a drink.
   Sana içecek alayım.   sa·*na* ee·che·jek a·la·*yuhm*

What would you like?
Ne alırsınız?　　　　　　　　ne a·*luhr*·suh·nuhz

I don't drink alcohol.
Alkol kullanmıyorum.　　　　al·*kol* kool·*lan*·muh·yo·room

It's my round.
Benim sıram.　　　　　　　　be·*neem* suh·*ram*

Do you serve meals here?
Yemek servisi　　　　　　　　ye·*mek* ser·vee·*see*
yapılıyor mu?　　　　　　　　ya·puh·*luh*·yor moo

drinking up

içerken

The drinks are on me.
İçkiler benden.　　　　　　　eech·kee·*ler* ben·*den*

Cheers!
Şerefe!　　　　　　　　　　　she·re·*fe*

This is hitting the spot.
Bu çok makbule geçti.　　　　boo chok mak·boo·*le* gech·*tee*

I feel fantastic!
Kendimi harika　　　　　　　ken·dee·*mee* ha·ree·*ka*
hissediyorum!　　　　　　　　hees·se·*dee*·yo·room

I think I've had one too many.
Sanırım çok içtim.　　　　　sa·*nuh*·ruhm chok eech·*teem*

---

listen for ...

Ne alırsınız? ne a·*luhr*·suh·nuhz	**What are you having?**
Sanırım yeterince içtin. sa·*nuh*·ruhm ye·te·reen·*je* eech·*teen*	**I think you've had enough.**
Son siparişler lütfen. son see·pa·reesh·*ler* lewt·*fen*	**Last orders.**

I'm feeling drunk.

Sarhoş oldum.   sar·*hosh* ol·doom

I'm pissed.

Zil zurna sarhoşum.   zeel zoor·*na* sar·*ho*·shoom

I feel ill.

Kendimi kötü   ken·dee·*mee* ker·*tew*

hissediyorum.   hees·se·*dee*·yo·room

Where's the toilet?

Tuvalet nerede?   too·va·*let* ne·re·de

I'm tired, I'd better go home.

Yorgunum, eve gitsem   yor·*goo*·noom e·*ve* geet·*sem*

daha iyi olur.   da·*ha* ee·*yee* o·*loor*

Can you call a taxi for me?

Bana bir taksi   ba·*na* beer tak·*see*

çağırır mısınız?   cha·uh·*ruhr* muh·suh·*nuhz*

I don't think you should drive.

Araba kullanmamalısın.   a·ra·*ba* kool·*lan*·ma·ma·luh·suhn

---

what a cucumber!

One Turkish word for 'dickhead' is *hıyar* huh·*yar*, which also means 'cucumber'.

buying food

yiyecek alırken

What's the local speciality?
*Bu yöreye has
yiyecekler neler?*
boo yer·re·ye has
yee·ye·jek·ler ne·ler

What's that?
Bu nedir?
boo ne·deer

What's *pestil*?
Pestil nedir?
pes·teel ne·deer

Can I taste it?
*Tadına bakabilir
miyim?*
ta·duh·na ba·ka·bee·leer
mee·yeem

How much (is a kilo of cheese)?
*(Bir kilo peynir)
Ne kadar?*
(beer kee·lo pay·neer)
ne ka·dar

I'd like ...	... istiyorum.	... ees·tee·yo·room
(200) grams	*(İkiyüz) gram*	(ee·kee·yewz) gram
half a dozen	*Yarım düzine*	ya·ruhm dew·zee·ne
a dozen	*Bir düzine*	beer dew·zee·ne
half a kilo	*Yarım kilo*	ya·ruhm kee·lo
a kilo	*Bir kilo*	beer kee·lo
(two) kilos	*(İki) kilo*	(ee·kee) kee·lo
a bottle	*Bir şişe*	beer shee·she
a jar	*Bir kavanoz*	beer ka·va·noz
a packet	*Bir paket*	beer pa·ket
a piece	*Bir parça*	beer par·cha
(three) pieces	*(Üç) parça*	(ewch) par·cha
a slice	*Bir dilim*	beer dee·leem
(six) slices	*(Altı) dilim*	(al·tuh) dee·leem
a tin	*Bir kutu*	beer koo·too

I'd like ...	... istiyorum.	... ees·tee·yo·room
(just) a little	(sadece) biraz	(sa·de·je) bee·raz
more	daha fazla	da·ha faz·la
some ...	biraz ...	bee·raz ...
that one	şunu	shoo·noo
this one	bunu	boo·noo

Less.	Daha az.	da·ha az
A bit more.	Biraz daha fazla.	bee·raz da·ha faz·la
Enough.	Yeterli.	ye·ter·lee

Do you have ...?	... var mı?	... var muh
anything	Daha ucuz	da·ha oo·jooz
cheaper	birşey	beer·shay
other kinds	Başka	bash·ka
	çeşitleriniz	che·sheet·le·ree·neez

Where can I find the ... section?	... reyonu nerede?	... re·yo·noo ne·re·de
dairy	Süt mamülleri	sewt ma·mewl·le·ree
fish	Balık	ba·luhk
frozen goods	Donmuş gıda	don·moosh guh·da
fruit and vegetable	Sebze meyve	seb·ze may·ve
meat	Et	et
poultry	Kümes	kew·mes
	hayvanları et	hai·van·la·ruh et

For food items, see the **menu decoder** and the **dictionary**.

food stuff

cooked	pişmiş	peesh·meesh
cured	terbiye edilmiş	ter·bee·ye e·deel·meesh
dried	kuru	koo·roo
fresh	taze	ta·ze
frozen	donmuş	don·moosh
raw	çiğ	chee
smoked	dumanda	doo·man·da
	kurutulmuş	koo·roo·tool·moosh

FOOD

170

Meze me·*ze* is the Turkish equivalent of Spanish tapas – a selection of small, tasty nibbles served in bars, restaurants and homes. Here's a list of some you're likely to find in your travels:

ançüez	an·chew·ez	pickled anchovy
barbunya pilaki	bar·*boon*·ya pee·*la*·kee	red bean salad
beyaz peynir	be·*yaz* pay·*neer*	white goat's cheese
beyin salatası	be·*yeen* sa·la·ta·*suh*	sheep's brain salad
biber dolması	bee·*ber* dol·ma·*suh*	stuffed capsicum
cacık	ja·*juhk*	yogurt with cucumber and mint
çerkez tavuğu	cher·*kez* ta·voo·*oo*	Circassian chicken, made with bread, walnuts, salt and garlic
enginar	en·gee·*nar*	cooked artichoke
fava	fa·*va*	mashed broad bean paste
haydari	hai·*da*·ree	yogurt with roasted eggplant and garlic
humus	hoo·*moos*	chickpea, tahini and lemon dip
kalamar	ka·la·*mar*	fried calamari
kısır	kuh·*suhr*	bulgur salad
lakerda	la·*ker*·da	sliced and salted tuna
mücver	mewj·*ver*	deep-fried zucchini fritters
pastırma	pas·tuhr·ma	air-dried beef
patlıcan kızartması	pat·luh·*jan* kuh·zart·ma·*suh*	fried eggplant with tomatoes
peynirli börek	pay·neer·*lee* ber·*rek*	cheese pastry
yaprak sarma	yap·*rak* sar·*ma*	vine leaves stuffed with rice, herbs and pine nuts

cooking utensils

Could I please borrow a ...?	Bir ... ödünç alabilir miyim lütfen?	beer ... er·dewnch a·la·bee·leer mee·yeem lewt·fen
chopping board	kesme tahtası	kes·me tah·ta·suh
frying pan	tava	ta·va
knife	bıçak	buh·chak
saucepan	tencere	ten·je·re

I need a ...	... ihtiyacım var.	... eeh·tee·ya·juhm var
chopping board	Kesme tahtasına	kes·me tah·ta·suh·na
frying pan	Tavaya	ta·va·ya
knife	Bıçağa	buh·cha·a
saucepan	Tencereye	ten·je·re·ye

For more cooking implements, see the **dictionary**.

---

listen for ...

Başka birşey var mı? bash·ka beer·shay var muh	**Anything else?**
Kalmadı. kal·ma·duh	**There isn't any.**
Ne arzu edersiniz? ne ar·zoo e·der·see·neez	**What would you like?**
Yardımcı olabilir miyim? yar·duhm·juh o·la·bee·leer mee·yeem	**Can I help you?**

vegetarian & special meals
vejeteryan & özel yemekler

ordering food

Where's a ... restaurant?	Buralarda ... restoran var mı?	boo·ra·lar·da ... res·to·ran var muh
Do you have ... food?	... yiyecekleriniz var mı?	... yee·ye·jek·le·ree·neez var muh
halal	helal	he·lal
kosher	koşer	ko·sher
vegetarian	vejeteryan	ve·zhe·ter·yan
I don't eat ...	... yemiyorum.	... ye·mee·yo·room
Is it cooked with ...?	İçinde ... var mı?	ee·cheen·de... var muh
butter	Tereyağ	te·re·ya
eggs	Yumurta	yoo·moor·ta
fish	Balık	ba·luhk
fish stock	Balık suyu	ba·luhk soo·yoo
meat stock	Et suyu	et soo·yoo
oil	Yağ	ya
pork	Domuz eti	do·mooz e·tee
poultry	Tavuk eti	ta·vook e·tee
red meat	Kırmızı et	kuhr·muh·zuh et

I can't eat meat.
  Et yiyemiyorum.   et yee·ye·mee·yo·room

Do you have any dishes without meat?
  Etsiz yemekleriniz var mı?   et·seez ye·mek·le·ree·neez var muh

---

asking about msg

Use the words *lezzet artırıcılar* lez·zet ar·tuh·ruh·juh·lar (flavour enhancers) to ask about MSG. The phrase *monosodyum glutamat* mo·no·sod·yoom gloo·ta·mat does exist but it isn't very well-known.

vegetarian & special meals

173

Is this ...?	Bu ...?	boo ...
decaffeinated	kafeinsiz mi	ka·fe·een·*seez* mee
free of animal produce	hayvansal ürünler içermiyor, değil mi	hai·van·*sal* ew·rewn·*ler* ee·*cher*·mee·yor de·*eel* mee
gluten-free	gluten içermiyor, değil mi	gloo·*ten* ee·*cher*·mee·yor de·*eel* mee
low in sugar	az şekerli mi	az she·ker·*lee* mee
organic	organik mi	or·ga·*neek* mee
salt-free	tuzsuz mu	tooz·*sooz* moo

special diets & allergies

özel diyetler & alerjiler

I'm a vegan.
Sadece bitkisel besinler yiyorum.
sa·de·*je* beet·kee·*sel* be·seen·*ler* yee·yo·room

I'm a(n) ...	Ben ...	ben ...
Buddhist	Budistim	boo·*dees*·teem
Hindu	Hinduyum	heen·*doo*·yoom
Jewish	Yahudiyim	ya·hoo·*dee*·yeem
Muslim	Müslümanım	mews·lew·*ma*·nuhm
vegetarian	vejeteryanım	ve·zhe·ter·*ya*·nuhm

I'm allergic to ...	... alerjim var.	... a·ler·*zheem* var
dairy produce	Süt ürünlerine	sewt ew·rewn·le·ree·*ne*
eggs	Yumurtaya	yoo·moor·ta·*ya*
gelatine	Jelatine	zhe·la·tee·*ne*
gluten	Glutene	gloo·te·*ne*
honey	Bala	ba·*la*
nuts	Çerezlere	che·rez·le·*re*
peanuts	Fıstığa	fuhs·tuh·*a*
seafood	Deniz ürünlerine	de·*neez* ew·rewn·le·ree·*ne*
shellfish	Kabuklu su ürünlerine	ka·book·*loo* soo ew·rewn·le·ree·*ne*

This miniguide to Turkish cuisine lists dishes and ingredients in Turkish alphabetical order. It's designed to help you get the most out of your gastronomic experience by providing you with food terms that you may see on menus. For certain dishes we've marked the region or city where they're most popular.

A

acı a·*juh* hot (spicy)
— **badem** ba·dem bitter almond
— **badem kurabiyesi** ba·dem koo·ra·bee·ye·see almond cookie
acur a·*joor* gherkin
Adana kebab a·*da*·na ke·*bab* spicy meat patty grilled on a poker (Adana)
ağ kabak a ka·*bak* squash
ağaç çileği a·*ach* chee·le·ee raspberry
ahlat ah·*lat* wild pear
ahtapot ah·ta·*pot* octopus
— **kavurma** ka·voor·ma fried octopus with lemon & parsley
ahtapotlu pilav ah·ta·pot·loo pee·*lav* rice pilau with sliced octopus (Muğla)
ahududu a·hoo·doo·doo raspberry
akciğer ak·jee·er lung
akıtma a·kuht·ma pancake dessert similar to **yassı kadayıf**
alacatane a·la·ja·ta·ne starter of onions with lentils & bulgur (Uşak)
alafranga a·la·*fran*·ga European-style
alaturka a·la·*toor*·ka Turkish-style
alinazik a·*lee*·na·zeek eggplant purée with yogurt & meat **köfte**
alkazar al·ka·*zar* red wine & lemon drink
Amerikan salatası a·me·ree·*kan* sa·la·ta·suh Turkish 'Russian salad' – with mayonnaise, chilli sauce & gherkins
ananas a·na·*nas* pineapple
ançüez an·chew·ez pickled anchovy
Ankara tavası an·ka·ra ta·va·suh lamb with pilau
Antalya piyazı an·*tal*·ya pee·ya·*zuh* type of **piyaz** with beans, tahini, capsicum & lemon (Antalya)
Antep fıstığı pilavı an·tep fuhs·tuh·uh pee·la·*vuh* pilau with pistachios

arabaşı çorbası a·rab·a·shuh chor·ba·suh spicy chicken soup
araka a·ra·ka large peas
armut ar·*moot* pear
Arnavut biberi ar·na·voot bee·be·ree cayenne • Albanian red capsicum
Arnavut ciğeri ar·na·voot jee·e·ree Albanian fried liver
arpa ar·pa barley
arpacık soğanı ar·pa·*juhk* so·a·nuh small onion used in soups or casseroles
asma kabağı as·ma ka·ba·uh squash
asma yaprağında sardalya as·ma yap·ra·uhn·da sar·dal·ya sardines in grapevine leaves
aşure a·shoo·re fruit pudding
av eti av e·tee game meat
av kuşu av koo·shoo game bird
ay çöreği ai cher·re·ee croissant
ayşekadın ai·she·ka·duhn green bean
ayşe kızın düğün çorbası ai·she kuh·*zuhn* dew·ewn chor·ba·suh soup of wheat, meat, yogurt & corn meal
ayva ai·va quince
az pişmiş az peesh·meesh rare (steak)

B

bacak ba·*jak* leg
badem ba·dem almond
— **ezmesi** ez·me·see almond paste • marzipan
— **şekeri** she·ke·ree sugared almonds
bademli ba·dem·lee with almonds
bakla bak·la broad bean
baklava bak·la·va triangular dessert of pastry stuffed with pistachio & walnuts
bakliyat bak·lee·yat legumes • pulses
bal bal honey
— **kabağı** ka·ba·uh pumpkin

balcan söğürmesi bal·jan ser·ewr·me·*see eggplant cooked over hot coals (Konya)*
balık ba·*luhk* fish
— buğulama boo·oo·la·*ma* steamed fish stew
— tavası ta·va·*suh* fried fish platter
— yahni yah·*nee* fish ragout
— yumurtası yoo·moor·ta·*suh* fish roe
bamya bam·*ya* okra
bamyalı tavuk bam·ya·*luh* ta·*vook* chicken with okra
barbunya bar·*boon*·ya pinto bean
— pilaki pee·*la*·kee red bean salad
— tava ta·*va* fried red mullets
bastı bas·*tuh* vegetable stew
bazlama baz·la·*ma* flat baked bread
beğendi be·en·*dee* puréed eggplant sauce
beğendili tas kebabı be·en·dee·*lee* tas ke·ba·*buh see* hünkar beğendi
beğendili tavuk be·en·dee·*lee* ta·*vook* chicken with puréed eggplant
benekli çorba be·nek·*lee* chor·*ba* lentil soup
benli pilav ben·*lee* pee·*lav* pilau dish of rice & lentils (Yozgat)
beyaz be·*yaz* white
— fıstık fuhs·*tuhk* pine nuts
— İspanyol şarabı ees·*pan*·yol sha·ra·*buh* sherry
— lahana la·*ha*·na white cabbage
— muhallebi moo·hal·le·*bee* white pudding
— peynir pay·*neer* white cheese like feta
— peynirli omlet pay·neer·*lee* om·*let* omelette with white cheese
— peynirli sandviç pay·neer·*lee* sand·*veech* white cheese sandwich
beyin be·*yeen* brain
beyti kebab bay·*tee* ke·*bab* Adana-style meat kebab, rolled in thin bread & sliced
bezelye be·*zel*·ye pea
bıldırcın buhl·duhr·*juhn* quail
— kebabı ke·ba·*buh* quail with potato, tomato & green capsicum (Bilecik)
— yumurtası yoo·moor·ta·*suh* quail eggs
biber bee·*ber* bell pepper • capsicum
— dolması dol·ma·*suh* stuffed capsicum
— gibi gee·*bee* hot • peppery
— kızartması kuh·zart·ma·*suh* fried capsicum
— tanesi ta·ne·*see* peppercorn
— turşusu toor·shoo·*soo* pickled capsicum
biftek beef·*tek* steak

bira bee·*ra* beer
bisküvi bees·kew·*vee* biscuit
bitkisel beet·kee·*sel* vegetable
— çay chai *herbal tea*
bizon bee·*zon* bison • buffalo
boğa bo·*a* bull
bonbon bon·*bon* candy • lollies • sweets
bonfile bon·fee·*le* sirloin steak
böbrek berb·*rek* kidney
böğürtlen ber·ewrt·*len* blackberry • dewberry
börek ber·*rek* various sweet or savoury dishes with a thin crispy pastry
— çorbası chor·ba·*suh* thick soup of mincemeat, bones, tomato & mint (Antep)
börülce ber·rewl·*je* black-eyed pea • cow pea
— pilavı pee·la·*vuh* pilau dish of rice & black-eyed peas (Aydın & Muğla)
— salatası sa·la·ta·*suh* salad of black-eyed peas, mushrooms, onion & parsley
— teletoru te·le·to·roo black-eyed pea salad with flour & lemon (Muğla)
bulamaç çorbası boo·la·*mach* chor·ba·*suh* soup of flour, semolina & margarine (Eskişehir)
bulgur bool·*goor* cracked wheat
— köftesi kerf·te·*see* meatballs of bulgur & mincemeat
— pilavı pee·la·*vuh* bulgur pilau
bumbar boom·*bar* sausage made of rice & meat stuffed in a large sheep or lamb gut
burma kadayıf boor·ma ka·da·*yuhf* shredded wheat bun with pistachios
Bursa kebabı boor·sa ke·ba·*buh* döner kebab with tomato & butter on pitta bread
bülbül yuvası bewl·*bewl* yoo·va·*suh* shredded wheat with pistachios & syrup

C

cacık ja·*juhk* yogurt, mint & cucumber mix
ceviz je·*veez* walnut
— gibi kabuklu bir yemiş gee·*bee* ka·book·loo beer ye·*meesh* pecan
cevizli bat je·veez·*lee* bat salad of bulgur, green lentils, tomato paste & walnuts
cevizli kek je·veez·*lee* kek walnut cake
cevizli sucuk je·veez·*lee* soo·*jook* walnuts on a string dipped in pekmez
cezeriye je·ze·ree·*ye* sweet of carrot & nuts
cızbız köfte juhz·*buhz* kerf·*te* grilled mincemeat ovals

Ç

çağanoz cha·a·noz *green crab*

çala *cha*·la *seasoned bread & cheese*

çalı fasulyesi cha·luh fa·sool·ye·*see string beans*

çamfıstığı *cham*·fuhs·tuh·uh *pine nut*

çarliston biber char·lees·ton bee·ber *long, light-green sweet capsicum*

çayüzümü chai·ew·zew·mew *blueberry*

çene çarpan çorbası che·*ne* char·pan chor·ba·suh *'jaw-bumping' soup of flour, water, egg, milk & lemon (Tekirdağ)*

Çerkez peyniri cher·kez pay·nee·ree *Circassian cheese, similar to dil peynir*

Çerkez tavuğu cher·kez ta·voo·oo *Circassian chicken with bread, walnuts & cayenne pepper (Sakarya & Adapazarı)*

çevirme che·veer·me *eggplant, chicken, rice, onion, pistachios & allspice dish*
— **çorbası** chor·ba·suh *soup of egg, rice, yogurt, butter & red capsicum (Kütahya)*

çılbır chuhl·*buhr* *eggs poached in vinegary water topped with yogurt sauce*

çıtırmak chuh·tuhr·mak *boiled honey & roasted sesame seed sweet (Muğla)*

çifte kavrulmuş lokum cheef·te kav·rool·moosh lo·koom *Turkish delight*

çiğ börek chee ber·*ek* *fried börek made with ground meat, onions & spices*

çiğ köfte chee kerf·te *raw lamb, bulgur, clove, cinnamon, black & red capsicum*

ciğer tava jee·er ta·va *fried liver & onions*

çilek chee·lek *strawberry*

çipura chee·*poo*·ra *sea bream*

çirli et cheer·lee et *dish of seasoned beef chunks & dried apricot (Sivas)*

çiroz chee·roz *kipper • mackerel*

çoban salatası cho·ban sa·la·ta·suh *salad of tomato, cucumber & capsicum*

çomak cho·mak *stuffed flat bazlama bread*

çorba chor·ba *soup*

çökelekli biber dolması cher·ke·lek·lee bee·ber dol·ma·suh *dolma dish of capsicums with cheese, & tomato (Antalya)*

çökelekli zeytin cher·ke·lek·lee zay·teen *cottage cheese & green olive salad (Hatay)*

çökelek peynir cher·ke·lek pay·neer *cottage cheese*

çökertme cher·kert·me *sliced steak served on potatoes with yogurt sauce (Muğla)*

çöp şiş kebap cherp sheesh ke·bab *meat-only kebab*

çörek cher·rek *sweet biscuit*

çullama chool·la·ma *pancake dish of sliced quail, butter & flour (Muğla)*

D

dağ domuzu da do·moo·zoo *mountain boar*

dağ keçisi da ke·chee·*see mountain goat*

dana eti da·na e·tee *veal*

delice de·lee·je *cockle*

deniz tarağı de·neez ta·ra·uh *clam • scallop*

deniz ürünü de·neez ew·rew·new *seafood*

dereotu de·re·o·too *dill*

dible deeb·le *cold vegetable dish with beans*

diken dutu dee·ken doo·too *blackberry*

dil deel *tongue*

dilber dudağı deel·ber doo·da·uh *sweet pastry in the shape of a lip*

dil peynir deel pay·neer *mozzarella-like cheese*

diş deesh *clove*

divriği alatlı pilavı deev·ree·ee a·lat·luh pee·la·vuh *pilau with rice, lamb, bouillon, chickpeas & seedless grapes (Sivas)*

dolma dol·ma *vine or cabbage leaves stuffed with rice*

domates do·ma·tes *tomato*

domatesli patlıcan kızartması do·ma·tes·lee pat·luh·jan kuh·zart·ma·suh *fried eggplant with tomato*

domatesli patlıcan çarliston biber kızartması do·ma·tes·lee pat·luh·jan char·lees·ton bee·ber kuh·zart·ma·suh *fried eggplant with tomato & capsicum*

domatesli pilav do·ma·tes·lee pee·*lav* *tomato pilau*

domatesli şehriye çorbası do·ma·tes·lee sheh·ree·ye chor·ba·suh *tomato soup with vermicelli*

domuz do·mooz *pig*
— **eti** e·tee *bacon • pork*
— **sosisi** so·see·see *pork sausages*

dondurma don·door·ma *ice cream*

döner der·ner *slices of meat stacked on a vertical skewer, grilled and shaved off*
— **kebab** ke·bab *kebab (usually lamb or chicken) cooked on a rotating spit*

dövme etli karalahana sarması derv·me et·lee ka·ra·la·ha·na sar·ma·suh *lamb strips, rice & tomato paste wrapped in karalahana leaves (Rize)*

dul avrat çorbası dool av·*rat* chor·ba·*suh*
'widow soup' of chickpeas, lentils, lamb,
tomato paste, capsicum & mint (Adana)

dut doot mulberry

düğün çorbası dew·*ewn* chor·ba·*suh*
wedding soup with ground meat, carrot &
lemon or vinegar

düğün pilavı dew·*ewn* pee·la·*vuh*
'wedding pilau' – rice, chickpeas & meat
(Kayseri) • chicken & *yarma* (Sakarya)

dürüm dew·*rewm* kebab in pitta bread

E

ekmek ek·*mek* bread
— **böreği** ber·re·*e* oven-baked stale
bread & melted *kaşar* cheese (İzmir)

ekmekkadayıf ek·*mek*·ka·da·*yuhf* dessert
of baked *kadayıf* bread rusks soaked in
thick syrup & topped with *kaymak*

ekşili ıspanak başı ek·shee·*lee* uhs·pa·*nak*
ba·*shuh* spinach & lentil stew (Tarsus)

ekşili nohutlu bamya ek·shee·*lee*
no·hoot·*loo* bam·*ya* mutton stew with
okra & chickpeas (Mersin & İçel)

ekşili patlıcan dolması ek·shee·*lee*
pat·luh·*jan* dol·ma·*suh* eggplant **dolma**

ekşili taraklık tavası ek·shee·*lee* ta·rak·*luhk*
ta·va·*suh* sour lamb cutlets with quince

elbasan el·ba·*san* open-faced pie with fried
lamb chunks, eggs & yogurt (Manisa)
— **dolması** dol·ma·*suh* **dolma** with
artichoke, rice & mincemeat
— **şarabı** sha·ra·*buh* apple cider

erik e·*reek* plum
— **aşı** a·*shuh* plum dish with prunes,
rice & sugar (Tekirdağ)

erikli biber dolması e·reek·*lee* bee·*ber*
dol·ma·*suh* capsicum stuffed with eggplant, tomato, walnuts & *kızılcık* (Bilecik)

erikli tavşan e·reek·*lee* tav·*shan* rabbit
with plums

erikli tavuk dolması e·reek·*lee* ta·*vook*
dol·ma·*suh* stuffed chicken with plums

erişte e·reesh·*te* noodles • pasta

Erzincan piyazı er·zeen·*jan* pee·ya·*zuh*
salad with cucumber, tomato, cheeses,
capsicum & herbs (Erzincan)

etli et·*lee* with meat
— **bohça böreği** boh·*cha* ber·re·*ee*
delicate **börek** filled with beef

— **bulgur pilavı** bool·*goor* pee·la·*vuh*
bulgur pilau with meat & chickpeas
— **dolma** dol·*ma* meat-stuffed vegetables
— **dövme pilavı** derv·*me* pee·la·*vuh*
pilau with chickpeas, bulgur & lamb
— **ekmek** ek·*mek* bread topped with meat
— **enginar** en·gee·*nar* stew of artichoke,
meat or lamb chunks, onion & tomato
— **enginar dolması** en·gee·*nar*
dol·ma·*suh* artichokes stuffed with meat
— **kabak dolması** ka·*bak* dol·ma·*suh*
zucchini stuffed with meat
— **kabak ve biber dolması** ka·*bak* ve
bee·*ber* dol·ma·*suh* zucchini & capsicum
stuffed with meat
— **kereviz dolması** ke·re·*veez*
dol·ma·*suh* celery stuffed with meat
— **kuru fasulye** koo·roo fa·sool·*ye*
haricot or butter beans & meat
— **lahana dolması** la·ha·na dol·ma·*suh*
cabbage leaves stuffed with meat
— **marul dolması** ma·rool dol·ma·*suh*
lettuce leaves stuffed with rice, tomato,
parsley, cumin & meat (Edirne)
— **nohut** no·*hoot* chickpeas in meat sauce
— **patlıcan dolması** pat·luh·*jan*
dol·ma·*suh* eggplant stuffed with meat
— **pide** pee·*de* Turkish 'pizza' with
ground meat
— **sebzeli güveç** seb·ze·lee gew·*vech*
stewed meat with vegetables
— **yaprak dolması** yap·rak dol·ma·*suh*
vine leaves with meat stuffing
— **yeşil mercimek** ye·sheel mer·jee·*mek*
lentils with meat, onion & tomato paste

etyemez et·ye·*mez* vegetarian

ezme lahana ez·me la·ha·na flat vegetable
'pie' made of **karalahana**, chard, suet,
cornflour, tomato & red capsicum (Rize)

ezme salata ez·me sa·la·*ta* tomato salad or
cold tomato soup, like gazpacho (Antep)

ezo gelin çorbası e·zo ge·*leen*
chor·ba·*suh* red lentil 'bride' soup

F

fasulye fa·sool·*ye* bean
— **filizi** fee·lee·*zee* beansprout

fındık fuhn·*duhk* hazelnut

fıstık fuhs·*tuhk* peanut

fosul fo·*sool* lamb or mutton kebab

francala fran·ja·la long narrow loaf of bread

G

gerdan dolması ger-*dan* dol-ma-*suh lamb neck stuffed with rice, mince, almonds, tomato paste & spiced **köfte** (Adana)

gerdaniye ger-*da*-nee-ye neck of lamb with plum & sugar (Edirne)

geyik eti ge-*yeek* e-*tee* venison

gökkuşağı salatası gerk-koo-sha-uh sa-la-ta-suh 'rainbow salad' – macaroni, capsicum, mushrooms, pickles & salami

gül reçeli gewl re-che-*lee* rose jam

gül şerbeti gewl sher-be-*tee* nonalcoholic drink of rose-water, water & sugar (Sivas)

gül tatlısı gewl tat-luh-suh fried rose-shaped pastry covered in lemon sherbet

güneşte kurutulmuş domates gew-nesh-te koo-roo-tool-*moosh* do-ma-tes sun-dried tomato

güveçte kıymalı yumurta gew-vech-*te* kuhy-ma-*luh* yoo-moor-ta casseroled eggs with minced meat

güveçte türlü gew-vech-*te* tewr-*lew* mixed vegetable casserole with chicken

güvercin gew-ver-*jeen* pigeon

H

Halep işi kebap ha-lep ee-*shee* ke-*bap* grilled meatballs, onions & spices

halim aşı ha-*leem* a-*shuh* soup of chickpeas, meaty bones, wheat & tomato

hamburger ekmeği ham-*boor*-ger ek-me-*ee* bread roll

hamsi ham-*see* anchovies

— **böreği** ber-re-*ee* layers of breaded fried anchovies & seasoned rice (Giresun)

— **buğulaması** boo-oo-la-ma-suh anchovies with tomato & capsicum

— **çorbası** chor-ba-suh anchovy & tomato soup (Trabzon)

— **ekşilisi** ek-shee-le-*see* 'anchovy sour' with capsicum & tomato salad (Rize)

— **ızgara** uhz-*ga*-ra grilled anchovies served with raw onion & lemon

— **kuşu** koo-*shoo* anchovies fried with tomato & green capsicum

— **salamura** sa-la-*moo*-ra pickled anchovy, rock salt & bay leaf

— **tatlısı** tat-luh-suh jellied sweet made from anchovy (Rize)

— **tava** ta-*va* fried, corn-breaded anchovies served with onion & lemon

hamsikoli ham-*see*-ko-lee bread with chard, mint, corn meal & anchovies (Rize)

hamsili pilav ham-see-lee pee-*lav* oven-baked anchovy pilau (Rize)

hamur işleri ha-*moor* eesh-le-*ree* pastries

hamur tatlısı ha-*moor* tat-luh-suh pastry

hamurlu çorba ha-moor-loo chor-ba dark soup of **erişte** dough, lentils & meat

hamurlu yeşil mercimek çorbası ha-moor-loo ye-*sheel* mer-jee-*mek* chor-ba-suh lentil soup with dumplings

hanibana ha-nee-ba-na **köfte** cooked with capsicum, carrot, tomato & peas

hardal har-*dal* mustard

hardallı patlıcan kızartması har-dal-*luh* pat-luh-*jan* kuh-zart-ma-suh fried eggplant & mustard

haşhaş hash-*hash* poppyseed

haşhaşlı gözleme hash-hash-*luh* gerz-le-me savoury pancake with poppy seed (Eskişehir & Edirne)

haşlama hash-la-*ma* steamed lamb & vegetables in broth

havuç ha-*vooch* carrot

havyar hav-*yar* caviar

haydari hai-*da*-ree yogurt with roasted eggplant & garlic

hırtlama köfte huhrt-la-*ma* kerf-*te* **köfte** of veal, cornflour & thyme (Trabzon)

hıyar huh-*yar* cucumber

hibeş hee-*besh* **meze** spread of tahini & red capsicum flakes (Antalya)

hindi heen-*dee* turkey

hindiba heen-dee-ba chicory • endive

Hindistan cevizi heen-dees-*tan* je-vee-zee coconut

hingel heen-*gel* dish of thin pastry layers & crumbled cottage cheese (Yozgat)

Hint cevizi heent je-vee-zee nutmeg

Hint fıstığı heent fuhs-tuh-*uh* cashew

Hint kirazı heent kee-ra-zuh mango

hörre her-*re* soup of butter, flour & tomato

höşmerim hersh-me-*reem* classic Anatolian pudding with walnuts & pistachios

humus hoo-*moos* humus – finely mashed chickpeas with sesame oil, lemon & spices

hurma hoor-ma date

— **tatlısı** tat-luh-suh semolina & date cake

hülüklü düğün çorbası hew-lewk-*lew* dew-*ewn* chor-ba-suh hearty soup with tripe, meatballs, chickpeas & rice (Adana)

hünkar beğendi hewn-*kar* be-en-*dee* 'sultan's delight' – lamb stew on eggplant

I

ısırganotu ezmesi uh·suhr·gan·o·too
ez·me·see *stinging nettle purée* (Rize)
ıslama uhs·la·ma *gravy from beef broth,
red capsicum & vegetable oil*
— **köfte** kerf·te *meat patties on toasted
bread, doused in* **ıslama** *juice* (Sakarya)
ıspanak uhs·pa·nak *spinach*
ızgara uhz·ga·ra *barbecue • grill*
— **köfte** kerf·te *grilled meatballs*

İ

içi dolmuş ee·chee dol·moosh *eggplant
with* **beyaz peynir,** *tomato & egg*
içli köfte eech·lee kerf·te **köfte** *with bulgur
covering* (Antep, Diyarbakır & Adana)
iç pilav eech pee·lav *rice with currants,
nuts & onions*
imambayıldı ee·mam·ba·yuhl·duh *'the
imam fainted' – famous dish of eggplant, tomato & onion*
incir een·jeer *fig*
— **uyuşturması** oo·yoosh·toor·ma·suh
'fig narcotic' – dessert of milk & figs
İnegöl köfte ee·ne·gerl kerf·te **köfte** *dish
made with mincemeat*
irmik eer·meek *semolina*
İskender kebab ees·ken·der ke·bab
döner *kebab on flat bread, covered with
tomato sauce & hot butter sauce*
isotreçeli ee·sot·re·che·lee *preserve made
of 'Urfa' capsicum & cinnamon* (Urfa)
istakoz ees·ta·koz *lobster*
istiridye ees·tee·reed·ye *oyster*
işkembe eesh·kem·be *tripe*
İzmir köfte eez·meer kerf·te **köfte** *with
mincemeat, egg, breadcrumbs & tomato*

K

kabak ka·bak *courgette • zucchini*
— **pane** pa·ne *crumbed fried zucchini*
— **tatlısı** tat·luh·suh *dessert of pumpkin,
sweet syrup & walnuts*
kabaklı pirinç çorbası ka·bak·luh pee·reench
chor·ba·suh *zucchini & rice soup*
kabuklular ka·book·loo·lar *shellfish*
kadayıf ka·da·yuhf *dessert of dough
soaked in syrup with a layer of* **kaymak**

kadınbudu köfte ka·duhn·boo·doo
kerf·te **köfte** *of ground meat mixed with
cooked rice & fried in batter* (İzmir)
kağıt kebabı ka·uht ke·ba·buh *lamb chunks
& vegetables baked in wax paper* (Manisa)
kağıtta barbunya ka·uht·ta bar·boon·ya
baked **barbunya**
kağıtta pastırma ka·uht·ta pas·tuhr·ma
pastırma *cooked in foil with vegetables*
kahırtlak hamuru ka·huhrt·lak ha·moo·roo
fried dough used in soup (Adana)
kalburabastı kal·boo·ra·bas·tuh *baked egg-
shaped dessert topped with lemon syrup*
kapalı kıymalı pide ka·pa·luh kuhy·ma·luh
pee·de **pide** *filled with mincemeat &
tomato* (Samsun, Bafra & Giresun)
kapama ka·pa·ma *boiled chicken & rice*
kaplumbağa kap·loom·ba·a *turtle*
kapuska ka·poos·ka *cold dish of onion,
tomato paste & cabbage* (Edirne)
karaçuval helvası ka·ra·choo·val
hel·va·suh *sweet potato-shaped pastries
served with* **pekmez** (Çorum)
karalahana ka·ra·la·ha·na *dark cabbage*
— **çorbası** chor·ba·suh **karalahana,**
carrot, zucchini, **çarliston biber** *&
potato soup* (Rize)
— **dible** deeb·le **karalahana,** *Albanian
red capsicum,* **barbunya** *& rice salad*
— **sarma karalahana** sar·ma
ka·ra·la·ha·na **karalahana** *with veal & rice
wrapped in* **karalahana** (Rize)
karaş ka·rash *pudding dessert of blackber-
ries, grapes & hazelnuts*
karides ka·ree·des *prawn*
karışık ızgara ka·ruh·shuhk uhz·ga·ra
mixed grill
karışık dolma ka·ruh·shuhk dol·ma **dolma**
of grape leaves, capsicum & eggplant
karışık meyve ka·ruh·shuhk may·ve
mixed fruit
karışık pide ka·ruh·shuhk pee·de *Turkish
'pizza' with tomato, green capsicum,
mincemeat,* **pastırma** *sausage &* **kaşar**
karnabahar kar·na·ba·har *cauliflower*
— **kızartması** kuh·zart·ma·suh *fried
cauliflower*
karnıyarık kar·nuh·ya·ruhk *'split belly' – eggplant stuffed with seasoned ground beef*
karpuz kar·pooz *watermelon*

kaşar ka·*shar* sheep's milk
— **peyniri** pay·nee·*ree* sheep's cheese similar to mild cheddar
— **peynirli omlet** pay·neer·*lee* om·*let* omelette with **kaşar peyniri**

kaşık börek çorbası ka·*shuhk* ber·*rek* chor·ba·*suh* egg, yogurt & tomato soup

katıklı aş ka·tuhk·*luh* ash soup of bulgur, water, butter & **süzme yoğurt** (Aksaray)

katmerli pazı böreği kat·mer·*lee* pa·zuh ber·re·*ee* savoury **börek** of flour, chard, onion, egg yolk & sesame seeds (Edirne)

katmerli sac böreği kat·mer·*lee* saj ber·re·*ee* **börek** of pitta bread filled with spinach, cheese & onion (Muğla)

kavun ka·*voon* melon · rockmelon

kavunağacı ka·voon·a·a·*juh* papaya

kavurma erişteşi pilavı ka·voor·ma e·reesh·te·*see* pee·la·*vuh* pilau dish of home-made noodles & rice (Sivas)

kayısı ka·yuh·*suh* apricot
— **yahnisi** yah·nee·*see* stew with apricots, meat chunks & **pekmez** (Nevşehir)

kaymak kai·*mak* sour cream

kaynamış kai·na·*muhsh* boiled

kaz kaz goose

kebab/kebap ke·bab/ke·bap skewered meat & vegetables cooked on an open fire

keçi ke·*chee* goat

kepekli ekmek ke·pek·*lee* ek·*mek* wholemeal bread

kepir dolması ke·peer dol·ma·*suh* **dolma** of kepir & mincemeat wrapped in **karalahana** & topped with yogurt (Ordu)

kerbel ker·*bel* fragrant herb from the parsley family used with fish & salads

kerevit ke·re·*veet* crawfish · crayfish · prawn

kereviz ke·re·*veez* celeriac · celery root

kesme çorbası kes·me chor·ba·*suh* black lentils, macaroni soup (Erzurum) · mincemeat & tomato soup (Kayseri) · ayran & salt soup (Erzincan)

kestane kes·ta·ne chestnut

kestaneli hindi kes·ta·ne·lee heen·*dee* roast turkey with chestnuts

kestane yemeği kes·ta·ne ye·me·*ee* dish of chestnuts & mincemeat (Sinop)

keşkek kesh·*kek* ground wheat · wedding dish of mutton & ground wheat (Denizli)

keşkül kesh·*kewl* pudding of ground almonds, coconut & milk

kete ke·*te* roll with spinach & nuts (Kars)

kiraz kee·*raz* cherry

kırmızı biber salatası kuhr·muh·*zuh* bee·*ber* sa·la·ta·*suh* capsicum, garlic, lemon & olive oil salad (Adana)

kırmızı turp kuhr·muh·*zuh* toorp radish

kısır kuh·*suhr* bulgur salad with onion, parsley, lemon, cucumber & tomato

kişniş hoşafı keesh·*neesh* ho·sha·*fuh* raisins, sugar & water drink (Sivas)

kıtır patlıcan kuh·*tuhr* pat·luh·*jan* crispy eggplant

kıvırcık salata kuh·vuhr·*juhk* sa·la·ta lettuce with very crinkly leaves

kıyma kuhy·ma ground meat · mincemeat

kızarmış kuh·zar·*muhsh* fried · roasted
— **ekmek** ek·*mek* toasted bread
— **patates** pa·ta·tes fried potato

kızılcık kuh·zuhl·*juhk* cranberry
— **tarhana çorbası** tar·ha·na chor·ba·*suh* soup of **tarhana** and **kızılcık**

kokoreç ko·ko·*rech* seasoned grilled lamb or mutton intestines (Tekirdağ)

kolay tatlı ko·*lai* tat·*luh* dessert with apricots & sugar water

kornişon kor·nee·*shon* gherkin

koyun ko·*yoon* mutton

koz helvası koz hel·va·*suh* nougat

köfte kerf·te small mincemeat or bulgur balls

köleş ker·*lesh* salad with cucumber, melon, tomato, capsicum & yogurt (Eskişehir)

köpek balığı ker·*pek* ba·luh·*uh* shark

köpüklü şarap ker·pewk·*lew* sha·rap sparkling wine

közleme biber salatası kerz·le·me bee·*ber* sa·la·ta·*suh* capsicum salad

Kudüs enginarı ko·dews en·gee·na·*ruh* Jerusalem artichoke

kulak çorbası koo·*lak* chor·ba·*suh* 'ear soup' – meat dumplings boiled in stock · chickpeas & meat (Antalya)

kurbağa koor·ba·a frog

kuru erik koo·roo e·reek prune

kuru köfte koo·roo kerf·te fried meat patty

kuru mantı koo·roo man·tuh meat dumplings with garlicky broth (Çorum)

kuru meyve koo·roo may·ve dried fruit

kuru üzüm koo·roo ew·zewm raisin

kuşkonmaz koosh·kon·*maz* asparagus

kuzu koo·*zoo* lamb · mutton

kümes hayvanları kew·mes hai·van·la·*ruh* poultry

menu decoder

181

L

labne *lab*-ne mild cream cheese
lahana la-*ha*-na cabbage
lahmacun lah-ma-*joon* Turkish 'pizza' (also **pide**)
lahusa şekeri la-*hoo*-sa she-ke-ree slabs of sugar flavoured with spices & dyed red
lahusa şerbeti la-*hoo*-sa sher-be-tee sherbet to celebrate a birth
lakerda la-*ker*-da salted tuna fish salad
lebeniyeli köfte le-be-nee-ye-*lee* kerf-te bulgur **köfte** stuffed with meat (Adana)
levrek lev-*rek* sea bass
loğusa tatlısı lo-oo-sa tat-luh-suh sweet of sugar, lemon powder & red food dye (see **lahusa şekeri**)
lokma lok-*ma* yeast fritters with syrup
lokum lo-*koom* Turkish delight • sweet pastry
— **pilavı** pee-la-*vuh* noodles & mincemeat
lop lop *'big, tender & round'* – sometimes used to describe a cut of meat like **nuar**
löbye lerb-ye cold bean salad (İstanbul)

M

maden suyu ma-*den* soo-yoo mineral water
madımak ma-duh-*mak* green vegetable
— **yemeği** ye-me-*ee* stew of **madımak**, **pastırma**, bulgur & spring onion
mafiş tatlısı ma-*feesh* tat-luh-suh savoury pastry dessert (Balıkesir)
mahaleb ma-ha-*leb* St Lucie cherry • cordial made from St Lucie cherry
mahallebi ma-hal-le-*bee* sweet rice flour & milk pudding
makarna ma-*kar*-na noodles • pasta
mandalina man-da-lee-na mandarin • tangerine
mantar man-*tar* mushroom
Maraş dondurması ma-*rash* don-door-ma-suh stringy, chewy & delicious ice cream
Maraş tarhanası ma-*rash* tar-ha-na-suh **tarhana** used in stuffing or as is' in soup
maraska ma-*ras*-ka sour cherry
marul ma-*rool* lettuce
menemen me-ne-*men* eggs with green capsicum, tomato & cheese
mercimek mer-jee-*mek* lentil
meşhur Karadeniz kavurması mesh-*hoor* ka-*ra*-de-neez ka-voor-ma-suh baked 'pizza' topped with fried meat

meyan me-*yan* liquorice
meyve may-*ve* fruit
meze me-*ze* Turkish hors d'oeuvres
mıhlama muh-la-*ma* egg dish • **pastırma**, onions & egg dish • cheese & corn dish
mısır muh-*suhr* corn
— **çorbası** chor-ba-*suh* soup of corn kernels, **barbunya** & meat chunks (Sinop)
midye meed-ye mussel
— **pilavı** pee-la-*vuh* pilau of rice, mussels, seedless grapes & nuts (Balıkesir)
misket limonu mees-*ket* lee-mo-noo lime
morina mo-ree-na cod
muammara moo-am-ma-*ra* **meze** or salad of walnuts, breadcrumbs & tahini (Adana)
musakka moo-sak-*ka* vegetable & ground meat pie
muska böreği moos-*ka* ber-re-ee **börek** of potato, cheese & mincemeat (Uşak)
muz mooz banana

N

nar nar pomegranate
nevzine nev-zee-*ne* savoury **börek** with eggs, tahini, yogurt & walnuts (Kayseri)
Niğde tavası nee-*de* ta-va-suh lamb with tomato, capsicum & rice (Niğde)
nohut no-*hoot* chickpea
nohutlu kuskus pilavı no-hoot-*loo* koos-*koos* pee-la-*vuh* couscous with boiled chickpeas & butter (İstanbul)
nokul no-*kool* meat pie with seasoned mincemeat, parsley & walnuts (Sinop)
nuar noo-*ar* tender cut of veal, boiled & sliced thinly for sandwiches & cold cuts

O

orfoz fileto or-foz fee-le-to fillet of groper garnished with rocket (Mediterranean)
orman kebabı or-*man* ke-ba-buh roast lamb & onions

Ö

öğmeç çorbası er-mech chor-ba-suh soup of flour, eggs & tomato paste (Burdur)
öküz er-*kewz* ox
ördek er-*dek* duck
örgülü makarna er-gew-lew ma-kar-na noodles, chicken, peas, carrot & almonds

P

paça çorbası pa-*cha* chor-ba-*suh* *sheep trotter soup*

pancar pan-*jar* *beetroot*
— **cacığı** ja-juh-*uh* *beet, bulgur, yogurt & garlic* **cacik** *(Yozgat)*

papaz yahnisi pa-*paz* yah-nee-*see* *'priest's stew' with beef, vinegar & cumin (İzmir)*

pastırma pas-*tuhr-ma* *pressed beef preserved in spices • Turkish pastrami*

pastırmalı kuru fasulye pas-tuhr-ma-*luh* koo-*roo* fa-*sool*-ye **pastırma** *& bean casserole*

pastırmalı omlet pas-tuhr-ma-*luh* om-*let* *omelette with* **pastırma**

pastırmalı sigara böreği pas-tuhr-ma-*luh* see-*ga*-ra ber-re-*ee* *pastry of yufka,* **pastırma***, tomato & capsicum (Kayseri)*

paşa pilavı pa-*sha* pee-la-*vuh* *'Sultan's pilau' – salad of potato, eggs & capsicum*

patates pa-*ta*-tes *potato*
— **kaygana** kai-ga-na *fried potato pancake • mixture of potato, parsley & red capsicum (Kastamonu)*

patlıcan pat-luh-*jan* *aubergine • eggplant*
— **biber tava** bee-*ber* ta-*va* *fried eggplant & capsicum with tomato paste*
— **böreği** ber-re-*ee* *sliced eggplant prepared with mincemeat & onion (Afyon)*
— **islim kebabı** ees-*leem* ke-ba-*buh* *baked lamb wrapped in eggplant*
— **karnıyarık** kar-nuh-ya-*ruhk* *eggplant stuffed with minced meat*
— **pane** pa-*ne* *fried eggplant covered with crumbled bread*
— **reçeli** re-che-*lee* *sweet eggplant preserves (Adana)*

patlıcanlı köfte pat-luh-jan-*luh* kerf-*te* *meatballs with eggplant*

patlıcanlı köy dolması pat-luh-jan-*luh* kay dol-ma-*suh* *mincemeat & bulgur served on eggplant slices (Karaman)*

patlıcanlı pilav pat-luh-jan-*luh* pee-*lav* *eggplant pilau*

pavruya pav-roo-*ya* *hermit crab*

pazı pa-*zuh* *chard*
— **kavurma** ka-voor-*ma* *fried eggs & chard, with onions & barbunya (Rize)*
— **kavurması** ka-voor-ma-*suh* *fried chard & onion served cold (Kastamonu)*
— **pilakisi** pee-la-kee-*see* **pilaki** *with chard, rice & salted anchovy (Trabzon)*

pekmez pek-*mez* *grape molasses*

peynir pay-*neer* *cheese*
— **helvası** hel-va-*suh* *dessert of cheese, flour, eggs, butter & granulated sugar*
— **tatlısı** tat-luh-*suh* *cheesecake • cookies*

peynirli börek pay-neer-*lee* ber-*rek* *pastry filled with* **peynir**

peynirli pide pay-neer-*lee* pee-*de* *cheese Turkish pizza*

pırasa puh-ra-*sa* *leek*
— **dolması** dol-ma-*suh* *leeks stuffed with mincemeat, rice & tomato (Kastamonu)*

pide pee-*de* *thin pitta-like bread used to make Turkish pizza or* **döner kebab**
— **ekmek** ek-*mek* *unleavened bread available during the month of Ramazan*

pilaki pee-la-*kee* *stew with vegetables & beans, black-eyed peas, rice or fish*

pilav pee-*lav* *pilau of rice, bulgur or lentils*

pilavlı hindi pee-lav-*luh* heen-*dee* *roast turkey with rice*

pilavlı tas kebabı pee-lav-*luh* tas ke-ba-*buh* *'kebab' with lamb chunks & red capsicum (Çorum)*

piliç pee-*leech* *chicken*

pirpirim çorbası peer-pee-*reem* chor-ba-*suh* *chickpea, bean & lentil soup*

piruhi pee-roo-*hee* *meat, flour & yogurt dish*

pirzola peer-zo-*la* *chops (lamb)*

pişmaniye peesh-*ma*-nee-ye *dessert made of sugar, flour & soapwort (Kocaeli)*

piyaz pee-*yaz* *white bean salad*

portakal por-ta-*kal* *orange (fruit or flavour)*

pürçüklü pewr-chewk-*lew* *purple carrot*

R

ravent ra-*vent* *rhubarb*

reçel re-*chel* *jam*

revani re-va-*nee* *sweet cake with semolina, vanilla & clotted cream*

ringa balığı reen-*ga* ba-luh-*uh* *herring*

S

saçaklı mantı sa-chak-*luh* man-*tuh* *chicken spread over seasoned pastry*

sahanda pirzola sa-han-*da* peer-zo-*la* *lamb cutlets with tomato sauce*

sakızlı bakla çorbası sa-kuhz-*luh* bak-*la* chor-ba-*suh* *soup with* **bakla** *(Bolu)*

salam sa-*lam* *salami*

salatalık sa-la-ta-*luhk* *cucumber*

salçalı köfte sal-cha-luh kerf-te meat patties in seasoned tomato sauce

samsa tatlısı sam-sa tat-luh-suh sweet pastry soaked in syrup (Isparta)

Samsun köfte sam-soon kerf-te meat loaf

samut salatası sa-moot sa-la-ta-suh salad with dill, parsley & red capsicum

sap kerevizi sap ke-re-vee-zee celery

sardalya sar-dal-ya sardine

sarmısak sar-muh-sak garlic
— **börülce salatası** ber-rewl-je sa-la-ta-suh black-eyed pea salad
— **köfte** kerf-te meatless köfte with tomato sauce (Adana)
— **tavuk dolması** ta-vook dol-ma-suh stuffed chicken with garlic

sebzeler seb-ze-ler vegetables

sebzeli pilavı seb-ze-lee bool-goor pee-la-vuh pilau of bulgur & vegetables

sebzeli kapama seb-ze-lee ka-pa-ma lamb & vegetable stew

sebzeli kuzu kızartma seb-ze-lee koo-zoo kuh-zart-ma roast lamb with vegetables

sebzeli piliç dolması seb-ze-lee pee-leech dol-ma-suh baked chicken with potato, peas, okra & tomato (İstanbul)

sebzeli tavuk çorbası seb-ze-lee ta-vook chor-ba-suh vegetable & chicken soup

sığır dili suh-uhr dee-lee ox tongue

sığır eti suh-uhr e-tee beef

sığır filetosu suh-uhr fee-le-to-soo sirloin

sıkıcık çorbası suh-kuh-juhk chor-ba-suh bulgur, tarhana & meat soup (Kütahya)

sıkma suhk-ma **börek** filled with onion, beyaz peynir & parsley (Adana)

sigara böreği see-ga-ra ber-re-ee cigar-shaped pastries filled with beyaz peynir

simit see-meet crispy roll with sesame seed

sinarit ızgara see-na-reet uhz-ga-ra grilled sea bream with dill & lemon juice sauce

sini köfte see-nee kerf-te bulgur & meat köfte

sirke seer-ke vinegar

soğan so-an onion
— **aşı** a-shuh dish with meaty bones, spring onion, potato & tomato (Tekirdağ)
— **kebabı** ke-ba-buh meat chunks with arpacık soğanı & tomato paste (Niğde)

soğanlama so-an-la-ma mincemeat with onion & tomato paste (Aksaray)

soğanlı et so-an-luh et meat & onion stew

soğuk çorba so-ook chor-ba cold soup of yogurt, rice & capsicum (Kayseri)

som balığı som ba-luh-uh salmon

somun ekmek so-moon ek-mek bread rolls

soya peyniri so-ya pay-nee-ree tofu

söğüş ser-ewsh boiled meat served cold • cold cuts • sliced uncooked vegetables

su soo water
— **böreği** ber-re-ee flaky pastry sometimes filled with mincemeat (Edirne)
— **kabağı** ka-ba-uh water squash
— **mahallebisi** ma-hal-le-bee-see milk pudding with rose-water
— **teresi** te-re-see watercress

sucuk soo-jook spicy sausage

susam soo-sam sesame

susamlı köfte soo-sam-luh kerf-te meatless köfte with bulgur & tomato

susamlı şeker soo-sam-luh she-ker sugar-coated peanuts & almonds • hazelnuts & walnuts covered in sesame seeds

susam yağı soo-sam ya-uh sesame oil

sülün sew-lewn pheasant

süt sewt milk
— **danası** da-na-suh veal

sütlaç sewt-lach rice pudding

süzme yoğurt sewz-me yo-oort yogurt strained to remove water

Ş

şalgam shal-gam swede • turnip
— **pilavı** pee-la-vuh pilau dish of turnip, mincemeat & bulgur (Sivas)

şamfıstığı sham-fuhs-tuh-uh pistachio

şeftali shef-ta-lee peach

şehriye sheh-ree-ye noodles used in soups

şeker she-ker sugar • candy • lollies • sweets
— **böreği** ber-re-ee sweet biscuit, taken with lemon sherbet (Niğde)

şekerpare she-ker-pa-re sweet biscuit topped with lemon & sugar syrup

şiş kebab sheesh ke-bab skewered meat prepared on an open fire

şiş köfte sheesh kerf-te grilled meatballs

T

tahinli lahana sarması ta-heen-lee la-ha-na sar-ma-suh cabbage with rice, chickpeas, tahini & tomato (Adana)

tahinli maydanoz ta-heen-lee mai-da-noz salad of parsley, garlic & tahini (Hatay)

tahinli patlıcan ta-heen-lee pat-luh-jan mashed eggplant & tahini salad (Hatay)

tahinli soğan ta-heen-lee so-an *onion, mayonnaise, lemon & tahini salad (Hatay)*

talaş böreği ta-lash ber-re-ee *meat pastry*

talaş kebabı ta-lash ke-ba-buh *meat pieces cooked then baked in pastry*

tandır kebabı tan-duhr ke-ba-buh *kebab roasted in an oven in a clay-lined pit*

tantuni kebab tan-too-nee ke-bab *dish of sliced veal & mutton on flat bread*

tarhana tar-ha-na *yogurt, onion, flour & chilli mix*

— **çorbası** chor-ba-suh *tarhana, yogurt, black-eyed pea & meat soup (Muğla)*

tas kebabı tas ke-ba-buh *veal & vegetable stew served on rice (Kütahya)*

tas kebaplı pilav tas ke-bap-luh pee-lav *lamb & vegetable stew (Samsun)*

tatlı biber tat-luh bee-ber *sweet capsicum*

tatlı mısır tat-luh muh-suhr *sweetcorn*

tatlı dürümü tat-luh dew-rew-mew *dessert of milk, yufka, walnuts & pekmez (Niğde)*

tatlıpatates tat-luh-pa-ta-tes *sweet potato*

tavşan tav-shan *hare • rabbit*

tavuk ta-vook *chicken*

— **dolması** dol-ma-suh *stuffed chicken*

— **göğsü** ger-sew *chicken breast*

— **kızartması** kuh-zart-ma-suh *roast chicken*

tavuklu zarf böreği ta-vook-loo zarf ber-re-ee *börek stuffed with chicken*

taze bezelye ta-ze be-zel-ye *snow pea*

Tekirdağ köftesi te-keer-da kerf-te-see *mincemeat with rice & capsicum*

tekke çorbası tek-ke chor-ba-suh *flour, meat, tomato & capsicum soup (Kütahya)*

telkadayıf tel-ka-da-yuhf *dessert of baked kadayıf dough with walnuts & kaymak*

tel şehriye tel sheh-ree-ye *thin delicate noodle, similar to vermicelli*

tel şehriyeli tavuk çorbası tel sheh-ree-ye-lee ta-vook chor-ba-suh *chicken vermicelli soup*

terbiye ter-bee-ye *sauce of lemon & egg*

terbiyeli ekşili köfte ter-bee-ye-lee ek-shee-lee kerf-te *meatballs with egg & lemon sauce*

terbiyeli işkembe çorbası ter-bee-ye-lee eesh-kem-be chor-ba-suh *tripe soup with terbiye*

terbiyeli kalkan balığı ter-bee-ye-lee kal-kan ba-luh-uh *turbot with sauce*

terbiyeli kuzu etli kereviz ter-bee-ye-lee koo-zoo et-lee ke-re-veez *celeriac with lamb in lemon sauce*

terbiyeli süt kuzusu kapaması ter-bee-ye-lee sewt koo-zoo-soo ka-pa-ma-suh *spring lamb with lettuce*

tere çorbası te-re chor-ba-suh *watercress & chicken broth soup (İzmir & Aydın)*

tereyağ te-re-ya *butter*

testi kebabı tes-tee ke-ba-buh *meat kebab in a mushroom & onion sauce (Anatolia)*

tıntış çorbası tuhn-tuhsh chor-ba-suh *corn meal soup (Zonguldak)*

ton balığı ton ba-luh-uh *tuna*

topik to-peek *chickpeas, pistachios, flour & currants topped with sesame sauce*

toyga çorbası toy-ga chor-ba-suh *soup of yogurt, hazelnut, rice, egg & mint (Konya)*

Trabzon hurması trab-zon hoor-ma-suh *persimmon*

Trabzon peynirlisi trab-zon pay-neer-lee-see *baked pizza made with 'Trabzon' cheese*

tulumba tatlısı too-loom-ba tat-luh-suh *fluted fritters served in sweet syrup*

turşu toor-shoo *pickled vegetable*

tuzlu domates ve fasulye kavurması tooz-loo do-ma-tes ve fa-sool-ye ka-voor-ma-suh *tomato & green beans*

tuzlu domuz eti tooz-loo do-mooz e-tee *salted pork*

türlü tewr-lew *stew*

U

un çorbası oon chor-ba-suh *'flour soup' – flour, meat, tomato & capsicum (Muğla)*

Urfa kebabı oor-fa ke-ba-buh *grilled lamb on skewers*

Ü

üzüm ew-zewm *grapes*

üzümlü kek ew-zewm-lew kek *cake or pie with dried grapes*

V

vartabit paçası var-ta-beet pa-cha-suh *seasoned white beans on Turkish bread*

vişneli ekmek tatlısı veesh-ne-lee ek-mek tat-luh-suh *cherry bread pudding*

Y

yaban havucu ya-*ban* ha-voo-*joo* *parsnip*
yabani pirinç ya-*ba*-nee pee-*reench* *wild rice*
yabani yeşil yapraklı sebzeler ya-*ba*-nee
  ye-*sheel* yap-rak-*luh* seb-*ze*-ler *wild greens*
yağsız ya-*suhz* *without fat • without beef*
— **kıyma** kuhy-*ma* *lean ground beef*
yahni yah-*nee* *meat & vegetable stew*
yarma yar-*ma* *coarsely ground wheat*
yassı kadayıf yas-*suh* ka-da-*yuhf* *baked
  kadayıf pancakes topped with kaymak*
yavan çorbası ya-*van* chor-ba-*suh* *'flavour-
  less soup' with wheat, chickpeas, lentils,
  beans, meat & capsicum (Malatya)*
yayla çorbası yai-*la* chor-ba-*suh*
  'highland' yogurt soup with mint
yaz türlüsü yaz tewr-lew-*sew* *summer
  vegetable stew*
yengeç yen-*gech* *crab*
yermantarı yer-man-ta-*ruh* *truffle*
yeşil ye-*sheel* *green*
— **biber** bee-*ber* *green capsicum*
— **mercimekli bulgur pilavı**
  mer-jee-mek-*lee* bool-*goor* pee-la-*vuh*
  pilau of green lentils & bulgur (Tokat)
— **mercimekli erişteli çorba**
  mer-jee-mek-*lee* e-reesh-te-*lee* chor-*ba*
  green lentil & noodle soup (Urfa)
— **salata** sa-la-*ta* *green salad*
— **soğan** so-*an* *chives • spring onion*
— **zeytin** zay-*teen* *green olive*
yeşillikler ye-sheel-leek-*ler* *mixed greens*
yılanbalığı yuh-*lan*-ba-luh-*uh* *eel*
yufka yoof-*ka* *dough used in sweets*
yoğurt yo-*oort* *yogurt*
— **çorbası** chor-ba-*suh* *yogurt soup*
yoğurtlu fıstıklı köfte yo-oort-*loo*
  fuhs-tuhk-*luh* kerf-*te* *köfte dish of
  bulgur, yogurt, tomato & capsicum flakes*
yoğurtlu patlıcan salatası yo-oort-*loo*
  pat-luh-*jan* sa-la-ta-*suh* *eggplant salad
  with yogurt*
yoğurtlu pazı yo-oort-*loo* pa-*zuh* *chard in
  garlicky yogurt sauce (Kastamonu)*
yörük kebabı yer-*rewk* ke-ba-*buh* *'nomad's
  kebab' – lamb, mushroom, capsicum,
  artichoke, tomato, beans & macaroni*
yulaf yoo-*laf* *oats*
yumurta yoo-moor-*ta* *egg*
yuvarlama yoo-var-la-*ma* *soup with
  chickpeas & small mince dumplings*

yüksük çorbası yewk-*sewk* chor-ba-*suh*
  soup of chickpeas & mincemeat
yüksük makarna yewk-*sewk* ma-kar-*na*
  short, fat macaroni
yürek yew-*rek* *heart*

Z

zerdali zer-da-*lee* *wild apricots*
zencefil zen-je-*feel* *ginger*
zerde zer-*de* *dessert of rice, almonds,
  pistachios & pomegranate*
zeytin zay-*teen* *olive*
— **piyazı** pee-ya-*zuh* *salad of green
  olives, walnuts, capsicum & pomegranate*
zeytinyağı zay-teen-ya-*uh* *olive oil*
zeytinyağlı biber dolması
  zay-teen-ya-*luh* bee-*ber* dol-ma-*suh*
  rice-stuffed capsicum
zeytinyağlı dolma içi zay-teen-ya-*luh*
  dol-*ma* ee-*chee* *seasoned rice used for
  stuffing vegetables*
zeytinyağlı domates dolması
  zay-teen-ya-*luh* do-ma-*tes* dol-ma-*suh*
  stuffed tomato with rice
zeytinyağlı pilaki zay-teen-ya-*luh*
  pee-la-kee *pilaki of black-eyed peas,
  spring onion, carrot & potato (Aydın)*
zeytinyağlı pırasa zay-teen-ya-*luh*
  puh-ra-sa *leeks in olive oil with carrot,
  rice, sugar, salt & lemon*
zeytinyağlı pırasa böreği zay-teen-ya-*luh*
  puh-ra-sa ber-re-*ee* *leek pie in olive oil*
zeytinyağlı taze bakla zay-teen-ya-*luh*
  ta-ze bak-*la* *whole broad beans in
  olive oil*
zeytinyağlı taze fasulye zay-teen-ya-*luh*
  ta-ze fa-sool-ye *green beans in olive oil*
zeytinyağlı yaprak dolması
  zay-teen-ya-*luh* yap-*rak* dol-ma-*suh*
  stuffed vine leaves with rice in olive oil
zeytinyağlı yaz türlüsü zay-teen-ya-*luh*
  yaz tewr-lew-sew *vegetables in olive oil*
zeytinyağlı yeşil fasulye zay-teen-ya-*luh*
  ye-sheel fa-sool-ye *string beans in
  olive oil*
zeytinyağlılar zay-teen-ya-luh-*lar* *cold
  vegetables in olive oil*
zile pekmezi zee-le pek-me-zee *pekmez
  whipped with egg white (Tokat)*
zırz zuhrz *salad with fresh onion, spinach,
  süzme yoğurt, olive oil & boiled eggs*

emergencies

acil durumlar

Help!	*İmdat!*	*eem*·dat
Stop!	*Dur!*	door
Go away!	*Git burdan!*	geet boor·*dan*
Thief!	*Hırsız var!*	huhr·*suhz* var
Fire!	*Yangın var!*	*yan*·guhn var
Watch out!	*Dikkat et!*	*deek*·kat et

Call the police.
Polis çağırın. po·*lees* cha·*uh*·ruhn

Call a doctor.
Doktor çağırın. dok·*tor* cha·*uh*·ruhn

Call an ambulance.
Ambulans çağırın. am·boo·*lans* cha·*uh*·ruhn

It's an emergency.
Bu acil bir durum. boo a·*jeel* beer *doo*·room

There's been an accident.
Bir kaza oldu. beer ka·*za* ol·*doo*

Could you please help?
Yardım edebilir yar·*duhm* e·*de*·bee·leer
misiniz lütfen? mee·see·*neez* lewt·fen

Can I use your phone?
Telefonunuzu te·le·fo·noo·noo·*zoo*
kullanabilir miyim? kool·la·*na*·bee·leer mee·*yeem*

signs

Acil Servis	a·*jeel* ser·*vees*	**Emergency Department**
Hastane	has·*ta*·ne	**Hospital**
Polis	po·*lees*	**Police**
Polis Karakolu	po·*lees* ka·ra·ko·*loo*	**Police Station**

essentials

187

I'm lost.
   Kayboldum.   kai·bol·*doom*

Where are the toilets?
   Tuvaletler nerede?   too·va·let·*ler* ne·re·de

Is it safe ...?	... güvenli mi?	... gew·ven·*lee* mee
at night	Geceleyin	ge·je·le·*yeen*
for gay	Homoseksüeller	ho·mo·sek·sew·el·*ler*
people	için	ee·*cheen*
for travellers	Seyahat edenler	se·ya·hat e·den·*ler*
	için	ee·*cheen*
for women	Bayanlar için	ba·yan·*lar* ee·*cheen*
on your own	Yalnız başına	yal·*nuhz* ba·shuh·na

police

polis

Where's the police station?
   Polis karakolu nerede?   po·*lees* ka·ra·ko·*loo* ne·re·de

Please telephone the Tourist Police.
   Lütfen turizm polisini   *lewt*·fen too·*reezm* po·lee·see·*nee*
   arayın.   a·*ra*·yuhn

I want to report an offence.
   Şikayette bulunmak   shee·ka·yet·*te* boo·loon·*mak*
   istiyorum.   ees·*tee*·yo·room

I've been ...	Ben ...	ben ...
assaulted	saldırıya uğradım	sal·duh·ruh·*ya* oo·ra·*duhm*
raped	tecavüze uğradım	te·ja·vew·*ze* oo·ra·*duhm*
robbed	soyuldum	so·yool·*doom*

He/She has been ...	O ...	o ...
assaulted	saldırıya uğradı	sal·duh·ruh·*ya* oo·ra·*duh*
raped	tecavüze uğradı	te·ja·vew·*ze* oo·ra·*duh*
robbed	soyuldu	so·yool·*doo*

He/She tried to ... me.	... çalıştı.	... cha·luhsh·*tuh*
assault	*Bana saldırmaya*	ba·*na* sal·duhr·ma·*ya*
rape	*Bana tecavüz etmeye*	ba·*na* te·ja·*vewz* et·me·*ye*
rob	*Beni soymaya*	be·*nee* soy·ma·*ya*

I've lost my ...	... kayıp.	... ka·*yuhp*
My ... was/were stolen.	... çalındı.	... cha·luhn·*duh*
backpack	*Sırt çantası*	suhrt chan·ta·*suh*
bags	*Çantalar*	chan·ta·*lar*
credit card	*Kredi kartı*	kre·dee kar·*tuh*
handbag	*El çantası*	el chan·ta·*suh*
jewellery	*Mücevherler*	mew·jev·her·*ler*
money	*Para*	pa·*ra*
papers	*Evraklar*	ev·rak·*lar*
travellers cheques	*Seyahat çekleri*	se·ya·*hat* chek·le·*ree*
passport	*Pasaport*	pa·sa·*port*
wallet	*Cüzdan*	jewz·*dan*

I've been drugged.
Bana uyuşturucu verildi. — ba·*na* oo·yoosh·too·roo·*joo* ve·reel·*dee*

He/She has been drugged.
Ona uyuşturucu verildi. — o·*na* oo·yoosh·too·roo·*joo* ve·reel·*dee*

It was him/her.
Oydu. — oy·doo

I have insurance.
Sigortam var. — see·gor·*tam* var

What am I accused of?
Neyle suçlanıyorum? — nay·le sooch·la·*nuh*·yo·room

I didn't realise I was doing anything wrong.
Yanlış birşey yaptığımın farkında değildim. — yan·*luhsh* beer·*shay* yap·tuh·uh·*muhn* far·kuhn·*da* de·*eel*·deem

I didn't do it.
Ben yapmadım. — ben *yap*·ma·duhm

the police may say …

… suçlanıyorsunuz.
… sooch·la·*nuh*·yor·soo·nooz — **You're charged with …**

… suçlanıyor.
… sooch·la·*nuh*·yor — **He/She is charged with …**

Hırsızlıkla	huhr·suhz·*luhk*·la	**theft**
Saldırıda bulunmakla	sal·duh·ruh·*da* boo·loon·*mak*·la	**assault**
Vize süresini aşmakla	vee·*ze* sew·re·see·*nee* ash·*mak*·la	**overstaying a visa**
Vizesiz seyahat etmekle	vee·ze·*seez* se·ya·*hat* et·*mek*·le	**not having a visa**
Yasa dışı uyuşturucu madde bulundurmakla	ya·*sa* duh·*shuh* oo·yoosh·too·roo·*joo* mad·*de* boo·loon·door·*mak*·la	**possession (of illegal substances)**

… cezası.	… je·za·*suh*	**It's a … fine.**
Hız	huhz	**speeding**
Park	park	**parking**

I want to contact my embassy/consulate.
Konsoloslukla görüşmek istiyorum. — kon·so·los·*look*·la ger·rewsh·*mek* ees·*tee*·yo·room

Can I make a phone call?
Bir telefon edebilir miyim? — beer te·le·*fon* e·*de*·bee·leer mee·*yeem*

Can I have a lawyer (who speaks English)?
(İngilizce konuşan) Bir avukat istiyorum. — (een·gee·*leez*·je ko·noo·*shan*) beer a·voo·*kat* ees·*tee*·yo·room

Can I pay an on-the-spot fine?
Cezayı hemen ödeyebilir miyim? — je·za·*yuh* he·*men* er·de·ye·bee·leer mee·*yeem*

I have a prescription for this drug.
Bu ilaç için reçetem var. — boo ee·*lach* ee·*cheen* re·che·*tem* var

doctor

doktorda

Where's the nearest ...?	*En yakın ...* *nerede?*	en ya·*kuhn* ... ne·re·de
dentist	*dişçi*	deesh·*chee*
doctor	*doktor*	dok·*tor*
emergency department	*acil servis*	a·*jeel* ser·*vees*
hospital	*hastane*	has·*ta*·ne
medical centre	*poliklinik*	po·*lee*·klee·neek
optometrist	*gözlükçü*	gerz·lewk·*chew*
(night) pharmacist	*(nöbetçi) eczane*	(ner·bet·*chee*) ej·*za*·ne

I need a doctor (who speaks English).
(İngilizce konuşan) (een·gee·*leez*·je ko·noo·*shan*)
Bir doktora ihtiyacım var. beer dok·to·*ra* eeh·tee·ya·*juhm* var

Could I see a female doctor?
Bayan doktora ba·*yan* dok·to·*ra*
görünebilir miyim? ger·rew·*ne*·bee·leer mee·*yeem*

Could the doctor come here?
Doktor buraya dok·*tor* boo·ra·*ya*
gelebilir mi? ge·*le*·bee·leer mee

Is there an after-hours emergency number?
Mesai saatleri harici acil me·sa·*ee* sa·at·le·*ree* ha·ree·*jee* a·*jeel*
telefon numarası var mı? te·le·*fon* noo·ma·ra·*suh* var muh

I've run out of my medication.
İlacım bitti. ee·la·*juhm* beet·tee

This is my usual medicine.
Bu benim daimi ilacım. boo be·*neem* da·ee·*mee* ee·la·*juhm*

My child weighs (20) kilos.
Çocuğumun ağırlığı cho·joo·oo·*moon* a·uhr·luh·*uh*
(yirmi) kilodur. (yeer·*mee*) kee·*lo*·door

If you're speaking to a medical professional, you can say *hepatit A/B/C* he·pa·*teet* a/be/je for 'hepatitis A/B/C'. For non-medical people, use the word *sarılık* sa·ruh·*luhk*, the general term for all three kinds of hepatitis.

What's the correct dosage?
Kullanılması gereken   kool·la·nuhl·ma·*suh* ge·re·*ken*
dozaj nedir?   do·*zazh* ne·deer

My prescription is …
Benim reçetem …   be·*neem* re·che·*tem* …

How much will it cost?
Ne kadar eder?   ne ka·*dar* e·der

Can I have a receipt for my insurance?
Sağlık sigortam için   sa·*luhk* see·*gor*·tam ee·*cheen*
makbuz alabilir miyim?   mak·*booz* a·la·bee·leer mee·*yeem*

I don't want a blood transfusion.
Kan nakli istemiyorum.   kan nak·*lee* ees·te·mee·yo·room

Please use a new syringe.
Lütfen yeni bir iğne   *lewt*·fen ye·*nee* beer ee·*ne*
kullanın.   kool·*la*·nuhn

I have my own syringe.
Benim kendi   be·*neem* ken·*dee*
şırıngam var.   shuh·ruhn·*gam* var

I've been	*Ben … aşısı*	ben … a·shuh·*suh*
vaccinated against …	*oldum.*	ol·*doom*
He/She has been	*O … aşısı*	o … a·shuh·*suh*
vaccinated against …	*oldu.*	ol·*doo*
tetanus	*tetanoz*	te·ta·*noz*
typhoid	*tifo*	tee·*fo*

I need new …	*Yeni …*	ye·*nee* …
	ihtiyacım var.	eeh·tee·ya·*juhm* var
contact	*kontakt*	kon·*takt*
lenses	*lenslere*	lens·le·*re*
glasses	*gözlüğe*	gerz·lew·*e*

symptoms & conditions

I'm sick.
Hastayım.　　　　　　　　has·*ta*·yuhm

My friend/child is (very) sick.
Arkadaşım/çocuğum　　　　ar·ka·da·*shuhm*/cho·joo·*oom*
(çok) hasta.　　　　　　　(chok) *has*·ta

He/She is	*O …*	o …
having a/an …		
allergic reaction	*alerjili*	a·ler·zhee·*lee*
asthma attack	*astım krizi*	as·*tuhm* kree·*zee*
	geçiriyor	ge·chee·*ree*·yor
baby	*doğurmak üzere*	do·oor·*mak* ew·ze·*re*
heart attack	*kalp krizi*	kalp kree·*zee*
	geçiriyor	ge·chee·*ree*·yor

I've been …	*Ben …*	ben …
bitten by	*bir hayvan*	beer hai·*van*
an animal	*tarafından*	ta·ra·fuhn·*dan*
	ısırıldım	uh·suh·ruhl·*duhm*
injured	*yaralandım*	ya·ra·lan·*duhm*
vomiting	*kusuyorum*	koo·*soo*·yo·room

He/She has been …	*O …*	o …
bitten by	*bir hayvan*	beer hai·*van*
an animal	*tarafından*	ta·ra·fuhn·*dan*
	ısırıldı	uh·suh·ruhl·*duh*
injured	*yaralandı*	ya·ra·lan·*duh*
vomiting	*kusuyor*	koo·*soo*·yor

---

sick as a dog

If you're not feeling well, try not to use the English word 'sick' – the Turkish word *sik* seek means 'fuck' or 'dick' so you could get a slightly unexpected response to your death-bed cries. Say *hastayım* has·*ta*·yuhm (lit: sick-I-am) instead, or 'I'm ill' if you can only choke out an English phrase.

health

193

the doctor may say ...

Ne şikayetiniz var?
ne shee·ka·ye·tee·*neez* var
What's the problem?

Nereniz ağrıyor?
ne·re·neez a·*ruh*·yor
Where does it hurt?

Ateşiniz var mı?
a·te·shee·*neez* var muh
Do you have a temperature?

Ne kadar zamandır bu durumdasınız?
ne ka·*dar* za·*man*·duhr boo doo·room·*da*·suh·nuhz
How long have you been like this?

Daha önce böyle bir şikayetiniz oldu mu?
da·*ha* ern·*je* bay·*le* beer shee·ka·ye·tee·*neez* ol·*doo* moo
Have you had this before?

Cinsel hayatınızda aktif misiniz?
jeen·*sel* ha·ya·tuh·nuhz·*da* ak·*teef* mee·see·*neez*
Are you sexually active?

Korunmasız cinsel ilişkide bulundunuz mu?
ko·roon·ma·*suhz* jeen·*sel* ee·leesh·kee·*de* boo·loon·doo·*nooz* moo
Have you had unprotected sex?

... kullanıyor musunuz?	... kool·la·*nuh*·yor moo·soo·*nooz*	**Do you ...?**
İçki	eech·*kee*	**drink**
Sigara	see·*ga*·ra	**smoke**
Uyuşturucu	oo·yoosh·too·roo·*joo*	**take drugs**

... var mı?	... var muh	**Are you ...?**
Herhangi birşeye alerjiniz	her·*han*·gee beer·she·*ye* a·ler·jee·*neez*	**allergic to anything**
Sürekli kullandığınız bir ilaç	sew·rek·*lee* kool·lan·duh·uh·*nuhz* beer ee·*lach*	**on medication**

Ne kadar zaman burada kalacaksınız?
ne ka·*dar* za·*man* boo·ra·*da* ka·la·*jak*·suh·nuhz
How long are you travelling for?

Ülkenize döndüğünüz zaman bir doktora görünmelisiniz.
ewl·ke·nee·ze dern·dew·ew·*newz* za·*man* beer dok·to·*ra* ger·rewn·me·*lee*·see·neez
You should have it checked when you go home.

Tedavi için ülkenize dönmeniz gerekli.
te·da·*vee* ee·*cheen* ewl·ke·nee·ze dern·me·*neez* ge·rek·*lee*
You should return home for treatment.

Hastaneye yatırılmanız gerekli.
has·ta·ne·*ye* ya·tuh·ruhl·ma·*nuhz* ge·rek·*lee*
You need to be admitted to hospital.

Çok evhamlısınız.
chok ev·ham·*luh*·suh·nuhz
You're a hypochondriac.

I feel ...	... hissediyorum.	... hees·se·dee·yo·room
anxious	*Endişeli*	en·dee·she·*lee*
better	*Daha iyi*	da·*ha* ee·*yee*
depressed	*Depresif*	dep·re·*seef*
dizzy	*Başımın döndüğünü*	ba·shuh·*muhn* dern·dew·ew·*new*
hot and cold	*Bir sıcak bir soğuk*	beer suh·*jak* beer so·*ook*
nauseous	*Kusacak gibi*	koo·sa·*jak* gee·*bee*
shivery	*Üşüdüğümü*	ew·shew·dew·ew·*mew*
strange	*Tuhaf*	too·*haf*
weak	*Halsiz*	hal·*seez*
worse	*Daha kötü*	da·*ha* ker·*tew*

It hurts here.
Burası ağrıyor.   boo·ra·*suh* a·*ruh*·yor

I'm dehydrated.
Vücudum susuz kaldı.   vew·joo·*doom* soo·*sooz* kal·*duh*

I can't sleep.
Uyuyamıyorum.   oo·yoo·*ya*·muh·yo·room

health

195

I think it's the medication I'm on.
Sanırım kullandığım
ilaçtan kaynaklanıyor.
sa·nuh·*ruhm* kool·lan·duh·*uhm*
ee·lach·*tan* kai·nak·la·*nuh*·yor

I'm on medication for …
… için ilaç
kullanıyorum.
… ee·*cheen* ee·*lach*
kool·la·*nuh*·yo·room

I have (a/an) …
Bende … var.
ben·*de* … var

He/She is on medication for …
O … için ilaç
kullanıyor.
o … ee·*cheen* ee·*lach*
kool·la·*nuh*·yor

He/She has (a/an) …
Onda … var.
on·*da* … var

asthma	astım	as·*tuhm*
cold n	soğuk algınlığı	so·*ook* al·guhn·luh·*uh*
constipation	kabızlık	ka·buhz·*luhk*
cough n	öksürük	erk·sew·*rewk*
diabetes	şeker hastalığı	she·*ker* has·ta·luh·*uh*
diarrhoea	ishal	ees·*hal*
fever	ateş	a·*tesh*
headache	baş ağrısı	bash a·ruh·*suh*
intestinal worms	bağırsak kurdu	ba·uhr·*sak* koor·*doo*
migraine	migren	meeg·*ren*
nausea	bulantı	boo·lan·*tuh*
pain	ağrı	a·*ruh*
sore throat	boğaz ağrısı	bo·*az* a·ruh·*suh*
sunburn	güneş yanığı	gew·*nesh* ya·nuh·*uh*

I've recently had …	Yakın zamanda … geçirdim.	ya·*kuhn* za·man·*da* … ge·cheer·*deem*
He/She has recently had …	O yakın zamanda … geçirdi.	o ya·*kuhn* za·man·*da* … ge·cheer·*dee*
(amoebic)	(amibik)	(a·mee·*beek*)
dysentery	dizanteri	dee·zan·te·*ree*
giardiasis	giardiyaz	gee·ar·dee·*yaz*
malaria	sıtma	suht·*ma*
rabies	kuduz	koo·*dooz*

women's health

(I think) I'm pregnant.
(Sanırım) Hamileyim.   (sa·*nuh*·ruhm) ha·mee·*le*·yeem

I'm on the pill.
Doğum kontrol hapı   do·*oom* kon·*trol* ha·*puh*
kullanıyorum.   kool·la·*nuh*·yo·room

I haven't had my period for (six) weeks.
(Altı) haftadır   (al·*tuh*) haf·ta·*duhr*
adet görmedim.   a·det *ger*·me·deem

I've noticed a lump here.
Burada bir şişlik   boo·ra·*da* beer sheesh·*leek*
fark ettim.   fark et·*teem*

Do you have something for (period pain)?
(Adet ağrısı) için   (a·det a·ruh·*suh*) ee·*cheen*
ilacınız var mı?   ee·la·juh·*nuhz* var muh

---

the doctor may say ...

Adet halinde misiniz?
a·det ha·leen·*de* mee·see·*neez*   **Are you menstruating?**

Doğum kontrol hapı kullanıyor musunuz?
do·*oom* kon·*trol* ha·*puh*
kool·la·*nuh*·yor moo·soo·*nooz*   **Are you using contraception?**

En son ne zaman adet gördünüz?
en son ne za·*man* a·det
ger·*dew*·newz   **When did you last have your period?**

Hamile misiniz?
ha·mee·*le* mee·see·*neez*   **Are you pregnant?**

Hamilesiniz.
ha·mee·*le*·see·neez   **You're pregnant.**

I have a ...	... var.	... var
urinary	İdrar yolları	eed·rar yol·la·ruh
tract infection	iltihabım	eel·tee·ha·buhm
yeast infection	Mantar	man·tar
	enfeksiyonum	en·fek·see·yo·noom

I need ...	... ihtiyacım var.	... eeh·tee·ya·juhm var
contraception	Doğum kontrol	do·oom kon·trol
	hapına	ha·puh·na
the morning-	İlişki sonrası	ee·leesh·kee son·ra·suh
after pill	kullanılabilen	kool·la·nuh·la·bee·len
	doğum kontrol	do·oom kon·trol
	ilacına	ee·la·juh·na
a pregnancy	Hamilelik	ha·mee·le·leek
test	testine	tes·tee·ne

allergies

I'm allergic to ...	... alerjim var.	... a·ler·zheem var
He/She is	... alerjisi var.	... a·ler·zhee·see var
allergic to ...		
antibiotics	Antibiyotiklere	an·tee·bee·yo·teek·le·re
anti-	Anti-	an·tee·
inflammatories	emflamatuarlara	em·fla·ma·too·ar·la·ra
aspirin	Aspirine	as·pee·ree·ne
bees	Arılara	a·ruh·la·ra
codeine	Kodeine	ko·de·ee·ne
penicillin	Penisiline	pe·nee·see·lee·ne
pollen	Polenlere	po·len·le·re
sulphur-based	Sülfür bazlı	sewl·fewr baz·luh
drugs	ilaçlara	ee·lach·la·ra

I have a skin allergy.
Alerjik bir cildim var.   a·ler·zheek beer jeel·deem var

If you suffer from food allergies, see **special diets & allergies**, page 174.

alternative treatments

alternatif tedavi yöntemleri

I don't use (Western medicine).
(Batı tıbbına) ait ilaç ve tedavi yöntemlerini kullanmıyorum.   (ba·*tuh* tuhb·buh·*na*) a·*eet* ee·*lach* ve te·da·*vee* yern·tem·le·ree·*nee* kool·*lan*·muh·yo·room

I prefer ...	... *tedavi yöntemini tercih ediyorum.*	... te·da·*vee* yern·te·mee·*nee* ter·*jeeh* e·*dee*·yo·room
Can I see someone who practises ...?	... *ile uğraşan birisini görebilir miyim?*	... ee·*le* oo·ra·*shan* bee·ree·see·*nee* ger·*re*·bee·leer mee·*yeem*
acupuncture	*Akupunktur*	a·koo·*poonk*·toor
naturopathy	*Natüropati*	na·tew·ro·pa·*tee*
reflexology	*Refleksoloji*	ref·lek·so·lo·*zhee*

parts of the body

My ... hurts.
Benim ... ağrıyor.
be·*neem* ... a·*ruh*·yor

I can't move my ...
... hareket ettiremiyorum.
... ha·re·*ket* et·tee·re·mee·yo·room

I have a cramp in my ...
... kramp girdi.
... kramp geer·*dee*

My ... is swollen.
... şişti.
... sheesh·*tee*

For other parts of the body, see the **dictionary**.

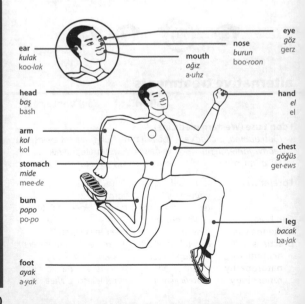

ear
kulak
koo·*lak*

nose
burun
boo·*roon*

eye
göz
gerz

mouth
ağız
a·*uhz*

head
baş
bash

hand
el
el

arm
kol
kol

chest
göğüs
ger·*ews*

stomach
mide
mee·*de*

bum
popo
po·*po*

leg
bacak
ba·*jak*

foot
ayak
a·*yak*

SAFE TRAVEL

200

pharmacist

I need something for (a headache).
(Baş ağrısı) için   (bash a·ruh·*suh*) ee·*cheen*
birşey almak istiyorum.   beer·*shay* al·*mak* ees·*tee*·yo·room

Do I need a prescription for (antihistamines)?
(Antihistamin) almak   (an·tee·hees·ta·meen) al·*mak*
için reçeteye   ee·*cheen* re·che·te·*ye*
ihtiyacım var mı?   eeh·tee·ya·*juhm* var muh

I have a prescription.
Reçetem var.   re·che·*tem* var

How many times a day?
Günde kaç kez almalıyım?   gewn·*de* kach kez al·ma·luh·*yuhm*

Will it make me drowsy?
Uyku verir mi?   ooy·*koo* ve·*reer* mee

antiseptic n	*antiseptik*	an·tee·sep·*teek*
gut blockers (for diarrhoea)	*müsil ilacı*	mew·*seel* ee·la·*juh*
painkillers	*ağrı kesici*	a·*ruh* ke·see·*jee*
thermometer	*termometre*	ter·mo·*met*·re
rehydration salts	*rehidrasyon tuzları*	re·heed·ras·*yon* tooz·la·*ruh*

---

the pharmacist may say ...

Bunu daha önce kullandınız mı?
boo·*noo* da·*ha* ern·je
kool·lan·*duh*·nuhz muh

Have you taken this before?

Günde iki kez (yemekle birlikte).
gewn·*de* ee·*kee* kez
(ye·*mek*·le beer·leek·*te*)

Twice a day (with food).

İlacı bitirene kadar kullanmalısınız.
ee·la·*juh* bee·tee·re·*ne* ka·*dar*
kool·lan·ma·*luh*·suh·nuhz

You must complete the course.

201

dentist

I have a ...	Dişim ...	dee·sheem ...
broken tooth	kırıldı	kuh·ruhl·duh
cavity	çürüdü	chew·rew·dew
toothache	ağrıyor	a·ruh·yor

I've lost a filling.
Dolgum düştü.　　　　dol·goom dewsh·tew

My dentures are broken.
Takma dişim kırıldı.　　tak·ma dee·sheem kuh·ruhl·duh

My gums hurt.
Damaklarım ağrıyor.　　da·mak·la·ruhm a·ruh·yor

I don't want it extracted.
Dişimin çekilmesini　　dee·shee·meen che·keel·me·see·nee
istemiyorum.　　　　　ees·te·mee·yo·room

I need (a/an) ...	... yaptırmam	... yap·tuhr·mam
	gerekli.	ge·rek·lee
anaesthetic	Anestezi	a·nes·te·zee
filling	Dolgu	dol·goo

---

the dentist may say ...

Hiç acımayacak.
　heech a·juh·ma·ya·jak　　　　　**This won't hurt a bit.**

Ağzınızı iyice açın.
　a·zuh·nuh·zuh ee·yee·je a·chuhn　**Open wide.**

Hareket etmeyin.
　ha·re·ket et·me·yeen　　　　　　**Don't move.**

Bunu ısırın.
　boo·noo uh·suh·ruhn　　　　　　**Bite down on this.**

Ağzınızı çalkalayın!
　a·zuh·nuh·zuh chal·ka·la·yuhn　**Rinse!**

Bitmedi, tekrar gelmelisiniz.
　beet·me·dee tek·rar　　　　　　**Come back, I haven't**
　gel·me·lee·see·neez　　　　　　**finished.**

SUSTAINABLE TRAVEL

Sustainability has become an important part of the travel vernacular. In practical terms, this means assessing our impact on the environment and local cultures and economies – and acting to make that impact as positive as possible. Here are some basic phrases to get you on your way …

communication & cultural differences

I'd like to learn some of your local dialects.
Bu yörelerin	boo yer·re·le·reen
şivesini öğrenmek	shee·ve·see·nee er·ren·mek
istiyorum.	is·tee·yo·room

Would you like me to teach you some English?
Size biraz İngilizce	see·ze bee·raz een·gee·leez·je
öğretmemi ister	er·ret·me·mee ees·ter
misiniz?	mee·see·neez

Is this a local or national custom?
Bu yerel mi,	boo ye·rel mee
yoksa ulusal	yok·sa oo·loo·sal
bir gelenek mi?	beer ge·le·nek mee

I respect your customs.
| Geleneklerinize saygı | ge·le·nek·le·ree·nee·ze sai·guh |
| duyuyorum. | doo·yoo·yo·room |

community benefit & involvement

What sorts of issues is this community facing?
Toplumun gündemini	top·loo·moon gewn·de·mee·nee
meşgul eden konular	mesh·gool e·den ko·noo·lar
nelerdir?	ne·ler·deer

drought	*kuraklık*	koo·rak·*luhk*
media control	*basın yayın*	ba·*suhn* ya·*yuhn*
	özgürlüğü	erz·gewr·lew·*ew*
political conflict	*politik görüş*	po·lee·*teek* ger·*rewsh*
	ayrılığı	ai·ruh·luh·*uh*
religious conflict	*dini görüş*	dee·*nee* ger·*rewsh*
	ayrılığı	ai·ruh·luh·*uh*

I'd like to volunteer my skills.

Gönüllü olarak	ger·newl·*lew* o·la·*rak*
çalışmak	cha·luhsh·*mak*
istiyorum.	ees·*tee*·yo·room

Are there any volunteer programs available in the area?

Bu bölgede gönüllü	boo berl·ge·*de* ger·newl·*lew*
hizmet programları	heez·*met* prog·ram·la·*ruh*
var mı?	var muh

environment

Where can I recycle this?

Bunu atabileceğim	boo·*noo* a·*ta*·bee·le·je·eem
geri dönüşüm	ge·*ree* der·new·*shewm*
kumbarası nerede var?	koom·ba·ra·*suh* ne·re·de var

transport

Can we get there by public transport?

Oraya toplu taşım	o·ra·*ya* top·*loo* ta·*shuhm*
aracıyla gidebilir	a·ra·*juhy*·la gee·*de*·bee·leer
miyiz?	mee·*yeez*

Can we get there by bike?

| *Oraya bisikletle* | o·ra·*ya* bee·seek·*let*·le |
| *gidebilir miyiz?* | gee·*de*·bee·leer mee·*yeez* |

I'd prefer to walk there.

| *Oraya yürümeyi* | o·ra·*ya* yew·rew·me·*yee* |
| *tercih ederim.* | ter·*jeeh* e·de·reem |

accommodation

I'd like to stay at a locally run hotel.

Yerel olarak işletilen bir	ye·rel o·la·rak eesh·le·tee·len beer
otelde kalmak istiyorum.	o·tel·de kal·mak ees·tee·yo·room

Can I turn the air conditioning off and open the window?

Klimayı kapatıp	klee·ma·yuh ka·pa·tuhp
pencereyi açabilir	pen·je·re·yee a·cha·bee·leer
miyim?	mee·yeem

Are there any ecolodges here?

Burada ekolojik	boo·ra·da e·ko·lo·zheek
konaklama yerleri var mı?	ko·nak·la·ma yer·le·ree var muh

There's no need to change my sheets.

Çarşaflarımın	char·shaf·la·ruh·muhn
değişmesine gerek yok.	de·eesh·me·see·ne ge·rek yok

shopping

Where can I buy locally produced goods?

Bu yöreye ait ürünler	boo yer·re·ye a·eet ew·rewn·ler
nereden alabilirim?	ne·re·den a·la·bee·lee·reem

Where can I buy locally produced souvenirs?

Bu yöreye ait	boo yer·re·ye a·eet
hediyelik eşyalar	he·dee·ye·leek esh·ya·lar
nereden alabilirim?	ne·re·den a·la·bee·lee·reem

Do you sell Fair Trade products?

Adil Ticaret ürünleri	a·deel tee·ja·ret ew·rewn·le·ree
satıyor musunuz?	sa·tuh·yor moo·soo·nooz

food

Do you sell ...?

	... satıyor musunuz?	... sa·tuh·yor moo·soo·nooz
locally produced food	Yöresel yiyecekler	yer·re·sel yee·ye·jek·ler
organic produce	Organic ürünler	or·ga·neek ew·rewn·ler

Can you tell me what traditional foods I should try?

Hangi geleneksel
yiyecekleri denememi
tavsiye edersiniz?

han·gee ge·le·nek·*sel*
yee·ye·jek·le·*ree* de·ne·me·*mee*
tav·see·*ye* e·*der*·see·neez

sightseeing

Does your company …?	*Firmanız …?*	feer·ma·*nuhz* …
donate money to charity	*hayır kurumlarına para bağışlıyor mu*	ha·*yuhr* koo·room·la·ruh·*na* pa·*ra* ba·uhsh·*luh*·yor moo
hire local guides	*yerel rehberler kiralıyor mu*	ye·*rel* reh·ber·*ler* kee·ra·*luh*·yor moo
visit local businesses	*yerel işletmelere uğruyor mu*	ye·*rel* eesh·let·me·le·*re* oo·*roo*·yor moo

Are cultural tours available?

Kültürel turlar
düzenliyor musunuz?

kewl·tew·*rel* toor·*lar*
dew·zen·lee·yor moo·soo·*nooz*

Does the guide speak local dialects?

Rehber yerel
şiveleri
konuşuyor mu?

reh·*ber* ye·*rel*
shee·ve·lee·*ree*
ko·noo·*shoo*·yor moo

… dialect	… *Şivesi*	… she·ve·*see*
Aegean	*Ege*	e·ge
Black Sea	*Karadeniz*	ka·*ra*·de·neez
Cyprus	*Kıbrıs*	*kuhb*·ruhs
Eastern Anatolia	*Doğu Anadolu*	do·*oo* a·*na*·do·loo
Middle Anatolia	*Orta Anadolu*	or·*ta* a·*na*·do·loo
Rumelia	*Rumeli*	roo·*me*·lee
Southeastern Anatolia	*Güneydoğu Anadolu*	gew·nay·do·*oo* a·*na*·do·loo
Thrace	*Trakya*	*trak*·ya

You'll find words marked as adjective a, noun n, verb v, singular sg, plural pl, informal inf and polite pol where necessary. All nouns are in the nominative case. Words which take suffixes (word endings), such as the Turkish words for 'to' and 'without', are shown with their different endings separated by a slash (/). To work out which one to use, see the **a–z phrasebuilder** and the box on **vowel harmony**, page 13.

A

aboard *-da/-de/-ta/-te* ·da/·de/·ta/·te
abortion *çocuk aldırma* cho·jook al·duhr·ma
about *etrafında* et·ra·fuhn·da
above *yukarısında* yoo·ka·ruh·suhn·da
abroad *yurt dışı* yoort duh·shuh
accident *kaza* ka·za
accommodation *kalacak yer* ka·la·jak yer
account n *hesap* he·sap
acropolis *akropolis* ak·ro·po·lees
across *karşısında* kar·shuh·suhn·da
activist *şiddet yanlısı* sheed·det yan·luh·suh
actor *oyuncu* o·yoon·joo
acupuncture *akupunktur* a·koo·poonk·toor
adaptor *adaptör* a·dap·ter
addiction *bağımlılık* ba·uhm·luh·luhk
address n *adres* ad·res
administration *yönetim* yer·ne·teem
admission (price) *giriş* gee·reesh
admit *kabul etmek* ka·bool et·mek
adult n *yetişkin* ye·teesh·keen
advertisement *ilan* ee·lan
advice *tavsiye* tav·see·ye
Aegean Sea *Ege Denizi* e·ge de·nee·zee
aerobics *ayrobik* ai·ro·beek
aeroplane *uçak* oo·chak
Africa *Afrika* af·ree·ka
after *sonra* son·ra
(this) afternoon *(bu) öğleden sonra* (boo) er·le·den son·ra
aftershave *traş losyonu* trash los·yo·noo
again *tekrar* tek·rar
age n *yaş* yash
(three days) ago *(üç gün) önce* (ewch gewn) ern·je
agora (open ground, town square) *büyük meydan* bew·yewk may·dan

agora (market place) *pazar yeri* pa·zar ye·ree
agree *aynı fikirde olmak* ai·nuh fee·keer·de ol·mak
agriculture *tarım* ta·ruhm
ahead *ileride* ee·le·ree·de
AIDS *AIDS* ayds
air n *hava* ha·va
air conditioning *klima* klee·ma
airline *hava yolları* ha·va yol·la·ruh
airmail *hava yoluyla* ha·va yo·looy·la
airplane *uçak* oo·chak
airport *havaalanı* ha·va·a·la·nuh
airport tax *toprak bastı* top·rak bas·tuh
aisle (on plane) *koridor* ko·ree·dor
alarm clock *çalar saat* cha·lar sa·at
alcohol *alkol* al·kol
all *hepsi* hep·see
allergy *alerji* a·ler·zhee
almond *badem* ba·dem
almost *hemen hemen* he·men he·men
alone *yalnız* yal·nuhz
already *zaten* za·ten
also *bir de* beer de
altar *sunak* soo·nak
altitude *yükseklik* yewk·sek·leek
always *her zaman* her za·man
ambassador *büyükelçi* bew·yewk·el·chee
ambulance *ambulans* am·boo·lans
American football *Amerikan futbolu* a·me·ree·kan foot·bo·loo
anaemia *kansızlık* kan·suhz·luhk
anarchist n *anarşist* a·nar·sheest
ancient a *tarihi* ta·ree·hee
and *ve* ve
angry *kızgın* kuhz·guhn
animal *hayvan* hai·van
ankle *ayak bileği* a·yak bee·le·ee
another *diğer* dee·er

answer n *cevap* je·vap
ant *karınca* ka·ruhn·ja
antibiotics *antibiyotik* an·tee·bee·yo·teek
antihistamines *antihistamin* an·tee·hees·ta·meen
antinuclear *antinükleer* an·tee·newk·le·er
antique n *antika* an·tee·ka
antiseptic n *antiseptik* an·te·sep·teek
any *herhangi bir* her·han·gee beer
apartment *apartman dairesi* a·part·man da·ee·re·see
appendix (body) *apandis* a·pan·dees
apple *elma* el·ma
appointment *randevu* ran·de·voo
apricot *kayısı* ka·yuh·suh
April *Nisan* nee·san
Arabic (language) *Arapça* a·rap·cha
archaeological *arkeolojik* ar·ke·o·lo·zheek
architect *mimar* mee·mar
architecture (art) *mimari yapı* mee·ma·ree ya·puh
architecture (profession) *mimarlık* mee·mar·luhk
argue *tartışmak* tar·tuhsh·mak
arm (body) *kol* kol
aromatherapy *aromaterapi* a·ro·ma·te·ra·pee
arrest v *tutuklamak* too·took·la·mak
arrivals *gelen yolcu* ge·len yol·joo
arrive *varmak* var·mak
art *sanat* sa·nat
art gallery *sanat galerisi* sa·nat ga·le·ree·see
artist *sanatçı* sa·nat·chuh
ashtray *kül tablası* kewl tab·la·suh
Asia *Asya* as·ya
ask (a question) v *sormak* sor·mak
ask (for something) v *istemek* ees·te·mek
asparagus *kuşkonmaz* koosh·kon·maz
aspirin *aspirin* as·pee·reen
asthma *astım* as·tuhm
at *-da/-de/-ta/-te* -da/-de/-ta/-te
athletics *atletizm* at·le·teezm
atmosphere *atmosfer* at·mos·fer
aubergine *patlıcan* pat·luh·jan
August *Ağustos* a·oos·tos
aunt (maternal) *teyze* tay·ze
aunt (paternal) *hala* ha·la
Australia *Avustralya* a·voos·tral·ya
Australian Rules Football *Avustralya futbolu* a·voos·tral·ya foot·bo·loo
Austria *Avusturya* a·voos·toor·ya
automated teller machine (ATM) *bankamatik* ban·ka·ma·teek

autumn *sonbahar* son·ba·har
avenue *cadde* jad·de
avocado *avokado* a·vo·ka·do
awful *korkunç* kor·koonch
Azerbaijan *Azerbaycan* a·zer·bai·jan

B

B&W film *siyah beyaz film* see·yah be·yaz feelm
baby n *bebek* be·bek
baby food *bebek maması* be·bek ma·ma·suh
baby powder *bebek pudrası* be·bek pood·ra·suh
babysitter *dadı* da·duh
back (body) *sırt* suhrt
back (position) *arka* ar·ka
backgammon *tavla* tav·la
backpack *sırt çantası* suhrt chan·ta·suh
bacon *domuz eti* do·mooz e·tee
bad *kötü* ker·tew
bag *çanta* chan·ta
baggage *bagaj* ba·gazh
baggage allowance *bagaj hakkı* ba·gazh hak·kuh
baggage claim *bagaj konveyörü* ba·gazh kon·ve·yer·rew
bait *yem* yem
bakery *fırın* fuh·ruhn
balance (account) *hesap bakiyesi* he·sap ba·kee·ye·see
balcony *balkon* bal·kon
ball (sport) n *top* top
ballet *bale* ba·le
banana *muz* mooz
band (music) *müzik gurubu* mew·zeek goo·roo·boo
bandage *bandaj* ban·dazh
Band-Aid *yara bandı* ya·ra ban·duh
bank n *banka* ban·ka
bank account *banka hesabı* ban·ka he·sa·buh
banknote *kağıt para* ka·uht pa·ra
baptism *vaftiz* vaf·teez
bar *bar* bar
bar work *bar işi* bar ee·shee
barber *berber* ber·ber
baseball *beysbol* bays·bol
basilica *büyük kilise* bew·yewk kee·lee·se
basket *sepet* se·pet
basketball *basketbol* bas·ket·bol
bath n *banyo* ban·yo

bathing suit *mayo* ma·yo
bathroom *banyo* ban·yo
battery (dry) *pil* peel
battery (car) *akü* a·kew
bazaar *pazar* pa·zar
be *olmak* ol·mak
beach *plaj* plazh
beach volleyball *plaj voleybolu*
   plazh vo·lay·bo·loo
bean *fasulye* fa·sool·ye
bean sprout *fasulye filizi*
   fa·sool·ye fee·lee·zee
beautiful *güzel* gew·zel
beauty salon *güzellik salonu*
   gew·zel·leek sa·lo·noo
because *çünkü* chewn·kew
bed *yatak* ya·tak
bed linen *çarşaf* char·shaf
bedding *yatak takımı* ya·tak ta·kuh·muh
bedroom *yatak odası* ya·tak o·da·suh
bee *arı* a·ruh
beef *sığır eti* suh·uhr e·tee
beer *bira* bee·ra
beerhall *birahane* bee·ra·ha·ne
beetroot *pancar* pan·jar
before *önce* ern·je
beggar *dilenci* dee·len·jee
behind *arkasında* ar·ka·suhn·da
Belgium *Belçika* bel·chee·ka
below *aşağısında* a·sha·uh·suhn·da
beside *yanında* ya·nuhn·da
best *a en iyi* en ee·yee
bet *n bahis* ba·hees
better *daha iyi* da·ha ee·yee
between *arasında* a·ra·suhn·da
Bible *incil* een·jeel
bicycle *bisiklet* bee·seek·let
big *büyük* bew·yewk
bigger *daha büyük* da·ha bew·yewk
biggest *en büyük* en bew·yewk
bike *bisiklet* bee·seek·let
bike chain *bisiklet zinciri*
   bee·seek·let zeen·jee·ree
bike lock *bisiklet kilidi*
   bee·seek·let kee·lee·dee
bike path *bisiklet yolu* bee·seek·let yo·loo
bike shop *bisikletçi* bee·seek·let·chee
bill (restaurant) *n hesap* he·sap
binoculars *dürbün* dewr·bewn
bird *kuş* koosh
birth certificate *doğum belgesi*
   do·oom bel·ge·see
birthday *doğum günü* do·oom gew·new

biscuit *bisküvi* bees·kew·vee
bite (dog) *n köpek ısırması*
   ker·pek uh·suhr·ma·suh
bite (insect) *n böcek ısırması*
   ber·jek uh·suhr·ma·suh
bitter *acı* a·juh
black *siyah* see·yah
Black Sea *Karadeniz* ka·ra·de·neez
bladder *mesane* me·sa·ne
blanket *battaniye* bat·ta·nee·ye
blind *a kör* ker
blister *kabarcık* ka·bar·juhk
blocked *tıkalı* tuh·ka·luh
blood *kan* kan
blood group *kan gurubu* kan goo·roo·boo
blood pressure *tansiyon* tan·see·yon
blood test *kan tahlili* kan tah·lee·lee
blue *mavi* ma·vee
board *v binmek* been·mek
boarding house *pansiyon* pan·see·yon
boarding pass *biniş kartı* bee·neesh kar·tuh
boat *vapur* va·poor
body *vücut* vew·joot
boiled *kaynamış* kai·na·muhsh
bone *kemik* ke·meek
book *n kitap* kee·tap
book (reserve) *v yer ayırtmak*
   yer a·yuhrt·mak
booked out (full) *dolu* do·loo
bookshop *kitapçı* kee·tap·chuh
boots *botlar* bot·lar
border *sınır* suh·nuhr
bored *canı sıkkın* ja·nuh suhk·kuhn
boring *sıkıcı* suh·kuh·juh
borrow *ödünç almak* er·dewnch al·mak
botanic garden *botanik bahçe*
   bo·ta·neek bah·che
both *her ikisi* her ee·kee·see
bottle *n şişe* shee·she
bottle opener *şişe açacağı*
   shee·she a·cha·ja·uh
bottle shop *tekel bayii* te·kel ba·yee·ee
bottom (body) *popo* po·po
bottom (position) *dipte* deep·te
bowl *n kase* ka·se
box *n kutu* koo·too
boxer shorts *bokser şort* bok·ser short
boxing *boks* boks
boy *oğlan* o·lan
boyfriend *erkek arkadaş* er·kek ar·ka·dash
bra *sütyen* sewt·yen
brakes *fren* fren
brandy *konyak* kon·yak

brave *cesur* je·*soor*
bread *ekmek* ek·*mek*
bread rolls *somun ekmek* so·*moon* ek·*mek*
break v *kırmak* kuhr·*mak*
break down v *bozulmak* bo·zool·*mak*
breakfast *kahvaltı* kah·val·*tuh*
breast *göğüs* ger·*ews*
breathe *nefes almak* ne·*fes* al·*mak*
bribe n *rüşvet* rewsh·*vet*
bridge (structure) *köprü* kerp·*rew*
briefcase *evrak çantası* ev·*rak* chan·ta·*suh*
bring *getirmek* ge·teer·*mek*
broccoli *brokoli* bro·ko·lee
brochure *broşür* bro·*shewr*
broken *kırık* kuh·*ruhk*
broken down *bozuk* bo·*zook*
bronchitis *bronşit* bron·*sheet*
brother *kardeş* kar·*desh*
brown *kahverengi* kah·ve·ren·gee
bruise n *çürük* chew·*rewk*
brush n *fırça* fuhr·*cha*
bucket *kova* ko·*va*
Buddhist *Budist* boo·*deest*
budget n *bütçe* bewt·*che*
buddy (dive) *dalış ortağı* da·*luhsh* or·ta·*uh*
buffet *büfe* bew·*fe*
bug n *böcek* ber·*jek*
build *inşa etmek* een·*sha* et·*mek*
builder *inşaatçı* een·sha·at·*chuh*
building *bina* bee·*na*
Bulgaria *Bulgaristan* bool·ga·rees·*tan*
bumbag *bel çantası* bel chan·ta·*suh*
burley *yem* yem
burn n *yanma* yan·*ma*
burnt *yanık* ya·*nuhk*
bus (city) *şehir otobüsü*
  she·*heer* o·to·bew·*sew*
bus (intercity) *şehirlerarası otobüs*
  she·*heer*·ler·a·ra·suh o·to·*bews*
bus station *otobüs terminali*
  o·to·*bews* ter·mee·na·lee
bus stop *otobüs durağı* o·to·*bews* doo·ra·*uh*
business n *iş* eesh
business class *business class* beez·*nuhs* klas
businessman *iş adamı* eesh a·da·*muh*
business trip *iş gezisi* eesh ge·zee·*see*
businesswoman *iş kadını* eesh ka·duh·*nuh*
busker *sokak çalgıcısı*
  so·*kak* chal·guh·juh·*suh*
busy *meşgul* mesh·*gool*
but *ama* a·*ma*
butcher *kasap* ka·*sap*
butter *tereyağ* te·re·ya

butterfly *kelebek* ke·le·*bek*
button *düğme* dew·*me*
buy v *satın almak* sa·*tuhn* al·*mak*

C

cabbage *lahana* la·*ha*·na
cable car *teleferik* te·le·fe·*reek*
café *kafe* ka·*fe*
cake *kek* kek
cake shop *pastane* pas·*ta*·ne
calculator *hesap makinesi*
  he·*sap* ma·kee·ne·*see*
calendar *takvim* tak·*veem*
call (telephone) v *aramak* a·ra·*mak*
call (shout) v *çağırmak* cha·uhr·*mak*
camera *kamera* ka·me·*ra*
camera shop *fotoğrafçı* fo·to·raf·*chuh*
camp v *kamp yapmak* kamp yap·*mak*
camping ground *kamp alanı* kamp a·la·*nuh*
camping store *kamp malzemeleri dükkanı*
  kamp mal·ze·me·le·*ree* dewk·ka·*nuh*
camp site *kamp yeri* kamp ye·*ree*
can (be able/have permission) v *-ebilmek/
  -abilmek* ·e·beel·*mek*/·a·beel·mek
can n *teneke kutu* te·ne·*ke* koo·*too*
can opener *konserve açacağı*
  kon·ser·*ve* a·cha·ja·*uh*
Canada *Kanada* ka·na·*da*
cancel *iptal etmek* eep·*tal* et·*mek*
cancer *kanser* kan·*ser*
candle *mum* moom
candy *şeker* she·*ker*
cantaloupe *kavun* ka·*voon*
capsicum *biber* bee·*ber*
car *araba* a·ra·*ba*
car hire *araba kiralama* a·ra·*ba* kee·ra·la·*ma*
car owner's title *araba yarışında birincilik*
  a·ra·*ba* ya·ruh·shuhn·*da* bee·reen·jee·*leek*
car park *otopark* o·to·*park*
car registration *plaka* pla·*ka*
caravan *karavan* ka·ra·*van*
caravanserai *kervansaray* ker·van·sa·rai
cardiac arrest *kalp krizi* kalp kree·*zee*
cards (playing) *oyun kağıdı*
  o·*yoon* ka·uh·*duh*
care (for someone) v *bakmak* bak·*mak*
caretaker *bakıcı* ba·kuh·*juh*
carpenter *marangoz* ma·ran·*goz*
carrot *havuç* ha·*vooch*
carry *taşımak* ta·shuh·*mak*
carton *karton* kar·*ton*
cash n *nakit* na·*keet*

cash (a cheque) *(çek) bozdurmak* (chek) boz·door·mak
cash register *yazar kasa* ya·zar ka·sa
cashew *Hint fıstığı* heent fuhs·tuh·uh
cashier *kasiyer* ka·see·yer
casino *gazino* ga·zee·no
cassette *kaset* ka·set
castle *kale* ka·le
casual work *geçici iş* ge·chee·jee eesh
cat *kedi* ke·dee
catamaran *katamaran* ka·ta·ma·ran
cathedral *katedral* ka·ted·ral
Catholic *Katolik* ka·to·leek
cauliflower *karnabahar* kar·na·ba·har
cave n *mağara* ma·a·ra
CD *CD* see·dee
celebration *kutlama* koot·la·ma
cell phone *cep telefonu* jep te·le·fo·noo
cemetery *mezarlık* me·zar·luhk
cent *sent* sent
centimetre *santimetre* san·tee·met·re
centre n *merkez* mer·kez
ceramics *seramik* se·ra·meek
cereal *tahıl ürünleri* ta·huhl ew·rewn·le·ree
certificate *sertifika* ser·tee·fee·ka
chain n *zincir* zeen·jeer
chair *sandalye* san·dal·ye
chairlift (skiing) *telesiyej* te·le·see·yezh
champagne *şampanya* sham·pan·ya
championships *şampiyona* sham·pee·yo·na
chance *şans* shans
change n *değişiklik* de·e·sheek·leek
change (coins) n *bozuk para* bo·zook pa·ra
change (money) v *(para) bozdurmak* (pa·ra) boz·door·mak
changing room *soyunma kabini* so·yoon·ma ka·bee·nee
charming *çekici* che·kee·jee
chat up v *sohbet etmek* soh·bet et·mek
cheap *ucuz* oo·jooz
cheat n *aldatma* al·dat·ma
check v *kontrol etmek* kon·trol et·mek
check (banking) n *çek* chek
check (bill) n *fatura* fa·too·ra
check-in desk *giriş* gee·reesh
checkpoint *kontrol noktası* kon·trol nok·ta·suh
cheese *peynir* pay·neer
cheese shop *peynirci* pay·neer·jee
chef *aşçıbaşı* ash·chuh·ba·shuh
cheque (banking) *çek* chek
cherry *kiraz* kee·raz
chess *satranç* sat·ranch

chess board *satranç tahtası* sat·ranch tah·ta·suh
chest (body) *göğüs* ger·ews
chestnut *kestane* kes·ta·ne
chewing gum *sakız* sa·kuhz
chicken *tavuk* ta·vook
chicken pox *su çiçeği* soo chee·che·ee
chickpea *nohut* no·hoot
child *çocuk* cho·jook
childminding *çocuk bakımı* cho·jook ba·kuh·muh
child seat *çocuk koltuğu* cho·jook kol·too·oo
children *çocuklar* cho·jook·lar
chilli *acı (biber)* a·juh (bee·ber)
chilli sauce *acı sos* a·juh sos
China *Çin* cheen
chiropractor *çıkıkçı* chuh·kuhk·chuh
chocolate *çikolata* chee·ko·la·ta
choose *seçmek* sech·mek
chopping board *kesme tahtası* kes·me tah·ta·suh
Christian n *Hiristiyan* huh·rees·tee·yan
Christian name *İlk ad* eelk ad
Christmas *Noel* no·el
Christmas Day *Noel yortusu* no·el yor·too·soo
Christmas Eve *Noel yortusu arifesi* no·el yor·too·soo a·ree·fe·see
church *kilise* kee·lee·se
cider *elma şarabı* el·ma sha·ra·buh
cigar *puro* poo·ro
cigarette *sigara* see·ga·ra
cigarette lighter *çakmak* chak·mak
cinema *sinema* see·ne·ma
circus *sirk* seerk
citadel *kale içi* ka·le ee·chee
citizenship *vatandaşlık* va·tan·dash·luhk
city *şehir* she·heer
city centre *şehir merkezi* she·heer mer·ke·zee
civil rights *medeni haklar* me·de·nee hak·lar
class (category) *kategori* ka·te·go·ree
class system *sınıf sistemi* suh·nuhf sees·te·mee
classical *klasik* kla·seek
clean a *temiz* te·meez
clean v *temizlemek* te·meez·le·mek
cleaning *temizlik* te·meez·leek
client *müşteri* mewsh·te·ree
cliff *uçurum* oo·choo·room
climb v *tırmanmak* tuhr·man·mak
cloakroom *vestiyer* ves·tee·yer
clock *saat* sa·at

close a yakın ya·kuhn
close v kapatmak ka·pat·mak
closed kapalı ka·pa·luh
clothesline çamaşır ipi cha·ma·shuhr ee·pee
clothing giyim gee·yeem
clothing store giyim mağazası
gee·yeem ma·a·za·suh
cloud n bulut boo·loot
cloudy bulutlu boo·loot·loo
clutch (car) debriyaj deb·ree·yazh
coach (bus) otobüs o·to·bews
coach (trainer) antrenör an·tre·ner
coat palto pal·to
cocaine kokain ko·ka·een
cockroach hamamböceği ha·mam·ber·je·ee
cocktail kokteyl kok·tayl
cocoa kakao ka·ka·o
coconut Hindistan cevizi
heen·dees·tan je·vee·zee
coffee kahve kah·ve
coins madeni para ma·de·nee pa·ra
cold n & a soğuk so·ook
colleague iş arkadaşı eesh ar·ka·da·shuh
collect call ödemeli telefon
er·de·me·lee te·le·fon
college kolej ko·lezh
colour n renk renk
comb n tarak ta·rak
come gelmek gel·mek
comedy komedi ko·me·dee
comfortable rahat ra·hat
commission n komisyon ko·mees·yon
communications (profession)
halkla ilişkiler halk·la ee·leesh·kee·ler
communion komünyon ko·mewn·yon
communist n komünist ko·mew·neest
companion arkadaş ar·ka·dash
company (firm) şirket sheer·ket
compass pusula poo·soo·la
complain şikayet etmek shee·ka·yet et·mek
complaint şikayet shee·ka·yet
complimentary (free) ikram eek·ram
computer bilgisayar beel·gee·sa·yar
computer game bilgisayar oyunu
beel·gee·sa·yar o·yoo·noo
concert konser kon·ser
concussion beyin sarsıntısı
be·yeen sar·suhn·tuh·suh
conditioner (hair) balsam bal·sam
condom prezervatif pre·zer·va·teef
conference (big) konferans kon·fe·rans
conference (small) görüşme ger·rewsh·me

confession (religious) günah çıkarma
gew·nah chuh·kar·ma
confirm (a booking) v teyit etmek
te·yeet et·mek
congratulations tebrikler teb·reek·ler
conjunctivitis konjonktivit iltihabı
kon·jonk·tee·veet eel·tee·ha·buh
connection (link) bağlantı ba·lan·tuh
connection (trip) aktarma ak·tar·ma
conservative n tutucu too·too·joo
constipation kabızlık ka·buhz·luhk
consulate konsolosluk kon·so·los·look
contact lens solution kontak lens
solüsyonu kon·tak lens so·lews·yo·noo
contact lenses kontak lens kon·tak lens
contraceptives doğum kontrol hapı
do·oom kon·trol ha·puh
contract n kontrat kon·trat
convenience store bakkal bak·kal
convent manastır ma·nas·tuhr
cook n aşçı ash·chuh
cook v pişirmek pee·sheer·mek
cookie kurabiye ko·ra·bee·ye
cooking yemek pişirme
ye·mek pee·sheer·me
cool (cold) a serin se·reen
cool (exciting) a hoş hosh
corkscrew tirbüşon teer·bew·shon
corn mısır muh·suhr
corner köşe ker·she
cornflakes mısır gevreği muh·suhr gev·re·ee
corrupt a bozuk bo·zook
cost v mal olmak mal ol·mak
cotton pamuk pa·mook
cotton balls pamuk yumağı
pa·mook yoo·ma·uh
cotton buds kulak temizleme çubuğu
koo·lak te·meez·le·me choo·boo·oo
cough v öksürmek erk·sewr·mek
cough medicine öksürük ilacı
erk·sew·rewk ee·la·juh
count v saymak sai·mak
counter (at bar) bar bar
country (nation) ülke ewl·ke
countryside şehir dışı she·heer duh·shuh
coupon kupon koo·pon
courgette kabak ka·bak
court (legal) mahkeme mah·ke·me
court (sport) kort kort
couscous kuskus koos·koos
cover charge fiks ücret feeks ewj·ret
cow inek ee·nek
crafts sanat sa·nat

crash n çarpışma char·puhsh·ma
crazy deli de·lee
cream (food) krema kre·ma
cream (lotion) krem krem
credit n kredi kre·dee
credit card kredi kartı kre·dee kar·tuh
cricket (sport) kriket kree·ket
crop (food) n ürün ew·rewn
cross (religious) n haç hach
crowded kalabalık ka·la·ba·luhk
cucumber salatalık sa·la·ta·luhk
cup fincan feen·jan
cupboard dolap do·lap
currency exchange döviz kuru
  der·veez koo·roo
current (electricity) akım a·kuhm
current affairs gündem gewn·dem
curry kari ka·ree
custom gelenek ge·le·nek
customs gümrük gewm·rewk
cut v kesmek kes·mek
cutlery çatal bıçak takımı
  cha·tal buh·chak ta·kuh·muh
CV özgeçmiş erz·gech·meesh
cycle v bisiklete binmek
  bee·seek·le·te been·mek
cycling bisiklet sporu bee·seek·let spo·roo
cyclist bisikletçi bee·seek·let·chee
Cyprus Kıbrıs kuhb·ruhs
cystitis sistit sees·teet

D

dad babacığım ba·ba·juh·uhm
daily günlük gewn·lewk
dance v dans etmek dans et·mek
dancing dans dans
dangerous tehlikeli teh·lee·ke·lee
dark (colour) koyu ko·yoo
dark (night) karanlık ka·ran·luhk
date (a person) v çıkmak chuhk·mak
date (appointment) n randevu ran·de·voo
date (day) n tarih ta·reeh
date (fruit) n hurma hoor·ma
date of birth doğum tarihi
  do·oom ta·ree·hee
daughter kız kuhz
dawn n şafak sha·fak
day gün gewn
day after tomorrow öbür gün er·bewr gewn
day before yesterday önceki gün
  ern·je·kee gewn
dead ölü er·lew

deaf sağır sa·uhr
deal (cards) v karmak kar·mak
December Aralık a·ra·luhk
decide karar vermek ka·rar ver·mek
deep derin de·reen
deforestation ormansızlaştırma
  or·man·suhz·lash·tuhr·ma
degrees (temperature) derece de·re·je
delay n gecikme ge·jeek·me
delicatessen şarküteri shar·kew·te·ree
deliver teslim etmek tes·leem et·mek
democracy demokrasi de·mok·ra·see
demonstration (protest) gösteri gers·te·ree
Denmark Danimarka da·nee·mar·ka
dental dam oral seks kondomu
  o·ral seks kon·do·moo
dental floss diş ipi deesh ee·pee
dentist dişçi deesh·chee
deodorant deodorant de·o·do·rant
depart ayrılmak ai·ruhl·mak
department store büyük mağaza
  bew·yewk ma·a·za
departure gidiş gee·deesh
departure gate gidiş kapısı
  gee·deesh ka·puh·suh
deposit (bank) depozito de·po·zee·to
derailleur bisiklet vites mekaniği
  bee·seek·let vee·tes me·ka·nee·ee
dervish derviş der·veesh
dervish ceremony derviş seramonisi
  der·veesh se·ra·mo·nee·see
descendent soy soy
desert n çöl cherl
design n desen de·sen
dessert tatlı tat·luh
destination gidilecek yer gee·dee·le·jek yer
details ayrıntı ai·ruhn·tuh
diabetes şeker hastalığı
  she·ker has·ta·luh·uh
dial tone çevir sesi che·veer se·see
diaper bebek bezi be·bek be·zee
diaphragm diyafram dee·yaf·ram
diarrhoea ishal ees·hal
diary günlük gewn·lewk
dice n zar zar
dictionary sözlük serz·lewk
die v ölmek erl·mek
diet diyet dee·yet
different farklı fark·luh
difficult zor zor
digital a dijital dee·zhee·tal
dining car yemekli vagon ye·mek·lee va·gon
dinner akşam yemeği ak·sham ye·me·ee

direct a *direk* dee-*rek*
direct-dial *direk arama* dee-*rek* a-ra-*ma*
direction *yön* yern
director *yönetmen* yer-net-*men*
dirty a *kirli* keer-*lee*
disabled *özürlü* er-zewr-*lew*
disco *disko* dees-ko
discount n *indirim* een-dee-*reem*
discrimination *ayrım* ai-*ruhm*
disease *hastalık* has-ta-*luhk*
dish n *yemek* ye-*mek*
disk (CD-ROM) *disk* deesk
disk (floppy) *disket* dees-*ket*
dive n *dalış* da-*luhsh*
dive v *dalmak* dal-*mak*
diving *dalış* da-*luhsh*
diving boat *dalış teknesi* da-*luhsh* tek-ne-*see*
diving course *dalış kursu* da-*luhsh* koor-*soo*
diving equipment *dalış malzemeleri*
    da-*luhsh* mal-ze-me-le-*ree*
divorced *boşanmış* bo-shan-*muhsh*
dizzy *başı dönen* ba-*shuh* der-*nen*
do *yapmak* yap-*mak*
doctor *doktor* dok-*tor*
documentary *belgesel* bel-ge-*sel*
dog *köpek* ker-*pek*
dole *sadaka* sa-da-*ka*
doll *oyuncak bebek* o-yoon-*jak* be-*bek*
dollar *dolar* do-*lar*
dome *kubbe* koob-*be*
door *kapı* ka-*puh*
down *aşağı* a-sha-*uh*
downhill *yokuş aşağı* yo-*koosh* a-sha-*uh*
dozen *düzine* dew-zee-ne
drama *dram* dram
drawing *çizim* chee-*zeem*
dream n *rüya* rew-*ya*
dress n *elbise* el-bee-*se*
dried *kuru* koo-roo
dried fruit *kuru meyve* koo-roo may-ve
drink (alcoholic) n *alkollü içecek*
    al-kol-*lew* ee-che-*jek*
drink (general) n *içecek* ee-che-*jek*
drink v *içmek* eech-*mek*
drive v *sürmek* sewr-*mek*
drivers licence *ehliyet* eh-lee-*yet*

drug (illegal) n *uyuşturucu*
    oo-yoosh-too-roo-*joo*
drug (medication) n *ilaç* ee-*lach*
drug addiction *uyuşturucu bağımlılığı*
    oo-yoosh-too-roo-*joo* ba-uhm-luh-luh-*uh*
drug dealer *uyuşturucu satıcısı*
    oo-yoosh-too-roo-*joo* sa-tuh-juh-*suh*
drug trafficking *uyuşturucu alış-verişi*
    oo-yoosh-too-roo-*joo* a-luhsh-ve-ree-*shee*
drug user *uyuşturucu bağımlısı*
    oo-yoosh-too-roo-*joo* ba-uhm-luh-*suh*
drum (music) n *davul* da-*vool*
drunk a *sarhoş* sar-*hosh*
dry a *kuru* koo-roo
dry v *kurulamak* koo-roo-la-*mak*
dry (clothes) v *kurutmak* koo-root-*mak*
duck *ördek* er-*dek*
dummy (pacifier) *emzik* em-*zeek*
Dutch (language) *Hollandaca*
    hol-*lan*-da-ja
duty-free *gümrüksüz satış*
    gewm-*rewk*-sewz sa-*tuhsh*
DVD *DVD* dee-vee-*dee*

E

each *her bir* her beer
ear *kulak* koo-*lak*
early *erken* er-*ken*
earn *kazanmak* ka-zan-*mak*
earplugs *kulak tıkacı* koo-*lak* tuh-ka-*juh*
earrings *küpe* kew-*pe*
Earth *yeryüzü* yer-yew-*zew*
earthquake *deprem* dep-*rem*
east *doğu* do-oo
Easter *Paskalya* pas-*kal*-ya
easy *kolay* ko-*lai*
eat *yemek yemek* ye-*mek* ye-*mek*
economy class *ekonomi sınıfı*
    e-ko-no-*mee* suh-nuh-*fuh*
ecstasy (drug) *ekstasi* eks-ta-*see*
eczema *egzama* eg-za-ma
editor *yazı işleri müdürü*
    ya-zuh eesh-le-ree mew-dew-*rew*
education *eğitim* e-ee-*teem*
egg *yumurta* yoo-moor-ta
eggplant *patlıcan* pat-luh-*jan*
election *seçim* se-*cheem*
electrical store *seçim bürosu*
    se-*cheem* bew-ro-soo
electricity *elektrik* e-lek-*treek*
elevator *asansör* a-san-*ser*
email n *e-posta* e-pos-ta

embarrassed *mahcup* mah·*joop*
embassy *elçilik* el·chee·*leek*
emergency *acil durum* a·*jeel* doo·room
emotional *duygusal* dooy·goo·*sal*
employee *çalışan* cha·luh·*shan*
employer *işveren* eesh·ve·*ren*
empty a *boş* bosh
end n *son* son
endangered species
    nesli tükenmekte olan hayvanlar
    nes·lee tew·ken·mek·te o·*lan* hai·van·*lar*
engaged (busy) *meşgul* mesh·*gool*
engaged (to marry) *nişanlı* nee·shan·*luh*
engagement (to marry) *nişan* nee·*shan*
engine *motor* mo·tor
engineer n *mühendis* mew·hen·*dees*
engineering *mühendislik*
    mew·hen·dees·*leek*
England *İngiltere* een·geel·te·re
English (language) *İngilizce* een·gee·*leez*·je
English (nationality) *İngiliz* een·gee·*leez*
enjoy (oneself) *eğlenmek* e·len·*mek*
enough *yeterli* ye·ter·*lee*
enter *girmek* geer·*mek*
entertainment guide *eğlence rehberi*
    e·len·je reh·be·*ree*
entry *giriş* gee·*reesh*
envelope *zarf* zarf
environment *çevre* chev·re
epilepsy *sara* sa·ra
equal opportunity *fırsat eşitliği*
    fuhr·*sat* e·sheet·lee·ee
equality *eşitlik* e·sheet·*leek*
equipment *teçhizat* tech·hee·*zat*
escalator *yürüyen merdiven*
    yew·rew·yen mer·dee·*ven*
estate agency *emlakçı* em·lak·*chuh*
euro *euro* yoo·ro
Europe *Avrupa* av·roo·pa
euthanasia *ötenazi* er·te·na·zee
evening *akşam* ak·sham
every *her* her
everyone *herkes* her·kes
everything *herşey* her·shay
exactly *tam olarak* tam o·la·rak
example *örnek* er·nek
excellent *mükemmel* mew·kem·mel
excess baggage *fazla yük* faz·la yewk
exchange n *değiş-tokuş* de·eesh·to·koosh
exchange (money) v *(para) bozdurmak*
    (pa·ra) boz·door·mak
exchange (general) v *değiştirmek*
    de·eesh·teer·mek

exchange rate *döviz kuru* der·veez koo·roo
excluded *hariç* ha·reech
exhaust (car) *egzoz* eg·zoz
exhibition *sergi* ser·gee
exit n *çıkış* chuh·kuhsh
expensive *pahalı* pa·ha·luh
experience n *deneyim* de·ne·yeem
expiry date *son kullanma tarihi*
    son kool·lan·ma ta·ree·hee
exploitation *sömürü* ser·mew·rew
express a *ekspres* eks·pres
express mail *ekspres posta* eks·pres pos·ta
extension (visa) *uzatma* oo·zat·ma
eye drops *göz damlası* gerz dam·la·suh
eyes *gözler* gerz·ler

F

fabric *kumaş* koo·mash
face *yüz* yewz
face cloth *yüz havlusu* yewz hav·loo·soo
factory *fabrika* fab·ree·ka
factory worker *fabrika işçisi*
    fab·ree·ka eesh·chee·see
fall (autumn) *sonbahar* son·ba·har
fall v *düşmek* dewsh·mek
family *aile* a·ee·le
family name *soyad* soy·ad
family room (home) *oturma odası*
    o·toor·ma o·da·suh
family room (restaurant) *aile bölümü*
    a·ee·le ber·lew·mew
family quarters *aile için kalacak yer*
    a·ee·le ee·cheen ka·la·jak yer
famous *ünlü* ewn·lew
fan (machine) *vantilatör* van·tee·la·ter
fan (sport, etc) *taraftar* ta·raf·tar
fanbelt *kayış* ka·yuhsh
far *uzak* oo·zak
fare *yol parası* yol pa·ra·suh
farm n *çiftlik* cheeft·leek
farmer *çiftçi* cheeft·chee
Farsi (Persian) *İranlı* ee·ran·luh
fashion n *moda* mo·da
fast a *hızlı* huhz·luh
fat a *şişman* sheesh·man
father *baba* ba·ba
father-in-law *kayınpeder* ka·yuhn·pe·der
faucet *musluk* moos·look
fault (someone's) *hata* ha·ta
faulty *bozuk* bo·zook
fax (document/machine) *faks* faks
February *Şubat* shoo·bat

feed v *beslemek* bes·le·*mek*
feel (touch) v *hissetmek* hees·set·*mek*
feeling (physical) *dokunma* do·koon·*ma*
feelings *duygular* dooy·goo·*lar*
female (animal) a *dişi* dee·*shee*
female (human) a *bayan* ba·*yan*
fence n *çit* cheet
fencing (sport) *eskrim* es·*kreem*
ferry n *feribot* fe·ree·bot
festival *festival* fes·tee·*val*
fever *ateş* a·*tesh*
few *birkaç* beer·*kach*
fiancé(e) *nişanlı* nee·shan·*luh*
fiction *roman* ro·*man*
fig *incir* een·*jeer*
fight n *kavga* kav·*ga*
fill v *doldurmak* dol·door·*mak*
fillet *fileto* fee·le·to
film (camera/cinema) n *film* feelm
film speed *film hızı* feelm huh·*zuh*
filtered *filtre edilmiş* feelt·re e·deel·*meesh*
find v *bulmak* bool·*mak*
fine *para cezası* pa·ra je·za·*suh*
fine a *iyi* ee·*yee*
finger *parmak* par·*mak*
finish n *bitiş* bee·*teesh*
finish v *bitirmek* bee·teer·*mek*
Finland *Finlandiya* feen·lan·dee·ya
fire (small fire under control) *ateş* a·*tesh*
fire (out of control) *yangın* yan·*guhn*
firewood *yakacak odun* ya·ka·jak o·*doon*
first a *ilk* eelk
first-aid kit *ilk yardım çantası* eelk yar·*duhm* chan·ta·*suh*
first class *birinci sınıf* bee·reen·jee suh·*nuhf*
first name *ilk ad* eelk ad
fish n *balık* ba·*luhk*
fishmonger *balıkçı* ba·luhk·*chuh*
fishing *balık avlama* ba·luhk av·la·ma
fishing line *misina* mee·see·na
fishing rod *olta* ol·ta
fish shop *balıkçı* ba·luhk·*chuh*
flag *bayrak* bai·*rak*
flannel (cloth for washing) *sabunluk* sa·boon·*look*
flare (fishing) *ışıltı* uh·shuhl·*tuh*
flash (camera) n *flaş* flash
flashlight (small torch) *cep feneri* jep fe·ne·*ree*
flat (apartment) n *apartman dairesi* a·part·*man* da·ee·re·see
flat a *düz* dewz
flea *pire* pee·*re*

fleamarket *bit pazarı* beet pa·za·*ruh*
flight *uçuş* oo·*choosh*
float (fishing) n *yüzmek* yewz·*mek*
flood n *sel* sel
floor (storey) *kat* kat
floor (surface) *yer* yer
florist *çiçekçi* chee·chek·*chee*
flour *un* oon
flower n *çiçek* chee·*chek*
flu *grip* greep
fly v *uçmak* ooch·*mak*
foggy *sisli* sees·*lee*
follow *takip etmek* ta·*keep* et·*mek*
food *yiyecek* yee·ye·*jek*
food supplies *erzak* er·*zak*
foot *ayak* a·*yak*
football (soccer) *futbol* foot·*bol*
footpath *patika* pa·tee·*ka*
foreign *yabancı* ya·ban·*juh*
forest *orman* or·*man*
forever *sonsuza dek* son·soo·za dek
forget *unutmak* oo·noot·*mak*
forgive *affetmek* af·fet·*mek*
fork n *çatal* cha·tal
fortnight *iki hafta* ee·kee haf·ta
fortune teller *falcı* fal·*juh*
foul (football) n *faul* fa·*ool*
fountain (natural) *pınar* puh·*nar*
fortress *kale* ka·*le*
foyer (hotel entry) *lobi* lo·*bee*
fragile *kırılabilir* kuh·ruh·*la*·bee·leer
France *Fransa* fran·sa
free (available) *boş* bosh
free (gratis) *ücretsiz* ewj·ret·*sez*
free (not bound) *serbest* ser·*best*
free kick *frikik* free·keek
freeze (to get cold) *donmak* don·*mak*
freeze (to make cold) *dondurmak* don·door·*mak*
French (language) *Fransızca* fran·*suhz*·ja
fresh *taze* ta·ze
Friday *Cuma* joo·ma
fridge *buzdolabı* booz·do·la·*buh*
fried *kızarmış* kuh·zar·*muhsh*
friend *arkadaş* ar·ka·*dash*
from -*dan*/-*den*/-*tan*/-*ten* -dan/-den/-tan/-ten
frost n *don* don
frozen *donmuş* don·*moosh*
fruit *meyve* may·*ve*
fruit picking *meyve toplama* may·ve top·la·ma
fry v *kızartmak* kuh·zart·*mak*

frying pan *kızartma tavası* kuh-zart-*ma* ta-va-*suh*
full (not empty) *dolu* do-*loo*
full (not hungry) *doymuş* doy-*moosh*
full-time *tam mesai* tam me-*sa*-ee
fun *eğlence* e-len-*je*
funeral *cenaze töreni* je-na-*ze* ter-re-*nee*
funny *komik* ko-*meek*
furniture *mobilya* mo-*beel*-ya
future n *gelecek* ge-le-*jek*

G

game (football) *maç* mach
game (sport) *oyun* o-*yoon*
garage *garaj* ga-*razh*
garbage *çöp* cherp
garbage can *çöp tenekesi* cherp te-ne-ke-*see*
garden n *bahçe* bah-*che*
gardener *bahçıvan* bah-chuh-*van*
gardening *bahçe işleri* bah-*che* eesh-le-*ree*
garlic *sarmısak* sar-muh-*sak*
gas (for cooking) *doğal gaz* do-*al* gaz
gas (petrol) *benzin* ben-*zeen*
gas cartridge *gaz tüpü* gaz tew-*pew*
gastroenteritis
  mide ve bağırsak enfeksiyonu
  mee-*de* ve ba-uhr-*sak* en-fek-see-yo-*noo*
gate (airport) *kapı* ka-*puh*
gauze *gazlı bez* gaz-*luh* bez
gay (homosexual) *eşcinsel* esh-jeen-*sel*
gearbox *vites kutusu* vee-*tes* koo-too-*soo*
gendarme *jandarma* zhan-dar-*ma*
Georgia *Gürcistan* gewr-jees-*tan*
German (language) *Almanca* al-*man*-ja
Germany *Almanya* al-*man*-ya
get *almak* al-*mak*
gift (present) *hediye* he-dee-*ye*
gift (talent) *yetenek* ye-te-*nek*
gig *eğlence* e-len-*je*
gin *cin* jeen
girl *kız* kuhz
girlfriend *kız arkadaş* kuhz ar-ka-*dash*
give *vermek* ver-*mek*
given name *İlk ad* eelk ad
glandular fever *glandüler ateş* glan-dew-*ler* a-*tesh*
glass (drinking) *bardak* bar-*dak*
glass (window) *cam* jam
glasses (spectacles) *gözlük* gerz-*lewk*
gloves (medical) *lateks eldiven* la-*teks* el-dee-*ven*

gloves (warm) *eldivenler* el-dee-ven-*ler*
glue n *tutkal* toot-*kal*
go *gitmek* geet-*mek*
go out *dışarıya çıkmak* duh-sha-ruh-*ya* chuhk-*mak*
go out with *ile çıkmak* ee-*le* chuhk-*mak*
go shopping *alış-verişe gitmek* a-luhsh-ve-ree-*she* geet-*mek*
goal (football) n *gol* gol
goalkeeper *kaleci* ka-le-*jee*
goat *keçi* ke-*chee*
god (general) *tanrı* tan-*ruh*
goggles (skiing) *kayak gözlüğü* ka-*yak* gerz-lew-*ew*
goggles (swimming) *deniz gözlüğü* de-*neez* gerz-lew-*ew*
gold n *altın* al-*tuhn*
golf ball *golf topu* golf to-*poo*
golf course *golf sahası* golf sa-ha-*suh*
good *iyi* ee-*yee*
government *devlet* dev-*let*
gram *gram* gram
grandchild *torun* to-*roon*
grandfather *büyükbaba* bew-*yewk*-ba-ba
grandmother *büyükanne* bew-*yewk*-an-ne
grandma *nine* nee-*ne*
grandpa *dede* de-*de*
grapefruit *greyfurt* gray-*foort*
grape(s) *üzüm* ew-*zewm*
grass (lawn) n *çim* cheem
grateful *müteşekkir* mew-te-shek-*keer*
grave n *mezar* me-*zar*
great (fantastic) *harika* ha-ree-*ka*
Greece *Yunanistan* yoo-na-nees-*tan*
green *yeşil* ye-*sheel*
greengrocer *manav* ma-*nav*
grey *gri* gree
grill n *ızgara* uhz-*ga*-ra
grocery *bakkal* bak-*kal*
grow *büyümek* bew-yew-*mek*
guaranteed *garantili* ga-ran-tee-*lee*
guess v *tahmin etmek* tah-*meen* et-*mek*
guesthouse *misafirhane* mee-sa-feer-ha-*ne*
guide (audio) *elektronik rehber* e-lek-tro-*neek* reh-*ber*
guide (person) n *rehber* reh-*ber*
guidebook *rehber kitap* reh-*ber* kee-*tap*
guide dog *rehber köpek* reh-*ber* ker-*pek*
guided tour *rehberli tur* reh-ber-*lee* toor
guilty *suçlu* sooch-*loo*
guitar *gitar* gee-*tar*
gum (chewing) *sakız* sa-*kuhz*
gun *silah* see-*lah*

gym (place) *jimnastik salonu* zheem·nas·*teek* sa·lo·noo
gymnastics *jimnastik* zheem·nas·*teek*
gynaecologist *jinekolog* zhee·ne·ko·*log*

H

hair *saç* sach
hairbrush *saç fırçası* sach fuhr·cha·*suh*
haircut *saç kestirme* sach kes·teer·*me*
hairdresser *kuaför* koo·a·*fer*
halal *helal* he·*lal*
half *yarım* ya·*ruhm*
hallucination *halüsinasyon* ha·lew·see·nas·yon
ham *jambon* zham·*bon*
hammer n *çekiç* che·*keech*
hammock *hamak* ha·*mak*
hand (body) *el* el
handbag *el çantası* el chan·ta·*suh*
handball *hentbol* hent·bol
handicrafts *el sanatları* el sa·nat·la·*ruh*
handkerchief *mendil* men·*deel*
handlebars *kulp* koolp
handmade *el işi* el ee·*shee*
handsome *yakışıklı* ya·kuh·shuhk·*luh*
happy *mutlu* moot·loo
harassment *taciz* ta·jeez
harbour n *liman* lee·man
hard (difficult) *zor* zor
hard (not soft) *sert* sert
hard-boiled *haşlanmış·katı* hash·lan·muhsh·ka·tuh
hardware store *hırdavatçı dükkanı* huhr·da·vat·chuh dewk·ka·nuh
hash (drug) *esrar* es·rar
hat *şapka* shap·ka
have *sahip olmak* sa·heep ol·mak
have a cold *üşütmek* ew·shewt·mek
have fun *eğlenmek* e·len·mek
hay fever *saman nezlesi* sa·man nez·le·see
hazelnut *fındık* fuhn·*duhk*
he o o
head n *baş* bash
headache *baş ağrısı* bash a·ruh·*suh*
headlights *farlar* far·lar
health *sağlık* sa·*luhk*
hear *duymak* dooy·mak
hearing aid *işitme cihazı* ee·sheet·me·jee·ha·zuh
heart (body) *kalp* kalp
heart attack *kalp krizi* kalp kree·zee

heart condition *kalp rahatsızlığı* kalp ra·hat·suhz·luh·*uh*
heat n *ısı* uh·*suh*
heated *ısıtılmış* uh·suh·tuhl·*muhsh*
heater *ısıtıcı* uh·suh·tuh·*juh*
heating *ısıtma* uh·suht·ma
heavy *ağır* a·*uhr*
helmet *kask* kask
help n *yardım* yar·duhm
help v *yardım etmek* yar·duhm et·mek
hepatitis (common term) *sarılık* sa·ruh·*luhk*
hepatitis (medical term) *hepatit* he·pa·*teet*
her (object) *onu* o·*noo*
her (possessive) *onun* o·*noon*
herb *bitki* beet·kee
herbalist *aktar* ak·tar
here *burada* boo·ra·da
heroin *eroin* e·ro·een
herring *ringa balığı* reen·ga ba·luh·*uh*
high *yüksek* yewk·sek
high school *lise* lee·se
highchair *mama sandalyesi* ma·ma san·dal·ye·see
highway *otoyol* o·to·yol
hike v *uzun yürüyüşe çıkmak* oo·zoon yew·rew·yew·she chuhk·mak
hiking *kırda uzun yürüyüş* kuhr·da oo·zoon yew·rew·yewsh
hiking boots *yürüyüş ayakkabısı* yew·rew·yewsh a·yak·ka·buh·suh
hiking route *yürüyüş güzergahı* yew·rew·yewsh gew·zer·ga·huh
hill *tepe* te·pe
him *onu* o·noo
Hindu *Hindu* heen·doo
hire v *kiralamak* kee·ra·la·mak
his *onun* o·noon
historical *tarihi* ta·ree·hee
history *tarih* ta·reeh
hitchhike *otostop yapmak* o·tos·top yap·mak
HIV *HIV* heev
hockey *hokey* ho·kay
holiday(s) *tatil* ta·teel
home *ev* ev
homeless *evsiz* ev·seez
homemaker *ev hanımı* ev ha·nuh·muh
homeopathy *homeopati* ho·me·o·pa·tee
homosexual *homoseksüel* ho·mo·sek·sew·el
honey *bal* bal
honeymoon *balayı* ba·la·yuh
hook(s) *olta iğnesi* ol·ta ee·ne·see
horoscope *yıldız falı* yuhl·duhz fa·luh

horse *at* at
horse riding *binicilik* bee·nee·jee·*leek*
hospital *hastane* has·ta·ne
hospitality *misafirperverlik*
mee·*sa*·feer·per·ver·leek
hot *sıcak* suh·*jak*
hot water *sıcak su* suh·*jak* soo
hotel *otel* o·*tel*
hour *saat* sa·at
house n *ev* ev
housework *ev işi* ev ee·*shee*
how *nasıl* na·suhl
hug v *sarılmak* sa·ruhl·*mak*
huge *kocaman* ko·ja·*man*
human resources *personel servisi*
per·so·*nel* ser·vee·*see*
human rights *insan hakları*
een·*san* hak·la·*ruh*
humanities *uygarlık tarihi*
ooy·gar·*luhk* ta·ree·*hee*
hundred *yüz* yewz
hungry *aç* ach
hunting *avlanma* av·lan·*ma*
hurt v *canı acımak* ja·nuh a·juh·*mak*
husband *koca* ko·*ja*
hydrofoil *deniz otobüsü*
de·*neez* o·to·bew·*sew*

I

I *ben* ben
ice *buz* booz
ice axe *buz kıracağı* booz kuh·ra·ja·*uh*
ice cream *dondurma* don·*door*·ma
ice-cream parlour *dondurmacı*
don·door·ma·*juh*
ice hockey *buz hokeyi* booz ho·ke·*yee*
identification *kimlik* keem·*leek*
identification card (ID) *kimlik kartı*
keem·*leek* kar·*tuh*
idiot *aptal* ap·*tal*
if *eğer* e·*er*
ill *hasta* has·*ta*
immigration *göç* gerch
important *önemli* er·nem·*lee*
impossible *imkansız* eem·kan·*suhz*
in *içinde* ee·cheen·*de*
in a hurry *acele ile* a·je·*le* ee·*le*
in front of *önünde* er·newn·*de*
included *dahil* da·*heel*
income tax *gelir vergisi* ge·*leer* ver·gee·*see*
India *Hindistan* heen·dees·*tan*
indicator (car) *gösterge* gers·ter·*ge*

indigestion *hazımsızlık*
ha·zuhm·suhz·*luhk*
indoor *içeride yapılan*
ee·che·ree·*de* ya·puh·*lan*
industry *endüstri* en·dews·*tree*
infection *enfeksiyon* en·fek·see·*yon*
inflammation *iltihap* eel·tee·*hap*
influenza *grip* greep
information *bilgi* beel·*gee*
ingredient *malzeme* mal·ze·*me*
inhaler *rahatlatıcı* ra·hat·la·tuh·*juh*
inject *iğne yapmak* ee·*ne* yap·*mak*
injection *iğne* ee·*ne*
injured *yaralı* ya·ra·*luh*
injury *yara* ya·*ra*
inner tube *iç lastik* eech las·*teek*
innocent *masum* ma·*soom*
inside *içeride* ee·che·ree·*de*
instructor *öğretmen* er·ret·*men*
insurance *sigorta* see·gor·*ta*
interesting *ilginç* eel·*geench*
intermission *ara* a·*ra*
international *uluslararası*
oo·loos·*lar*·a·ra·suh
Internet *internet* een·ter·*net*
Internet café *internet kafe* een·ter·*net* ka·*fe*
interpreter *tercüman* ter·jew·*man*
interview n *mülakat* mew·la·*kat*
invite v *davet etmek* da·vet et·*mek*
Iran *İran* ee·*ran*
Iraq *Irak* uh·*rak*
Ireland *İrlanda* eer·*lan*·da
iron (clothes) n *ütü* ew·*tew*
island *ada* a·*da*
Israel *İsrail* ees·ra·*eel*
it o o
IT *ET (enformasyon teknolojisi)*
e·*te* (en·for·mas·*yon* tek·no·lo·jee·*see*)
Italian (language) *İtalyanca* ee·tal·*yan*·ja
Italy *İtalya* ee·*tal*·ya
itch n *kaşıntı* ka·shuhn·*tuh*
itemised *ayrıntılı yazılmış*
ay·ruhn·tuh·*luh* ya·zuhl·*muhsh*
itinerary *yolculukta izlenecek yol*
yol·joo·*look*·ta eez·le·ne·*jek* yol
IUD *rahim içi araç* ra·*heem* ee·*chee* a·*rach*

J

jacket *ceket* je·*ket*
jail n *hapishane* ha·pees·*ha*·ne
jam n *marmelat* mar·me·*lat*
January *Ocak* o·*jak*

Japan *Japonya* zha-*pon*-ya
Japanese (language) *Japonca* zha-*pon*-ja
jar *kavanoz* ka-va-*noz*
jaw *çene* che-*ne*
jealous *kıskanç* kuhs-*kanch*
jeans *kot pantolon* kot pan-to-*lon*
jeep *cip* jeep
jet lag *yol yorgunluğu* yol yor-*goon*-loo-oo
jewellery *mücevherler* mew-jev-her-*ler*
Jewish *Yahudi* ya-hoo-*dee*
job *meslek* mes-*lek*
jogging *yavaş koşu* ya-*vash* ko-*shoo*
joke n *şaka* sha-*ka*
journalist *gazeteci* ga-ze-te-*jee*
journey n *yolculuk* yol-joo-*look*
judge n *yargıç* yar-*guhch*
juice *suyu* soo-*yoo*
July *Temmuz* tem-*mooz*
jump v *atlamak* at-la-*mak*
jumper (sweater) *kazak* ka-*zak*
jumper leads *akü takviye kablosu*
  a-*kew* tak-vee-ye kab-lo-*soo*
June *Haziran* ha-zee-*ran*

K

kayaking *kayak yapmak* ka-*yak* yap-*mak*
ketchup *ketçap* ket-*chap*
key n *anahtar* a-nah-*tar*
keyboard *klavye* klav-*ye*
kick v *tekmelemek* tek-me-le-*mek*
kidney *böbrek* berb-*rek*
kilogram *kilogram* kee-log-*ram*
kilometre *kilometre* kee-*lo*-met-re
kind (nice) *kibar* kee-*bar*
kindergarten *ana okulu* a-na o-koo-*loo*
king *kral* kral
kiosk *satış kulübesi* sa-*tuhsh* koo-lew-be-*see*
kiss n *öpücük* er-pew-*jewk*
kiss v *öpmek* erp-*mek*
kitchen *mutfak* moot-*fak*
kiwifruit *kivi* kee-*vee*
knee *diz* deez
knife n *bıçak* buh-*chak*
know *bilmek* beel-*mek*
kosher *koşer* ko-*sher*

L

labourer *işçi* eesh-*chee*
lace *dantel* dan-*tel*
lake *göl* gerl
lamb *kuzu* koo-*zoo*

land n *toprak parçası* top-*rak* par-cha-*suh*
landlady/lord *mülk sahibi* mewlk sa-hee-*bee*
language *lisan* lee-*san*
laptop *diz üstü bilgisayar*
  deez ews-*tew* beel-gee-sa-*yar*
large *iri* ee-*ree*
last (final) *son* son
last (previous) *önceki* ern-je-*kee*
last (week) *geçen (hafta)* ge-*chen* (haf-*ta*)
late *geç* gech
later *sonra* son-*ra*
laugh v *gülmek* gewl-*mek*
launderette *çamaşırhane*
  cha-ma-shuhr-*ha*-ne
laundry (clothes) *çamaşır* cha-ma-*shuhr*
laundry (room) *çamaşırlık*
  cha-ma-shuhr-*luhk*
law *kanun* ka-*noon*
law (study, profession) *hukuk* hoo-*kook*
lawyer *avukat* a-voo-*kat*
laxative *müsil ilacı* mew-*seel* ee-la-*juh*
lazy *tembel* tem-*bel*
leader *lider* lee-*der*
leaf n *yaprak* yap-*rak*
learn *öğrenmek* er-ren-*mek*
leather *deri* de-*ree*
Lebanon *Lübnan* lewb-*nan*
lecturer *okutman* o-koot-*man*
ledge *çıkıntı* chuh-kuhn-*tuh*
leek *pırasa* puh-ra-*sa*
Lefkosia *Lefkoşa* lef-ko-*sha*
left (direction) *sol* sol
left luggage *emanet* e-ma-*net*
left-luggage office *emanet bürosu*
  e-ma-*net* bew-ro-*soo*
left-wing *sol-kanat* sol-ka-*nat*
leg (body) *bacak* ba-*jak*
legal *yasal* ya-*sal*
legislation *yasama* ya-sa-*ma*
legume *bakliyat* bak-lee-*yat*
lemon *limon* lee-*mon*
lemonade *limonata* lee-mo-na-*ta*
lens *lens* lens
lentil *mercimek* mer-jee-*mek*
lesbian n *lezbiyen* lez-bee-*yen*
less *daha az* da-ha az
letter (mail) *mektup* mek-*toop*
lettuce *marul* ma-*rool*
liar *yalancı* ya-lan-*juh*
library *kütüphane* kew-tewp-*ha*-ne
lice *bit* beet
licence n *ehliyet* eh-lee-*yet*
license plate number *plaka* pla-*ka*

lie (not stand) *uzanmak* oo·zan·mak
lie (not tell the truth) v *yalan söylemek* ya·lan say·le·mek
life n *hayat* ha·yat
life jacket *can yeleği* jan ye·le·ee
lift (elevator) *asansör* a·san·ser
light (colour) a *açık* a·chuhk
light (weight) a *hafif* ha·feef
light bulb *ampül* am·pewl
light meter *ışık ölçer* uh·shuhk erl·cher
lighter (cigarette) *çakmak* chak·mak
like v *sevmek* sev·mek
lime n *misket limonu* mees·ket lee·mo·noo
linen (material) *yatak takımı* ya·tak ta·kuh·muh
linen (sheets etc) *çarşaf* char·shaf
lip balm *nemlendirici ruj* nem·len·dee·ree·jee roozh
lips *dudaklar* doo·dak·lar
lipstick *ruj* roozh
liquor store *tekel bayii* te·kel ba·yee·ee
listen to *dinlemek* deen·le·mek
little a *küçük* kew·chewk
little n *az* az
live (somewhere) v *oturmak* o·toor·mak
liver *karaciğer* ka·ra·jee·er
lizard *kertenkele* ker·ten·ke·le
local a *yerel* ye·rel
lock n *kilit* kee·leet
lock v *kilitlemek* kee·leet·le·mek
locked *kilitli* kee·leet·lee
lollies *şeker* she·ker
long a *uzun* oo·zoon
look v *bakmak* bak·mak
look after *bakımını yapmak* ba·kuh·muh·nuh yap·mak
look for *aramak* a·ra·mak
lookout *gözlem yeri* gerz·lem ye·ree
loose a *serbest* ser·best
loose change *bozuk para* bo·zook pa·ra
lose *kaybetmek* kai·bet·mek
lost *kayıp* ka·yuhp
lost-property office *kayıp eşya bürosu* ka·yuhp esh·ya bew·ro·soo
(a) lot *çok* chok
loud *yüksek ses* yewk·sek ses
love n *aşk* ashk
love (fall in) v *aşık olmak* a·shuhk ol·mak
lover *sevgili* sev·gee·lee
low *alçak* al·chak
lubricant *yağlayıcı madde* ya·la·yuh·juh mad·de

luck *şans* shans
lucky *şanslı* shans·luh
luggage *bagaj* ba·gazh
luggage lockers *kilitli eşya dolabı* kee·leet·lee esh·ya do·la·buh
luggage tag *bagaj etiketi* ba·gazh e·tee·ke·tee
lump *yumru* yoom·roo
lunch *öğle yemeği* er·le ye·me·ee
lung *akciğer* ak·jee·er
lure (fishing) n *yem* yem
luxury a *lüks* lewks

M

machine *makine* ma·kee·ne
magazine *dergi* der·gee
mail (letters) n *mektup* mek·toop
mail (postal system) n *posta* pos·ta
mailbox *posta kutusu* pos·ta koo·too·soo
main a *esas* e·sas
main road *anayol* a·na·yol
make *yapmak* yap·mak
make-up *makyaj* mak·yazh
male a *erkek* er·kek
mammogram *meme röntgeni* me·me rernt·ge·nee
man *adam* a·dam
manager (business) *müdür* mew·dewr
manager (sport) *menejer* me·ne·zher
Mandarin (language) *Çince* cheen·je
mandarin *mandalina* man·da·lee·na
mango *mango* man·go
mansion *konak* ko·nak
manual worker *amele* a·me·le
many *çok* chok
map (of country) *ülke haritası* ewl·ke ha·ree·ta·suh
map (of town) *kasaba haritası* ka·sa·ba ha·ree·ta·suh
March *Mart* mart
margarine *margarin* mar·ga·reen
marijuana *marihuana* ma·ree·hoo·a·na
marital status *medeni hal* me·de·nee hal
market n *pazar* pa·zar
marmalade *marmelat* mar·me·lat
marriage *evlilik* ev·lee·leek
married *evli* ev·lee
marry v *evlenmek* ev·len·mek
martial arts *savunma sporları* sa·voon·ma spor·la·ruh
mass (Catholic) *ekmek ve şarap ayini* ek·mek ve sha·rap a·yee·nee

massage n *masaj* ma·*sazh*
masseur *masör* ma·*ser*
masseuse *masöz* ma·*serz*
mat *paspas* pas·*pas*
match (sports) *maç* mach
matches (for lighting) *kibrit* keeb·*reet*
mattress *şilte* sheel·*te*
May *Mayıs* ma·*yuhs*
maybe *belki* bel·kee
mayonnaise *mayonez* ma·yo·*nez*
mayor *belediye başkanı*
    be·le·dee·ye bash·ka·nuh
me *beni* be·nee
me (obj) *bana* ba·*na*
meal *yemek* ye·*mek*
measles *kızamık* kuh·za·*muhk*
meat *et* et
mechanic (car) *araba tamircisi*
    a·ra·ba ta·meer·jee·see
media *basın* ba·*suhn*
medicine (medication) *ilaç* ee·*lach*
medicine (study, profession) *tıp* tuhp
meditation *meditasyon* me·dee·tas·yon
Mediterranean Sea *Akdeniz* ak·de·neez
meet (first time) v *tanışmak* ta·nuhsh·*mak*
meet (get together) v *buluşmak*
    boo·loosh·*mak*
melon *kavun* ka·*voon*
member *üye* ew·ye
men's quarters *erkekler bölümü*
    er·kek·ler ber·lew·mew
menstruation *adet* a·*det*
menu *yemek listesi* ye·*mek* lees·te·see
message n *mesaj* me·*sazh*
metal n *metal* me·tal
metre *metre* met·re
metro (train) *metro* met·ro
metro station *metro istasyonu*
    met·ro ees·tas·yo·noo
microwave oven *mikrodalga*
    meek·ro·dal·ga
midday *gün ortası* gewn or·ta·suh
midnight *gece yarısı* ge·je ya·ruh·suh
migraine *migren* meeg·ren
military n *askeriye* as·ke·ree·ye
military service *askerlik hizmeti*
    as·ker·leek heez·me·tee
milk *süt* sewt
millimetre *milimetre* mee·lee·met·re
million *milyon* meel·yon
minaret *minare* mee·na·re
mince n *kıyma* kuhy·ma
mineral water *maden suyu* ma·den soo·yoo

minute *dakika* da·kee·ka
mirror *ayna* ai·na
miscarriage *düşük* dew·shewk
miss (feel absence of) *özlemek* erz·le·mek
mistake n *hata* ha·ta
mix v *karıştırmak* ka·ruhsh·tuhr·mak
mobile phone *cep telefonu* jep te·le·fo·noo
modem *modem* mo·dem
modern *modern* mo·dern
moisturiser *nemlendirici*
    nem·len·dee·ree·jee
monastery *manastır* ma·nas·tuhr
Monday *Pazartesi* pa·zar·te·see
money *para* pa·ra
monk *keşiş* ke·sheesh
month *ay* ai
monument *anıt* a·nuht
moon *ay* ai
more *daha fazla* da·ha faz·la
morning *sabah* sa·bah
morning sickness *sabah bulantıları*
    sa·bah boo·lan·tuh·la·ruh
mosque *cami* ja·mee
mosquito *sivrisinek* seev·ree·see·nek
mosquito coil *spiral sinek kovar*
    spee·ral see·nek ko·var
mosquito net *cibinlik* jee·been·leek
motel *motel* mo·tel
mother *anne* an·ne
mother-in-law *kayınvalide*
    ka·yuhn·va·lee·de
motorbike *motosiklet* mo·to·seek·let
motorboat *motorbot* mo·tor·bot
motorway (tollway) *paralı yol* pa·ra·luh yol
mountain *dağ* da
mountain bike *dağ bisikleti*
    da bee·seek·le·tee
mountain path *dağ yolu* da yo·loo
mountain range *sıra dağlar* suh·ra da·lar
mountaineering *dağcılık* da·juh·luhk
mouse (animal) *fare* fa·re
mouth *ağız* a·uhz
movie *film* feelm
Mr *Bay* bai
Mrs/Ms/Miss *Bayan* ba·yan
mud *çamur* cha·moor
muesli *musli* moos·lee
mum *anneciğim* an·ne·jee·eem
mumps *kabakulak* ka·ba·koo·lak
murder n *cinayet* jee·na·yet
murder v *cinayet işlemek*
    jee·na·yet eesh·le·mek
muscle *kas* kas

museum *müze* mew-ze
mushroom *mantar* man-tar
music *müzik* mew-zeek
music shop *müzik mağazası*
  mew-zeek ma-a-za-suh
musician *müzisyen* mew-zees-yen
Muslim *Müslüman* mews-lew-man
Muslim cleric *Müslüman din adamı*
  mews-lew-man deen a-da-muh
mussel *midye* meed-ye
mustard *hardal* har-dal
mute (person) *dilsiz* deel-seez
my *benim* be-neem

N

nail clippers *tırnak makası*
  tuhr-nak ma-ka-suh
name n *ad* ad
napkin *peçete* pe-che-te
nappy *bebek bezi* be-bek be-zee
nappy rash *pişik* pee-sheek
national park *milli park* meel-lee park
nationality *milliyet* meel-lee-yet
nature *doğa* do-a
naturopathy *naturapati* na-too-ra-pa-tee
nausea *bulantı* boo-lan-tuh
near *yakında* ya-kuhn-da
nearby *yakın* ya-kuhn
nearest *en yakın* en ya-kuhn
necessary *gerekli* ge-rek-lee
neck *boyun* bo-yoon
necklace *kolye* kol-ye
nectarine *nektarin* nek-ta-reen
need v *ihtiyacı olmak*
  eeh-tee-ya-juh ol-mak
needle (sewing) *dikiş iğnesi*
  dee-keesh ee-ne-see
needle (syringe) *şırınga* shuh-ruhn-ga
negative a *olumsuz* o-loom-sooz
neighbourhood *mahalle* ma-hal-le
neither *hiçbiri* heech-bee-ree
net n *ağ* a
Netherlands *Hollanda* hol-lan-da
never *asla* as-la
new *yeni* ye-nee
New Year's Day *Yeni Yıl* ye-nee yuhl
New Year's Eve *Yeni Yıl arifesi*
  ye-nee yuhl a-ree-fe-see
New Zealand *Yeni Zelanda* ye-nee ze-lan-da
news *haberler* ha-ber-ler
newsstand *gazete satış kulübesi*
  ga-ze-te sa-tuhsh koo-lew-be-see

newsagency *gazete bayii* ga-ze-te ba-yee-ee
newspaper *gazete* ga-ze-te
next (month) *gelecek (ay)* ge-le-jek (ai)
next to *yanında* ya-nuhn-da
nice *hoş* hosh
nickname n *lakap* la-kap
night *gece* ge-je
night dive n *gece dalışı* ge-je da-luh-shuh
night out *akşam gezmesi*
  ak-sham gez-me-see
nightclub *gece kulübü* ge-je koo-lew-bew
Nikosia (Lefkosia) *Lefkoşa* lef-ko-sha
no *hayır* ha-yuhr
noisy *gürültülü* gew-rewl-tew-lew
none *hiçbiri* heech-bee-ree
nonsmoking *sigara içilmeyen*
  see-ga-ra ee-cheel-me-yen
noodles *erişte* e-reesh-te
noon *öğle* er-le
north *kuzey* koo-zay
Norway *Norveç* nor-vech
nose *burun* boo-roon
not *değil* de-eel
notebook *not defteri* not def-te-ree
nothing *hiç birşey* heech beer-shay
November *Kasım* ka-suhm
now *şimdi* sheem-dee
nuclear energy *nükleer enerji*
  newk-le-er e-ner-jee
nuclear testing *nükleer deneme*
  newk-le-er de-ne-me
nuclear waste *nükleer atık* newk-le-er a-tuhk
number (general) *sayı* sa-yuh
number (house/street) *numara* noo-ma-ra
numberplate *plaka* pla-ka
nun *rahibe* ra-hee-be
nurse *hemşire* hem-shee-re
nut *çerez* che-rez

O

oar(s) *kürek* kew-rek
oats *yulaf* yoo-laf
ocean *okyanus* ok-ya-noos
October *Ekim* e-keem
off (spoiled) *bozuk* bo-zook
office *ofis* o-fees
office worker *memur* me-moor
often *sık sık* suhk suhk
oil (food) *yağ* ya
oil (petrol) *benzin* ben-zeen
old (object) *eski* es-kee
old (person) *yaşlı* yash-luh

olive n *zeytin* zay·*teen*
olive oil *zeytinyağı* zay·*teen*·ya·uh
Olympic Games *Olimpiyat Oyunları*
o·leem·pee·yat o·yoon·la·*ruh*
omelette *omlet* om·*let*
on *-da/-de/-ta/-te* da/·de/·ta/·te
on time *zamanında* za·ma·nuhn·*da*
once *bir kez* beer kez
one *bir* beer
one-way a *gidiş* gee·*deesh*
onion *soğan* so·*an*
only *sadece* sa·de·je
open a *açık* a·*chuhk*
open v *açmak* ach·*mak*
opening hours *açılış saatleri*
a·chuh·*luhsh* sa·at·le·ree
opera *opera* o·pe·ra
opera house *opera binası*
o·pe·ra bee·na·suh
operation (medical) *ameliyat* a·me·lee·yat
operator *operatör* o·pe·ra·ter
opinion *fikir* fee·keer
opposite *karşısında* kar·shuh·suhn·da
optometrist *gözlükçü* gerz·lewk·chew
or *veya* ve·ya
orange n *portakal* por·ta·kal
orange (colour) *turuncu* too·roon·joo
orange juice *portakal suyu*
por·ta·kal soo·yoo
orchestra *orkestra* or·kes·tra
order n *sipariş* see·pa·reesh
order v *sipariş vermek* see·pa·reesh ver·mek
ordinary *sıradan* suh·ra·dan
orgasm *orgazm* or·gazm
original *orijinal* o·ree·zhee·nal
other *diğer* dee·er
our *bizim* bee·zeem
out of order *bozuk* bo·zook
outside *dışarıda* duh·sha·ruh·da
ovarian cyst *yumurtalık tümörü*
yoo·moor·ta·luhk tew·mer·rew
ovary *yumurtalık* yoo·moor·ta·luhk
oven *fırın* fuh·ruhn
overcoat *palto* pal·to
overdose n *aşırı doz* a·shuh·ruh doz
overnight *bir gecelik* beer ge·je·leek
overseas *yurt dışı* yoort duh·shuh
owe *borcu olmak* bor·joo ol·mak
owner *sahip* sa·heep
oxygen *oksijen* ok·see·zhen
oyster *istiridye* ees·tee·reed·ye
ozone layer *ozon tabakası*
o·zon ta·ba·ka·suh

P

pacemaker *kalp pili* kalp pee·lee
pacifier (dummy) *emzik* em·zeek
package *ambalaj* am·ba·lazh
packet *paket* pa·ket
padlock *asma kilit* as·ma kee·leet
page n *sayfa* sai·fa
pain n *ağrı* a·ruh
painful *ağrılı* a·ruh·luh
painkiller *ağrı kesici* a·ruh ke·see·jee
painter (artist) *ressam* res·sam
painter (occupation) *boyacı* bo·ya·juh
painting (a work) *tablo* tab·lo
painting (the art) *ressamlık* res·sam·luhk
pair (two) *çift* cheeft
Pakistan *Pakistan* pa·kees·tan
palace *saray* sa·rai
pan *tava* ta·va
pants (trousers) *pantolon* pan·to·lon
panty liners *kadın bağı* ka·duhn ba·uh
pantyhose *külotlu çorap*
kew·lot·loo cho·rap
pap smear *rahim ağzı kanser tarama testi*
ra·heem a·zuh kan·ser ta·ra·ma tes·tee
paper *kağıt* ka·uht
paperwork *kağıt işlemleri*
ka·uht eesh·lem·le·ree
paraplegic *felçli* felch·lee
parcel *paket* pa·ket
parents *ana baba* a·na ba·ba
park n *park* park
park (a car) v *park etmek* park et·mek
parliament *parlamento* par·la·men·to
part (component) *parça* par·cha
part-time a *yarım gün* ya·ruhm gewn
party (night out/politics) *parti* par·tee
pass v *geçmek* gech·mek
passenger *yolcu* yol·joo
passport *pasaport* pa·sa·port
passport number *pasaport numarası*
pa·sa·port noo·ma·ra·suh
past n *geçmiş* gech·meesh
pasta *makarna* ma·kar·na
pastry *hamur işi* ha·moor ee·shee
pastry shop *börekçi* ber·rek·chee
path *patika* pa·tee·ka
pavillion *büyük çadır* bew·yewk cha·duhr
pay v *ödemek* er·de·mek
payment *ödeme* er·de·me
pea *bezelye* be·zel·ye
peace *barış* ba·ruhsh
peach *şeftali* shef·ta·lee

peak (mountain) *zirve* zeer·ve
peanut *fıstık* fuhs·tuhk
pear *armut* ar·moot
pedal n *pedal* pe·dal
pedestrian *yaya* ya·ya
pedestrian crossing *yaya geçidi*
  ya·ya ge·chee·dee
pen (ballpoint) *tükenmez kalem*
  tew·ken·mez ka·lem
penalty (football) *penaltı* pe·nal·tuh
pencil *kurşun kalem* koor·shoon ka·lem
penicillin *penisilin* pe·nee·see·leen
penis *penis* pe·nees
penknife *çakı* cha·kuh
pensioner *emekli* e·mek·lee
people *kişi(ler)* kee·shee·(ler)
pepper (bell) *biber* bee·ber
pepper (black) *kara biber* ka·ra bee·ber
per (day) *(gün) başına (gewn)* ba·shuh·na
per cent *yüzde* yewz·de
perfect a *mükemmel* mew·kem·mel
performance *gösteri* gers·te·ree
perfume n *parfüm* par·fewm
period pain *adet ağrısı* a·det a·ruh·suh
permission *izin* ee·zeen
permit n *ruhsat* rooh·sat
person *kişi* kee·shee
petrol *benzin* ben·zeen
petrol station *benzin istasyonu*
  ben·zeen ees·tas·yo·noo
pharmacist *eczacı* ej·za·juh
pharmacy *eczane* ej·za·ne
phone book *telefon rehberi*
  te·le·fon reh·be·ree
phone box *telefon kulübesi*
  te·le·fon koo·lew·be·see
phone call *telefon konuşması*
  te·le·fon ko·noosh·ma·suh
phone card *telefon kartı* te·le·fon kar·tuh
phone number *telefon numarası*
  te·le·fon noo·ma·ra·suh
photo *fotoğraf* fo·to·raf
photographer *fotoğrafçı* fo·to·raf·chuh
photography *fotoğrafçılık*
  fo·to·raf·chuh·luhk
phrasebook *pratik konuşma kılavuzu*
  pra·teek ko·noosh·ma kuh·la·voo·zoo
pickaxe *kazma* kaz·ma
pickles *turşu* toor·shoo
picnic n *piknik* peek·neek
piece n *parça* par·cha
pig *domuz* do·mooz
pill *hap* hap

the pill *doğum kontrol hapı*
  do·oom kon·trol ha·puh
pillow *yastık* yas·tuhk
pillowcase *yastık kılıfı* yas·tuhk kuh·luh·fuh
pineapple *ananas* a·na·nas
pink *pembe* pem·be
pistachio *şamfıstığı* sham·fuhs·tuh·uh
place n *yer* yer
place of birth *doğum yeri* do·oom ye·ree
plane *uçak* oo·chak
planet *gezegen* ge·ze·gen
plant n *bitki* beet·kee
plastic a *plastik* plas·teek
plate *tabak* ta·bak
plateau *plato* pla·to
platform (train) *peron* pe·ron
play cards v *kağıt oynamak*
  ka·uht oy·na·mak
play guitar v *gitar çalmak* gee·tar chal·mak
play (theatre) *n oyun* o·yoon
player *oyuncu* o·yoon·joo
plug (bath) n *tapa* ta·pa
plug (electricity) n *fiş* feesh
plum *erik* e·reek
poached *suda pişmiş* soo·da peesh·meesh
pocket *cep* jep
pocketknife *çakı* cha·kuh
poetry *şiir* shee·eer
point (decimal/dot) n *nokta* nok·ta
point (score) n *puan* poo·an
point v *göstermek* gers·ter·mek
poisonous *zehirli* ze·heer·lee
police *polis* po·lees
police officer *polis memuru*
  po·lees me·moo·roo
police station *polis karakolu*
  po·lees ka·ra·ko·loo
policy *politika* po·lee·tee·ka
politician *politikacı* po·lee·tee·ka·juh
politics *politika* po·lee·tee·ka
pollen *polen* po·len
pollution *kirlilik* keer·lee·leek
pool (game) *bilardo* bee·lar·do
pool (swimming) *yüzme havuzu*
  yewz·me ha·voo·zoo
poor *fakir* fa·keer
popular *popüler* po·pew·ler
pork *domuz eti* do·mooz e·tee
port (sea) *liman* lee·man
Portugal *Portekiz* por·te·keez
positive a *olumlu* o·loom·loo
possible *muhtemel* mooh·te·mel
postage *posta ücreti* pos·ta ewj·re·tee

postcard *kartpostal* kart·pos·*tal*
post code *posta kodu* pos·ta ko·doo
post office *postane* pos·ta·ne
poster *poster* pos·ter
pot (ceramics) *toprak kap* top·rak kap
potato *patates* pa·ta·tes
pottery *çömlekçilik* cherm·lek·chee·*leek*
pound (money) *sterlin* ster·*leen*
pound (weight) *libre* leeb·re
poverty *yoksulluk* yok·sool·*look*
powder n *pudra* pood·ra
power n *güç* gewch
prawn *karides* ka·ree·des
prayer *dua* doo·a
prayer book *dua kitabı* doo·a kee·ta·buh
prefer *tercih etmek* ter·jeeh et·mek
pregnancy test kit *gebelik test çubuğu*
  ge·be·*leek* test choo·boo·oo
pregnant *hamile* ha·mee·le
premenstrual tension *adet öncesi gerginlik*
  a·det ern·je·se·gi ger·geen·*leek*
prepare *hazırlamak* ha·zuhr·la·mak
prescription *reçete* re·che·te
present (gift) *hediye* he·dee·ye
present (time) *şimdiki zaman*
  sheem·dee·kee za·man
president *başkan* bash·kan
pressure n *basınç* ba·suhnch
pretty *hoş* hosh
previous *önceki* ern·je·kee
price n *fiyat* fee·yat
priest *papaz* pa·paz
prime minister *başbakan* bash·ba·kan
printer (computer) *printer* preen·ter
prison *cezaevi* je·za·e·vee
prisoner *mahkum* mah·koom
private a *özel* er·zel
produce v *üretmek* ew·ret·mek
profit n *kar* kar
program n *program* prog·ram
projector *projektör* pro·zhek·ter
promise v *söz vermek* serz ver·mek
prostitute n *fahişe* fa·hee·she
protect *korumak* ko·roo·mak
protected (species) *koruma altına alınmış*
  ko·roo·ma al·tuh·na a·luhn·muhsh
protest n *protesto* pro·tes·to
protest v *protesto etmek* pro·tes·to et·mek
provisions *erzak* er·zak
prune n *kuru erik* koo·roo e·reek
pub (bar) *bar* bar
public baths *hamam* ha·mam
public gardens *park* park

public relations *halkla ilişkiler*
  halk·la ee·leesh·kee·ler
public telephone *umumi telefon*
  oo·moo·mee te·le·fon
public toilet *umumi tuvalet*
  oo·moo·mee too·va·let
pull v *çekmek* chek·mek
pump n *pompa* pom·pa
pumpkin *bal kabağı* bal ka·ba·uh
puncture n *patlak* pat·lak
pure *saf* saf
purple *mor* mor
purse n *cüzdan* jewz·dan
push v *itmek* eet·mek
put *koymak* koy·mak

Q

quadriplegic *her iki kolu ve bacağı felçli*
  her ee·kee ko·loo ve ba·ja·uh felch·lee
qualifications *nitelikler* nee·te·leek·ler
quality *kalite* ka·lee·te
quarantine *karantina* ka·ran·tee·na
quarter *çeyrek* chay·rek
quay *rıhtım* ruh·tuhm
queen *kraliçe* kra·lee·che
question n *soru* so·roo
queue n *sıra* suh·ra
quick a *çabuk* cha·book
quiet a *sakin* sa·keen
quit *bırakmak* buh·rak·mak

R

rabbit *tavşan* tav·shan
race (sport) n *yarış* ya·ruhsh
racetrack *yarış pisti* ya·ruhsh pees·tee
racing bike *yarış bisikleti*
  ya·ruhsh bee·seek·le·tee
racism *ırkçılık* uhrk·chuh·luhk
racquet *raket* ra·ket
radiator *radyatör* rad·ya·ter
radio n *radyo* rad·yo
radish *kırmızı turp* kuhr·muh·zuh toorp
railway station *tren istasyonu*
  tren ees·tas·yo·noo
rain n *yağmur* ya·moor
raincoat *yağmurluk* ya·moor·look
raisin *kuru üzüm* koo·roo ew·zewm
Ramadan *Ramazan* ra·ma·zan
rape n *tecavüz* te·ja·vewz
rare (food) *az pişmiş* az peesh·meesh

are (uncommon) *az bulunur*
az boo·loo·*noor*
ash *isilik* ee·see·*leek*
aspberry *ahududu* a·hoo·doo·doo
at *sıçan* suh·*chan*
ave n *rave parti* rayv par·*tee*
aw *çiğ* chee
azor *traş makinesi* trash ma·kee·ne·*see*
azor blade *jilet* jee·*let*
ead v *okumak* o·koo·*mak*
eading *okuma* o·koo·*ma*
eady *hazır* ha·*zuhr*
eal estate agent *emlakçı* em·lak·*chuh*
ealistic *gerçekçi* ger·chek·*chee*
ear (location) *geri* ge·*ree*
eason n *sebep* se·*bep*
eceipt *makbuz* mak·*booz*
ecently *yakın zamanda* ya·*kuhn* za·man·*da*
ecommend *tavsiye etmek* tav·see·*ye* et·*mek*
ecord v *kaydetmek* kai·det·*mek*
ecording *kayıt* ka·*yuht*
ecyclable *yeniden kazanılabilir*
ye·nee·*den* ka·za·nuh·*la*·bee·leer
ecycle *yeniden kazanmak*
ye·nee·*den* ka·za·*nmak*
ed *kırmızı* kuhr·muh·*zuh*
eferee *hakem* ha·*kem*
eference n *referans* re·fe·*rans*
eflexology *refleksoloji* ref·lek·so·lo·*zhee*
efrigerator *buzdolabı* booz·do·la·*buh*
efugee *mülteci* mewl·te·*jee*
efund n *para iadesi* pa·*ra* ee·a·de·*see*
efuse v *reddetmek* red·det·*mek*
egional *bölgesel* berl·ge·*sel*
egistered mail/post *taahhütlü posta*
ta·ah·hewt·*lew* pos·*ta*
ehydration salts *rehidrasyon tuzu*
re·heed·ras·*yon* too·*zoo*
eiki *reiki* re·ee·*kee*
elationship (family) *akrabalık* ak·ra·ba·*luhk*
elationship (general) *ilişki* ee·*leesh*·kee
elax v *dinlenmek* deen·len·*mek*
elic *eski eser* es·*kee* e·*ser*
eligion *din* deen
eligious *dini* dee·*nee*
emote a *uzak* oo·*zak*
emote control *uzaktan kumanda*
oo·zak·*tan* koo·man·*da*
ent v *kiralamak* kee·ra·la·*mak*
epair v *tamir etmek* ta·*meer* et·*mek*
epublic *cumhuriyet* joom·hoo·ree·*yet*
eservation n *rezervasyon* re·zer·vas·*yon*
est v *dinlenmek* deen·len·*mek*

restaurant *restoran* res·to·*ran*
résumé *özgeçmiş* erz·gech·*meesh*
retired *emekli* e·mek·*lee*
return (come back) v *geri dönmek*
ge·*ree* dern·*mek*
return a *gidiş-dönüş* gee·deesh·der·*newsh*
review n *yeniden gözden geçirme*
ye·nee·*den* gerz·*den* ge·cheer·*me*
rhythm *ritim* ree·*teem*
rib *kaburga* ka·boor·*ga*
rice (cooked) *pilav* pee·*lav*
rice (uncooked) *pirinç* pee·*reench*
rich (wealthy) *zengin* zen·*geen*
ride n *binmek* been·*mek*
ride (horse) v *ata binmek* a·*ta* been·*mek*
right (correct) a *doğru* do·*roo*
right (direction) a *doğru yön* do·*roo* yern
right-wing *sağ-kanat* sa·ka·*nat*
ring (on finger) *yüzük* yew·*zewk*
ring (phone) v *çalmak* chal·*mak*
rip-off n *kazıklama* ka·zuhk·la·*rna*
risk n *risk* reesk
river *nehir* ne·*heer*
road *yol* yol
road map *yol haritası* yol ha·ree·ta·*suh*
rob *soymak* soy·*mak*
rock n *kaya* ka·*ya*
rock (music) *rok* rok
rock climbing *kaya tırmanışı*
ka·*ya* tuhr·ma·nuh·*shuh*
rock group *rok grubu* rok goo·roo·*boo*
rockmelon *kavun* ka·*voon*
roll (bread) *hamburger ekmeği*
ham·*boor*·ger ek·me·*ee*
rollerblading *paten* pa·*ten*
Romania *Romanya* ro·man·*ya*
romantic *romantik* ro·man·*teek*
room n *oda* o·*da*
room number *oda numarası*
o·*da* noo·ma·ra·*suh*
rope n *ip* eep
round a *yuvarlak* yoo·var·*lak*
roundabout *trafik adası* tra·*feek* a·da·*suh*
route n *rota* ro·*ta*
rowing *kürek çekme* kew·*rek* chek·*me*
rubbish n *çöp* cherp
rubella *kızamıkçık* kuh·za·muhk·*chuhk*
rug *kilim* kee·*leem*
rugby *ragbi* rag·*bee*
ruins *harabeler* ha·ra·be·*ler*
rule n *kural* koo·*ral*
rum *rom* rom
run v *koşmak* kosh·*mak*

running *koşu* ko-*shoo*
runny nose *burun akıntısı*
  boo-*roon* a-kuhn-tuh-*suh*
Russia *Rusya* roos-ya
Russian (language) *Rusça* roos-cha

S

sad *üzgün* ewz-*gewn*
saddle n *eyer* e-*yer*
safe n *kasa* ka-*sa*
safe a *emniyetli* em-nee-yet-*lee*
safe sex *güvenli seks* gew-ven-*lee* seks
sailing boat *yelkenli tekne* yel-ken-*lee* tek-ne
saint *aziz* a-*zeez*
salad *salata* sa-la-*ta*
salami *salam* sa-*lam*
salary *maaş* ma-*ash*
sale n *indirimli satış*
  een-dee-reem-*lee* sa-*tuhsh*
sales tax *satış vergisi* sa-*tuhsh* ver-gee-*see*
salmon *som balığı* som ba-luh-*uh*
salt *tuz* tooz
same *aynı* ai-*nuh*
sand n *kum* koom
sandal *sandalet* san-da-*let*
sanitary napkin *hijyenik kadın bağı*
  heezh-ye-*neek* ka-duhn ba-*uh*
Saturday *Cumartesi* joo-mar-te-*see*
sauce n *sos* sos
saucepan *sos tenceresi* sos ten-je-re-*see*
sauna *sauna* sa-oo-na
sausage *sosis* so-*sees*
say v *söylemek* say-le-*mek*
scalp n *kafa derisi* ka-fa de-ree-*see*
scarf *atkı* at-*kuh*
school *okul* o-*kool*
science *bilim* bee-*leem*
scientist *bilim adamı* bee-*leem* a-da-*muh*
scissors *makas* ma-*kas*
score v *puan* poo-*an*
scoreboard *puan tahtası* poo-*an* tah-ta-*suh*
Scotland *İskoçya* ees-koch-ya
scrambled *karıştırılmış*
  ka-ruhsh-tuh-ruhl-*muhsh*
scuba diving *aletli dalış* a-let-*lee* da-*luhsh*
sculpture *heykel* hay-*kel*
sea *deniz* de-*neez*
seasick *deniz tutmuş* de-*neez* toot-*moosh*
seaside n *deniz kenarı* de-*neez* ke-na-*ruh*
season *mevsim* mev-*seem*
seat (place) *yer* yer

seatbelt *emniyet kemeri*
  em-nee-*yet* ke-me-*ree*
second (time) n *saniye* sa-nee-*ye*
second a *ikinci* ee-keen-*jee*
second class n *ikinci sınıf*
  ee-keen-*jee* suh-*nuhf*
second-hand a *ikinci el* ee-keen-*jee* el
second-hand shop *eskici* es-kee-*jee*
secretary *sekreter* sek-re-*ter*
see *görmek* ger-*mek*
self service *self-servis* self-ser-vees
self-employed *serbest çalışan*
  ser-*best* cha-luh-*shan*
selfish *bencil* ben-*jeel*
sell *satmak* sat-*mak*
send *göndermek* gern-der-*mek*
sensible *makul* ma-*kool*
sensual *erotik* e-ro-*teek*
separate a *ayrı* ai-*ruh*
September *Eylül* ay-*lewl*
serious *ciddi* jeed-*dee*
service n *servis* ser-vees
service charge *hizmet ücreti*
  heez-*met* ewj-re-*tee*
service station *benzin istasyonu*
  ben-*zeen* ees-tas-yo-noo
serviette *peçete* pe-che-*te*
several *birkaç* beer-*kach*
sew *dikiş dikmek* dee-*keesh* deek-*mek*
sex (gender) *cinsiyet* jeen-see-*yet*
sex (intercourse) *seks* seks
sexism *cinsiyet ayrımı*
  jeen-see-*yet* ai-ruh-*muh*
sexy *seksi* sek-*see*
shade n *gölge* gerl-*ge*
shadow n *gölge* gerl-*ge*
shadow-puppet theatre *gölge oyunu*
  gerl-*ge* o-yoo-noo
shampoo *şampuan* sham-poo-*an*
shape n *biçim* bee-*cheem*
share v *paylaşmak* pai-lash-*mak*
share with v *ile paylaşmak*
  ee-*le* pai-lash-*mak*
shave v *tıraş olmak* tuh-*rash* ol-*mak*
shaving cream *tıraş kremi* tuh-*rash* kre-*mee*
she *o* o
sheep *koyun* ko-*yoon*
sheet (bed) *çarşaf* char-*shaf*
shelf *raf* raf
shiatsu *akupresyon* a-koo-pres-yon
shingles (illness) *zona* zo-na
ship n *gemi* ge-*mee*
shirt *gömlek* germ-*lek*

shoe shop *ayakkabıcı* a·yak·ka·buh·*juh*
shoes *ayakkabılar* a·yak·ka·buh·*lar*
shoot v *ateş etmek* a·*tesh* et·*mek*
shop n *dükkan* dewk·*kan*
shop v *alış-veriş yapmak*
  a·luhsh·ve·*reesh* yap·*mak*
shopping *alış-veriş* a·luhsh·ve·*reesh*
shopping centre *alış-veriş merkezi*
  a·luhsh·ve·*reesh* mer·ke·zee
short (height) *kısa* kuh·*sa*
shortage *eksiklik* ek·seek·*leek*
shorts *şort* short
shoulder *omuz* o·mooz
shout v *bağırmak* ba·uhr·*mak*
show n *gösteri* gers·te·ree
show v *göstermek* gers·ter·*mek*
shower n *duş* doosh
shrine *tapınak* ta·puh·*nak*
shut a *kapalı* ka·pa·*luh*
shy *utangaç* oo·tan·*gach*
sick *hasta* has·ta
side n *kenar* ke·nar
sign n *işaret* ee·sha·ret
sign v *imzalamak* eem·za·la·*mak*
signature *imza* eem·za
silk *ipek* ee·pek
silver n *gümüş* gew·mewsh
SIM card *SİM kart* seem kart
similar *benzer* ben·zer
simple *basit* ba·seet
since (May) *(Mayıs)tan beri*
  (ma·yuhs)·tan be·ree
sing *şarkı söylemek* shar·kuh say·le·*mek*
Singapore *Singapur* seen·ga·poor
singer *şarkıcı* shar·kuh·*juh*
single (not married) *bekar* be·kar
single room *tek kişilik oda*
  tek kee·shee·leek o·da
singlet *atlet* at·let
sinker (fishing) *olta kurşunu*
  ol·ta koor·shoo·noo
sister (kız) *kardeş* (kuhz) kar·desh
sit *oturmak* o·toor·mak
size n *beden* be·den
skate v *patenle kaymak* pa·ten·le kai·mak
skateboarding *kay-kay* kai·kai
ski v *kayak yapmak* ka·yak yap·mak
skiing *kayak* ka·yak
skim milk *az yağlı süt* az ya·luh sewt
skin n *cilt* jeelt
skirt *etek* e·tek
skull *kafatası* ka·fa·ta·suh
sky *gökyüzü* gerk·yew·zew

sled n *kızak* kuh·zak
sleep v *uyumak* oo·yoo·mak
sleeping bag *uyku tulumu*
  ooy·koo too·loo·moo
sleeping berth *yatak* ya·tak
sleeping car *yataklı vagon* ya·tak·luh va·gon
sleeping pills *uyku hapı* ooy·koo ha·puh
sleepy *uykulu* ooy·koo·loo
slice n *dilim* dee·leem
slide (film) *slayt* slait
slow a *yavaş* ya·vash
slowly *yavaşça* ya·vash·cha
small *küçük* kew·chewk
smaller *daha küçük* da·ha kew·chewk
smallest en *küçük* en kew·chewk
smell n *koku* ko·koo
smile v *gülümsemek* gew·lewm·se·mek
smoke v *sigara içmek* see·ga·ra eech·mek
snack n *hafif yemek* ha·feef ye·mek
snail *salyangoz* sal·yan·goz
snake *yılan* yuh·lan
snorkelling *şnorkelli dalış*
  shnor·kel·lee da·luhsh
snow n *kar* kar
snowboarding *board kayağı* bord ka·ya·uh
snow pea *taze bezelye* ta·ze be·zel·ye
soap *sabun* sa·boon
soap opera *pembe dizi* pem·be dee·zee
soccer *futbol* foot·bol
social welfare *toplum refahı*
  top·loom re·fa·huh
socialist a *sosyalist* sos·ya·leest
socks *çoraplar* cho·rap·lar
soft-boiled *az haşlanmış* az hash·lan·muhsh
soft drink *meşrubat* mesh·roo·bat
soldier n *asker* as·ker
some *biraz* bee·raz
someone *birisi* bee·ree·see
something *birşey* beer·shay
sometimes *bazen* ba·zen
son *oğul* o·ool
song *şarkı* shar·kuh
soon *yakında* ya·kuhn·da
sore *ağrılı* a·ruh·luh
soup *çorba* chor·ba
sour cream *kaymak* kai·mak
south *güney* gew·nay
souvenir *hediyelik eşya*
  he·dee·ye·leek esh·ya
souvenir shop *hediyelik eşya dükkanı*
  he·dee·ye·leek esh·ya dewk·ka·nuh
soy milk *soya sütü* so·ya sew·tew

S

english–turkish

229

soy sauce *soya sosu* so-*ya* so-*soo*
space (place) *yer* yer
space (universe) *uzay* oo-*zai*
Spain *İspanya* ees-*pan*-ya
Spanish (language) *İspanyolca* ees-pan-*yol*-ja
sparkling wine *köpüklü şarap* ker-*pewk*-lew sha-*rap*
speak *konuşmak* ko-noosh-*mak*
special a *özel* er-zel
specialist *uzman* ooz-*man*
speed (velocity) n *hız* huhz
speed limit *hız sınırı* huhz suh-nuh-*ruh*
speedometer *hız göstergesi* huhz gers-ter-ge-*see*
spider *örümcek* er-rewm-*jek*
spinach *ıspanak* uhs-pa-nak
spoilt (person) *şımarık* shuh-ma-*ruhk*
spoke n *tekerlek parmaklığı* te-ker-lek par-mak-luh-*uh*
spoon n *kaşık* ka-*shuhk*
sport n *spor* spor
sports store *spor malzemeleri mağazası* spor mal-ze-me-le-*ree* ma-a-za-*suh*
sportsperson *sporcu* spor-*joo*
sprain n *burkulma* boor-kool-*ma*
spring (coil) n *yay* yai
spring (season) *ilkbahar* eelk-ba-har
spring water *memba suyu* mem-*ba* soo-yoo
square (town) *meydan* may-*dan*
stadium *stadyum* stad-*yoom*
stairway *merdiven* mer-dee-*ven*
stale *bayat* ba-*yat*
stamp (postage) *pul* pool
stand-by a *açık* a-*chuhk*
star *yıldız* yuhl-*duhz*
(four-)star (*dört*) *yıldızlı* (dert) yuhl-duhz-*luh*
start n *başlangıç* bash-lan-*guhch*
start v *başlamak* bash-la-*mak*
station *istasyon* ees-tas-*yon*
stationer's *kırtasiyeci* kuhr-ta-see-ye-*jee*
statue *heykel* hay-*kel*
stay (at a hotel) v (*otelde*) *kalmak* (o-tel-*de*) kal-*mak*
stay (in one place) v *durmak* door-*mak*
steak (beef) *biftek* beef-*tek*
steal v *çalmak* chal-*mak*
steep a *sarp* sarp
step n *adım* a-*duhm*
stereo n *stereo* ster-yo
still water *durgun su* door-goon soo
stock (food) *stok* stok

stockings *çorap* cho-*rap*
stolen *çalıntı* cha-luhn-*tuh*
stomach *mide* mee-*de*
stomachache *mide ağrısı* mee-de a-ruh-*suh*
stone n *taş* tash
stoned (drugged) *uyuşturucu etkisi altında* oo-yoosh-too-roo-joo et-kee-see al-tuhn-*da*
stop (bus etc) n ... *durağı* ... doo-ra-*uh*
stop (cease) v *durmak* door-*mak*
stop (prevent) v *durdurmak* door-door-*mak*
storm *fırtına* fuhr-*tuh*-na
story *hikaye* hee-*ka*-ye
stove *ocak* o-*jak*
straight a *düz* dewz
strange *acayip* a-ja-*yeep*
stranger *yabancı* ya-ban-*juh*
strawberry *çilek* chee-*lek*
stream *akıntı* a-kuhn-*tuh*
street *sokak* so-*kak*
street market *semt pazarı* semt pa-za-*ruh*
strike (stop work) n *grev* grev
striker (football) *golcü* gol-*jew*
string *ip* eep
stroke (health) *felç* felch
stroller *puset* poo-*set*
strong *güçlü* gewch-*lew*
stubborn *inatçı* ee-nat-*chuh*
student *öğrenci* er-ren-*jee*
studio *stüdyo* stewd-*yo*
stupid *aptal* ap-*tal*
style *tarz* tarz
subtitles *altyazı* alt-ya-*zuh*
suburb *bölge* berl-*ge*
subway (pedestrian) *alt geçit* alt ge-*cheet*
subway (train) *metro* met-ro
sugar *şeker* she-ker
suitcase *bavul* ba-*vool*
sultana *kuru üzüm* koo-roo ew-*zewm*
summer *yaz* yaz
sun *güneş* gew-nesh
sunblock *güneşten koruma kremi* gew-nesh-ten ko-roo-ma kre-mee
sunburn *güneş yanığı* gew-nesh ya-nuh-*uh*
Sunday *Pazar* pa-*zar*
sunglasses *güneş gözlüğü* gew-nesh gerz-lew-*ew*
sunny *güneşli* gew-nesh-*lee*
sunrise *gün doğumu* gewn do-oo-*moo*
sunset *gün batımı* gewn ba-tuh-*muh*
sunstroke *güneş çarpması* gew-nesh charp-ma-*suh*
supermarket *süpermarket* sew-per-mar-ket

superstition *batıl inanç* ba·*tuhl* ee·*nanch*
supporter (politics/sport) *taraftar* ta·raf·*tar*
surf v *sörf yapmak* serf yap·*mak*
surface mail (land) *kara yoluyla gönderi* ka·*ra* yo·*looy*·la gern·de·ree
surface mail (sea) *deniz yoluyla gönderi* de·*neez* yo·*looy*·la gern·de·ree
surfboard *sörf tahtası* serf tah·ta·*suh*
surfing *sörf* serf
surname *soyad* soy·ad
surprise n *sürpriz* sewrp·reez
sweater *kazak* ka·zak
Sweden *İsveç* ees·vech
sweet a *tatlı* tat·luh
sweets *şeker* she·ker
swelling *şişlik* sheesh·leek
swim v *yüzmek* yewz·mek
swimming (sport) *yüzme* yewz·me
swimming pool *yüzme havuzu* yewz·me ha·voo·zoo
swimsuit *mayo* ma·yo
Switzerland *İsviçre* ees·veech·re
synagogue *havra* hav·ra
synthetic *sentetik* sen·te·teek
Syria *Suriye* soo·ree·ye

T

table n *masa* ma·sa
table tennis *masa tenisi* ma·sa te·nee·see
tablecloth *masa örtüsü* ma·sa er·tew·sew
tail n *kuyruk* kooy·rook
tailor *terzi* ter·zee
take v *almak* al·mak
take a photo *fotoğraf çekmek* fo·to·raf chek·mek
talk v *konuşmak* ko·noosh·mak
tall (person) *uzun boylu* oo·zoon boy·loo
tampon *tampon* tam·pon
tanning lotion *güneş yağı* gew·nesh ya·uh
tap *musluk* moos·look
tap water *çeşme suyu* chesh·me soo·yoo
tasty *lezzetli* lez·zet·lee
tax n *vergi* ver·gee
taxi *taksi* tak·see
taxi rank *taksi durağı* tak·see doo·ra·uh
tea *çay* chai
tea garden *çay bahçesi* chai bah·che·see
tea glass *çay bardağı* chai bar·da·uh
teapot *çaydanlık* chai·dan·luhk
teaspoon *çay kaşığı* chai ka·shuh·uh
tea urn *semaver* se·ma·ver

teacher *öğretmen* er·ret·men
team *takım* ta·kuhm
technique *teknik* tek·neek
teeth *dişler* deesh·ler
telegram n *telgraf* tel·graf
telephone n *telefon* te·le·fon
telephone v *telefon etmek* te·le·fon et·mek
telephone box *telefon kulübesi* te·le·fon koo·lew·be·see
telephone centre *telefon santralı* te·le·fon san·tra·luh
telescope *teleskop* te·les·kop
television *televizyon* te·le·veez·yon
tell *anlatmak* an·lat·mak
temperature (fever) *ateş* a·tesh
temperature (weather) *derece* de·re·je
temple *tapınak* ta·puh·nak
tennis *tenis* te·nees
tennis court *tenis kortu* te·nees kor·too
tent *çadır* cha·duhr
tent peg *çadır kazığı* cha·duhr ka·zuh·uh
terrible *korkunç* kor·koonch
test n *test* test
thank v *teşekkür etmek* te·shek·kewr et·mek
that (one) *şunu/onu* shoo·noo/o·noo
theatre *tiyatro* tee·yat·ro
their *onların* on·la·ruhn
them *onları* on·la·ruh
there *orada* o·ra·da
thermal bath *kaplıca hamamı* kap·luh·ja ha·ma·muh
thermal spring *kaplıca* kap·luh·ja
they *onlar* on·lar
thick *kalın* ka·luhn
thief *hırsız* huhr·suhz
thin a *ince* een·je
think v *düşünmek* dew·shewn·mek
third a *üçüncü* ew·chewn·jew
thirsty *susamış* soo·sa·muhsh
this (month) *bu (ay)* boo (ai)
this (one) *bunu* boo·noo
thread *iplik* eep·leek
throat *boğaz* bo·az
thrush (health) *pamukçuk* pa·mook·chook
thunderstorm *fırtına* fuhr·tuh·na
Thursday *Perşembe* per·shem·be
ticket *bilet* bee·let
ticket booth *bilet gişesi* bee·let gee·she·see
ticket collector *biletçi* bee·let·chee
ticket machine *bilet makinesi* bee·let ma·kee·ne·see
ticket office *bilet gişesi* bee·let gee·she·see
tide *dalga* dal·ga

tight *sıkı* suh-*kuh*
time n *zaman* za-*man*
time difference *zaman farkı* za-*man* far-*kuh*
timetable *tarife* ta-ree-fe
tin (can) *teneke kutu* te-ne-ke koo-*too*
tin opener *konserve açacağı*
 kon-*ser*-ve a-*cha*-ja-*uh*
tiny *küçücük* kew-chew-*jewk*
tip (gratuity) *bahşiş* bah-*sheesh*
tire *lastik* las-*teek*
tired *yorgun* yor-*goon*
tissues *kağıt mendil* ka-*uht* men-*deel*
to *-a/-e/-ya/-ye -a/-e/-ya/-ye*
toast n *kızarmış ekmek*
 kuh-*zar*-muhsh ek-*mek*
toaster *ekmek kızartma makinesi*
 ek-mek kuh-zart-ma ma-kee-ne-see
tobacco *tütün* tew-*tewn*
tobacconist *tütüncü* tew-tewn-*jew*
tobogganing *tobagan* to-ba-*gan*
today *bugün* boo-*gewn*
toe *ayak parmağı* a-*yak* par-ma-*uh*
tofu *soya peyniri* so-ya pay-nee-*ree*
together *birlikte* beer-leek-te
toilet *tuvalet* too-va-*let*
toilet paper *tuvalet kağıdı*
 too-va-let ka-uh-*duh*
tomato *domates* do-*ma*-tes
tomato sauce *domates sosu*
 do-*ma*-tes so-*soo*
tomb *mezar* me-*zar*
tomorrow *yarın* ya-*ruhn*
tomorrow afternoon *yarın öğleden sonra*
 ya-ruhn er-le-den son-ra
tomorrow evening *yarın akşam*
 ya-ruhn ak-*sham*
tomorrow morning *yarın sabah*
 ya-ruhn sa-*bah*
tonight *bu gece* boo ge-je
too (expensive etc) *çok* chok
tooth *diş* deesh
toothache *diş ağrısı* deesh a-ruh-*suh*
toothbrush *diş fırçası* deesh fuhr-cha-*suh*
toothpaste *diş macunu* deesh ma-joo-*noo*
toothpick *kürdan* kewr-*dan*
torch (flashlight) n *el feneri* el fe-ne-ree
touch v *dokunmak* do-koon-*mak*
tour n *tur* toor
tourist *turist* too-*reest*
tourist office *turizm bürosu*
 too-reezm bew-ro-*soo*
towel *havlu* hav-*loo*
tower n *kule* koo-le

toxic waste *zararlı atık* za-rar-*luh* a-*tuhk*
toy shop *oyuncakçı* o-yoon-jak-*chuh*
track (path) *patika* pa-tee-*ka*
track (sport) *yarış pisti* ya-*ruhsh* pees-*te*
trade n *ticaret* tee-ja-*ret*
tradesperson *tüccar* tewj-*jar*
traffic n *trafik* tra-*feek*
traffic light *trafik ışığı* tra-feek uh-shuh-*uh*
trail n *patika* pa-tee-*ka*
train n *tren* tren
train station *tren istasyonu*
 \tren ees-tas-yo-noo
tram *tramvay* tram-*vai*
transit lounge *transit yolcu salonu*
 tran-*seet* yol-joo sa-lo-noo
translate *çevirmek* che-veer-*mek*
transport n *ulaşım* oo-la-*shuhm*
travel v *seyahat* se-ya-*hat*
travel agency *seyahat acentesi*
 seya-*hat* a-jen-te-*see*
travel sickness *araç tutması*
 a-*rach* toot-ma-*suh*
travellers cheque *seyahat çeki*
 se-ya-hat che-*kee*
tree *ağaç* a-*ach*
trip (journey) *gezi* ge-*zee*
trolley *trolli* trol-*lee*
trousers *pantolon* pan-to-*lon*
truck *kamyon* kam-*yon*
trust v *güvenmek* gew-ven-*mek*
try (attempt) v *teşebbüs etmek*
 te-sheb-*bews* et-*mek*
try on v *denemek* de-ne-*mek*
T-shirt *tişört* tee-shert
tube (tyre) *iç lastik* eech las-*teek*
Tuesday *Salı* sa-*luh*
tumour *tümör* tew-*mer*
tuna *ton balığı* ton ba-luh-*uh*
tune n *melodi* me-lo-*dee*
turkey *hindi* heen-*dee*
Turkey *Türkiye* tewr-kee-ye
Turkish (language) *Türkçe* tewrk-che
Turkish bath *hamam* ha-*mam*
Turkish delight *lokum* lo-koom
Turkish Republic of
 Northern Cyprus (TRNC)
 Kuzey Kıbrıs Türk Cumhuriyeti (KKTC)
 koo-*zay* kuhb-*ruhs* tewrk
 joom-hoo-ree-ye-tee (ka-ka-te-je)
turn v *çevirmek* che-veer-*mek*
TV *TV* te-ve
tweezers *cımbız* juhm-*buhz*
twice *iki kez* ee-kee kez

twin beds *çift yatak* cheeft ya-*tak*
twins *ikiz* ee-*keez*
two *iki* ee-*kee*
type n *çeşit* che-*sheet*
typical *tipik* tee-*peek*
tyre *lastik* las-*teek*

U

ultrasound *ultrason* ool-tra-*son*
umbrella *şemsiye* shem-see-ye
uncomfortable *rahatsız* ra-hat-suhz
understand *anlamak* an-la-mak
underwear *iç çamaşırı*
eech cha-ma-shuh-ruh
unemployed *işsiz* eesh-seez
unfair *haksız* hak-suhz
uniform n *üniforma* ew-nee-for-ma
universe *kainat* ka-ee-nat
university *üniversite* ew-nee-ver-see-te
unleaded *kurşunsuz* koor-shoon-sooz
unsafe *tehlikeli* teh-lee-ke-lee
until (Friday) *(Cuma)ya kadar*
(joo-ma)-ya ka-dar
unusual *alışılmadık* a-luh-shuhl-ma-duhk
up *yukarı* yoo-ka-ruh
uphill *yokuş yukarı* yo-koosh yoo-ka-ruh
urgent *acil* a-jeel
urinary infection *idrar yolları enfeksiyonu*
eed-rar yol-la-ruh en-fek-see-yo-noo
USA *ABD (Amerika Birleşik Devletleri)* a-be-de
(a-me-ree-ka beer-le-sheek dev-let-le-ree)
useful *yararlı* ya-rar-luh

V

vacancy *yer* yer
vacant *boş* bosh
vacation *tatil* ta-teel
vaccination *aşı* a-shuh
vagina *vajina* va-zhee-na
validate *geçerli kılmak* ge-cher-lee kuhl-mak
valley *vadi* va-dee
valuable *değerli* de-er-lee
value n *değer* de-er
van *van* van
veal *dana eti* da-na e-tee
vegetable n *sebze* seb-ze
vegetarian n & a *vejeteryan* ve-zhe-ter-yan
vein *damar* da-mar
venereal disease *zührevi hastalık*
zewh-re-vee has-ta-luhk

venue *toplantı yeri* top-lan-tuh ye-ree
very *çok* chok
video camera *video kamera*
vee-de-o ka-me-ra
video recorder *video kayıt cihazı*
vee-de-o ka-yuht jee-ha-zuh
video tape *video kaset* vee-de-o ka-set
view n *manzara* man-za-ra
villa *villa* veel-la
village *köy* kay
vine *asma* as-ma
vinegar *sirke* seer-ke
vineyard *bağ* ba
virus *virüs* vee-rews
visa *vize* vee-ze
visit v *ziyaret etmek* zee-ya-ret et-mek
vitamins *vitaminler* vee-ta-meen-ler
voice *ses* ses
volleyball (sport) *voleybol* vo-lay-bol
volume *ses* ses
vote v *oy vermek* oy ver-mek

W

wage n *maaş* ma-ash
wait for *beklemek* bek-le-mek
waiter *garson* gar-son
waiting room *bekleme odası*
bek-le-me o-da-suh
wake up v *uyandırmak* oo-yan-duhr-mak
Wales *Galler* gal-ler
walk v *yürümek* yew-rew-mek
wall *duvar* doo-var
want v *istemek* ees-te-mek
war n *savaş* sa-vash
wardrobe *gardırop* gar-duh-rop
warm a *ılık* uh-luhk
warn *uyarmak* oo-yar-mak
wash (oneself) *yıkanmak* yuh-kan-mak
wash (something) *yıkamak* yuh-ka-mak
wash cloth (flannel) *sabunluk* sa-boon-look
washing machine *çamaşır makinesi*
cha-ma-shuhr ma-kee-ne-see
watch n *saat* sa-at
watch v *izlemek* eez-le-mek
water n *su* soo
water bottle *su şişesi* soo shee-she-see
water bottle (hot) *termofor* ter-mo-for
waterfall *şelale* she-la-le
watermelon *karpuz* kar-pooz
water-pipe (Turkish) *nargile* nar-gee-le
waterproof *su geçirmez* soo ge-cheer-mez

water-skiing *su kayağı* soo ka·ya·*uh*
wave (sea) *dalga* dal·*ga*
way *yol* yol
we *biz* beez
weak *zayıf* za·*yuhf*
wealthy *zengin* zen·*geen*
wear v *giymek* geey·*mek*
weather *hava* ha·*va*
wedding *düğün* dew·*ewn*
wedding cake *düğün pastası*
  dew·*ewn* pas·ta·*suh*
wedding present *düğün hediyesi*
  dew·*ewn* he·dee·ye·*see*
Wednesday *Çarşamba* char·sham·*ba*
(this) week *(bu) hafta* (boo) haf·*ta*
weekend *hafta sonu* haf·*ta* so·*noo*
weigh *tartmak* tart·*mak*
weight(s) *ağırlık* a·uhr·*luhk*
welcome v *hoş geldiniz* hosh gel·*dee*·neez
welfare *refah* re·*fah*
well a *iyi* ee·*yee*
west *batı* ba·*tuh*
wet a *ıslak* uhs·*lak*
what *ne* ne
wheel *tekerlek* te·ker·*lek*
wheelchair *tekerlekli sandalye*
  te·ker·lek·*lee* san·dal·*ye*
when *ne zaman* ne za·*man*
where *nerede* ne·re·*de*
which *hangi* han·*gee*
white *beyaz* be·*yaz*
who *kim* keem
wholemeal bread *kepekli ekmek*
  ke·pek·*lee* ek·*mek*
why *neden* ne·*den*
wide *geniş* ge·*neesh*
wife *karı* ka·*ruh*
win v *kazanmak* ka·zan·*mak*
wind n *rüzgar* rewz·*gar*
window *pencere* pen·je·*re*
windscreen *oto ön camı* o·to ern ja·*muh*
windsurfing *rüzgar sörfü* rewz·gar ser·*few*
wine *şarap* sha·*rap*
winehall *meyhane* may·ha·*ne*
wine shop *şarap dükkanı*
  sha·*rap* dewk·ka·*nuh*
winner *galip* ga·*leep*
winter *kış* kuhsh
wish v *dilemek* dee·le·*mek*
with *ile* ee·*le*
within (an hour) *(bir saat) içinde*
  (beer sa·*at*) ee·cheen·*de*

without *-sız/-siz/-suz/-süz*
  ·*suhz*/·*seez*/·*sooz*/·*sewz*
wok *çin tavası* cheen ta·va·*suh*
woman *kadın* ka·*duhn*
women's quarters *kadınlar bölümü*
  ka·duhn·*lar* ber·lew·*mew*
wonderful *şahane* sha·ha·*ne*
wood *odun* o·*doon*
wool *yün* yewn
word n *kelime* ke·lee·*me*
work n *iş* eesh
work v *çalışmak* cha·luhsh·*mak*
work experience *deneyim* de·ne·*yeem*
workout n *egzersiz* eg·zer·*seez*
work permit *çalışma izni*
  cha·luhsh·*ma* eez·*nee*
workshop *atölye* a·terl·*ye*
world *dünya* dewn·*ya*
World Cup *Dünya Kupası*
  dewn·*ya* koo·pa·*suh*
worms *solucanlar* so·loo·jan·*lar*
worried v *endişeli* en·dee·she·*lee*
worship v *ibadet etmek* ee·ba·det et·*mek*
wreck n *batık* ba·*tuhk*
wrist *el bileği* el bee·le·*ee*
write *yazı yazmak* ya·zuh yaz·*mak*
writer *yazar* ya·*zar*
wrong *yanlış* yan·*luhsh*

Y

yacht (general) *yat* yat
yacht (traditional Turkish) *gulet* goo·*let*
(this) year *(bu) yıl* (boo) yuhl
yellow *sarı* sa·*ruh*
yes *evet* e·*vet*
yesterday *dün* dewn
yoga *yoga* yo·*ga*
yogurt *yoğurt* yo·*oort*
you sg inf *sen* sen
you sg pol & pl inf/pol *siz* seez
young *genç* gench
your *senin* se·*neen*
youth hostel *gençlik hosteli* gench·*leek* hos·te·*lee*

Z

zip(per) *fermuar* fer·moo·*ar*
zodiac *burçlar* boorch·*lar*
zoo *hayvanat bahçesi*
  hai·va·*nat* bah·che·*see*
zucchini *kabak* ka·*bak*

You'll find the English words marked as adjective a, noun n, verb v, singular sg, plural pl, informal inf and polite pol where necessary. All verbs are provided in the infinitive, and all nouns are in the nominative case. For any food items, refer to the **menu decoder**.

A

ABD (Amerika Birleşik Devletleri) a-be-*de* (a-me-ree-ka beer-le-*sheek* dev-let-le-*ree*) *USA*

acayip a-ja-*yeep strange*

acele ile a-je-*le* ee-*le in a hurry*

acı a-*juh bitter*

acil a-*jeel urgent*
    — **durum** doo-*room emergency*

aç ach *hungry*

açık a-*chuhk light (colour)* a • *open* a
    — **bilet** bee-*let stand-by ticket*

açılış saatleri a-chuh-*luhsh* sa-at-le-*ree opening hours*

açmak ach-*mak open* v

ad ad *name* n

ada a-*da island*

adam a-*dam man*

adaptör a-dap-*ter adaptor*

adet a-*det menstruation*
    — **ağrısı** a-ruh-*suh period pain*
    — **öncesi gerginlik** ern-je-*see* ger-geen-*leek premenstrual tension*

adım a-*duhm step* n

adres ad-*res address* n

affetmek af-fet-*mek forgive*

ağ a *net* n

ağaç a-*ach tree*

ağır a-*uhr heavy*

ağırlık a-uhr-*luhk weight(s)*

ağız a-*uhz mouth*

ağrı a-*ruh pain* n
    — **kesici** ke-see-*jee painkiller*

ağrılı a-ruh-*luh painful* • *sore* a

aile a-ee-*le family*
    — **bölümü** ber-lew-*mew family room (restaurant)*
    — **için kalacak yer** ee-*cheen* ka-la-*jak yer family quarters*

akciğer ak-jee-*er lung*

Akdeniz ak-de-*neez Mediterranean Sea*

akım a-*kuhm current (electricity)*

akıntı a-kuhn-*tuh stream*

akrabalık ak-ra-ba-*luhk relationship (family)*

akşam ak-*sham evening*
    — **gezmesi** gez-me-*see night out*
    — **yemeği** ye-me-*ee dinner*

aktar ak-*tar herbalist*

aktarma ak-tar-*ma connection (trip)*

akupresyon a-koo-pres-*yon shiatsu*

akü a-*kew battery (car)*
    — **takviye kablosu** tak-vee-*ye* ka-blo-*soo jumper leads*

alçak al-*chak low*

aldatma al-dat-*ma cheat* n

alışılmadık a-luh-*shuhl*-ma-duhk *unusual*

alış-veriş a-luhsh-ve-*reesh shopping*
    — **merkezi** mer-ke-*zee shopping centre*

alış-verişe gitmek a-luhsh-ve-ree-*she* geet-*mek go shopping*

almak al-*mak get* • *take*

Almanca al-man-*ja German (language)*

Almanya al-man-*ya Germany*

alt geçit alt ge-*cheet subway*

altın al-*tuhn gold* n

altyazı alt-ya-*zuh subtitles*

ama a-*ma but*

ambalaj am-ba-*lazh package*

amele a-me-*le manual worker*

ameliyat a-me-lee-*yat operation (medical)*

ampül am-*pewl light bulb*

ana baba a-*na* ba-*ba parents*

ana cadde a-*na* jad-*de main road*

anahtar a-nah-*tar key* n

anayol a-na-*yol main road*

anıt a-*nuht monument*

anlamak an-la-*mak understand*

anlatmak an-lat-*mak tell*

anne an-*ne mother*

anneciğim an-ne-jee-*eem mum*

apandis a-pan-*dees appendix (body)*

apartman dairesi a·part·man da·ee·re·see apartment • flat n
aptal ap·tal idiot
ara a·ra intermission
araba a·ra·ba car
— **kiralama** kee·ra·la·ma car hire
— **tamircisi** ta·meer·jee·see mechanic
— **yarışında birincilik** ya·ruh·shuhn·da bee·reen·jee·leek car owner's title
araç tutması a·rach toot·ma·suh travel sickness
Aralık a·ra·luhk December
aramak a·ra·mak call (telephone) v • look for
Arapça a·rap·cha Arabic (language)
arasında a·ra·suhn·da between
arı a·ruh bee
arka ar·ka back (position)
arkadaş ar·ka·dash companion • friend
arkasında ar·ka·suhn·da behind
asansör a·san·ser elevator • lift
asker as·ker soldier n
askeriye as·ke·ree·ye military n
askerlik hizmeti as·ker·leek heez·me·tee military service
asla as·la never
asma as·ma vine
asma kilit as·ma kee·leet padlock
astım as·tuhm asthma
aşağı a·sha·uh down
aşağısında a·sha·uh·suhn·da below
aşçı ash·chuh cook n
aşçıbaşı ash·chuh·ba·shuh chef
aşı a·shuh vaccination
aşık olmak a·shuhk ol·mak fall in love v
aşırı doz a·shuh·ruh doz overdose n
aşk ashk love n
at at horse
ata binmek a·ta been·mek ride a horse v
ateş a·tesh fever • small fire under control
— **etmek** et·mek shoot v
atkı at·kuh scarf
atlamak at·la·mak jump v
atlet at·let singlet
atölye a·terl·ye workshop
avlanma av·lan·ma hunting
Avrupa av·roo·pa Europe
avukat a·voo·kat lawyer
ay ai month • moon
ayak a·yak foot
— **bileği** bee·le·ee ankle
— **parmağı** par·ma·uh toe
ayakkabıcı a·yak·ka·buh·juh shoe shop
ayakkabılar a·yak·ka·buh·lar shoes

ayna ai·na mirror
aynı ai·nuh same
— **fikirde olmak** fee·keer·de ol·mak agree
ayrı ai·ruh separate a
ayrılmak ai·ruhl·mak depart
ayrım ai·ruhm discrimination
ayrıntı ai·ruhn·tuh details
ayrıntılı yazılmış ay·ruhn·tuh·luh ya·zuhl·muhsh itemised
az az little n • least a
— **bulunur** boo·loo·noor rare
aziz a·zeez saint

B

baba ba·ba father
babacığım ba·ba·juh·uhm dad
bacak ba·jak leg (body)
bağ ba·ruh vineyard
bagaj ba·gazh baggage • luggage
— **etiketi** e·tee·ke·tee luggage tag
— **hakkı** hak·kuh baggage allowance
— **konveyörü** kon·ve·yer·rew baggage claim
bağımlılık ba·uhm·luh·luhk addiction
bağırmak ba·uhr·mak shout v
bağlantı ba·lan·tuh connection (link)
bahçe bah·che garden n
— **işleri** eesh·le·ree gardening
bahçıvan bah·chuh·van gardener
bahis ba·hees bet n
bakıcı ba·kuh·juh caretaker
bakımını yapmak ba·kuh·muh·nuh yap·mak look after
bakkal bak·kal convenience store • grocery
bakliyat bak·lee·yat legume
bakmak bak·mak care (for someone) v • look v
balayı ba·la·yuh honeymoon
bale ba·le ballet
balık ba·luhk fish n
— **avlama** av·la·ma fishing
balıkçı ba·luhk·chuh fishmonger • fish shop
balsam bal·sam hair conditioner
bana ba·na me
bandaj ban·dazh bandage
banka hesabı ban·ka he·sa·buh bank account
bankamatik ban·ka·ma·teek ATM
banyo ban·yo bath • bathroom
bardak bar·dak drinking glass
bar işi bar ee·shee bar work

barış ba-*ruhsh peace*
basın ba-*suhn media*
basınç ba-*suhnch pressure* n
basit ba-*seet simple*
baş bash *head* n
— **ağrısı** a-ruh-*suh headache*
başbakan bash-ba-kan *prime minister*
başı dönen ba-*shuh der-nen dizzy*
(gün) başına (gewn) ba-shuh-*na per (day)*
başkan bash-*kan president*
başlamak bash-la-*mak start* v
başlangıç bash-lan-*guhch start* n
batı ba-*tuh west*
batıl inanç ba-*tuhl ee-nanch superstition*
battaniye bat-*ta-nee-ye blanket*
bavul ba-*vool suitcase*
Bay bai *Mr/Sir*
Bayan ba-*yan Mrs/Ms/Miss/Madam*
bayan ba-*yan female (human)* a
bayrak bai-*rak flag*
bazen ba-*zen sometimes*
bebek be-*bek baby* n
— **bezi** be-*zee diaper • nappy*
— **maması** ma-ma-*suh baby food*
— **pudrası** pood-ra-*suh baby powder*
beden be-*den size* n
bekar be-*kar single (not married)*
bekleme odası bek-le-me o-da-*suh*
   waiting room
beklemek bek-le-*mek wait for*
bel çantası bel chan-ta-*suh*
   bumbag • fanny sack
belediye başkanı be-le-dee-ye
   bash-ka-nuh *mayor*
belgesel bel-ge-*sel documentary*
belki bel-*kee maybe*
ben ben *I*
bencil ben-*jeel selfish*
beni be-*nee me*
benim be-*neem my*
benzer ben-*zer similar*
benzin ben-*zeen gas • oil • petrol*
— **istasyonu** ees-tas-yo-*noo*
   petrol station • service station
beri be-*ree since*
beslemek bes-le-*mek feed* v
beyaz be-*yaz white*
beyin sarsıntısı be-*yeen sar-suhn-tuh-suh*
   concussion
bıçak buh-*chak knife* n
bırakmak buh-rak-*mak quit*
biçim bee-*cheem shape* n
bilardo bee-*lar-do pool (game)*

bilet bee-*let ticket*
— **gişesi** gee-she-*see*
   ticket booth • ticket office
biletçi bee-let-*chee ticket collector*
bilgi beel-*gee information*
bilgisayar beel-gee-sa-*yar computer*
bilgisayar oyunu beel-gee-sa-*yar*
   o-yoo-*noo computer game*
bilim bee-*leem science*
— **adamı** a-da-*muh scientist*
bilmek beel-*mek know*
bina bee-*na building*
binicilik bee-nee-jee-*leek horse riding*
biniş kartı bee-*neesh kar-tuh boarding pass*
binmek been-*mek board* v • *ride* n
bir beer *one*
— **de** de *also*
— **gecelik** ge-je-*leek overnight*
bira bee-*ra beer*
birahane bee-ra-ha-*ne beerhall*
biraz bee-*raz some*
birinci sınıf bee-reen-jee suh-*nuhf first class*
birisi bee-ree-*see someone*
birkaç beer-*kach few • several*
bir kez beer kez *once*
birlikte beer-leek-*te together*
birşey beer-*shay something*
bisiklet bee-seek-*let bicycle*
— **kilidi** kee-lee-dee *bike lock*
— **sporu** spo-*roo cycling*
— **yolu** yo-*loo bike path*
— **zinciri** zeen-jee-*ree bike chain*
bisikletçi bee-seek-let-*chee*
   bike shop • cyclist
bisiklete binmek bee-seek-le-*te*
   been-*mek cycle* v
bit beet *lice*
— **pazarı** pa-za-*ruh fleamarket*
bitirmek bee-teer-*mek finish* v
bitiş bee-*teesh finish* n
bitki beet-*kee herb • plant*
biz beez *we*
bizim bee-*zeem our*
board kayağı bord ka-ya-uh *snowboarding*
boğaz bo-*az throat*
borcu olmak bor-joo ol-*mak owe*
boş bosh *available • empty • vacant*
boşanmış bo-shan-*muhsh divorced*
botlar bot-*lar boots*
boyacı bo-ya-*juh painter (occupation)*
boyun bo-*yoon neck (body)*

bozuk bo-*zook* *broken down* • *corrupt* • *faulty* • *off (spoiled)* • *out of order*
— **para** pa-*ra*
change (coins) • *loose change*
bozulmak bo-*zool-mak* *break down* v
böbrek berb-*rek* *kidney*
böcek ber-*jek* *bug* n
— **ısırması** uh-suhr-ma-*suh* *bite (insect)* n
bölge berl-*ge* *suburb*
bölgesel berl-*ge-sel* *regional*
börekçi ber-rek-*chee* *pastry shop*
bronşit bron-*sheet* *bronchitis*
bu boo *this*
— **gece** ge-*je* *tonight*
bugün boo-*gewn* *today*
bulantı boo-lan-*tuh* *nausea*
Bulgaristan bool-ga-rees-*tan* *Bulgaria*
bulmak bool-*mak* *find* v
buluşmak boo-loosh-*mak*
meet (get together) v
bulut boo-*loot* *cloud* n
bulutlu boo-loot-*loo* *cloudy*
bunu boo-*noo* *this one*
burada boo-ra-*da* *here*
burçlar boorch-*lar* *zodiac*
burkulma boor-kool-*ma* *sprain* n
burun boo-*roon* *nose*
— **akıntısı** a-kuhn-tuh-*suh* *runny nose*
buz booz *ice*
— **kıracağı** kuh-ra-ja-*uh* *ice axe*
buzdolabı booz-do-la-*buh* *refrigerator*
bütçe bewt-*che* *budget* n
büyük bew-*yewk* *big*
— **çadır** cha-*duhr* *pavillion*
— **kilise** kee-lee-*se* *basilica*
— **mağaza** ma-a-*za* *department store*
— **meydan** may-*dan*
agora (open ground, town square)
büyükanne bew-yewk-an-*ne* *grandmother*
büyükbaba bew-yewk-ba-*ba* *grandfather*
büyükelçi bew-yewk-el-*chee* *ambassador*
büyümek bew-yew-*mek* *grow*

C

cadde jad-*de* *avenue*
cam jam *glass (window)*
cami ja-*mee* *mosque*
canı acımak ja-nuh a-juh-*mak* *hurt* v
canı sıkkın ja-nuh suhk-*kuhn* *bored*
can yeleği jan ye-le-e-*ee* *life jacket*
ceket je-*ket* *jacket*

cenaze töreni je-na-ze ter-re-*nee* *funeral*
cep jep *pocket*
— **feneri** fe-ne-*ree* *flashlight* • *torch*
— **telefonu** te-le-fo-*noo*
cell phone • *mobile phone*
cesur je-*soor* *brave*
cevap je-*vap* *answer* n
cezaevi je-za-e-*vee* *prison*
cımbız juhm-*buhz* *tweezers*
cibinlik jee-been-*leek* *mosquito net*
ciddi jeed-*dee* *serious*
cilt jeelt *skin* n
cin jeen *gin*
cinayet jee-na-*yet* *murder* n
— **işlemek** eesh-le-*mek* *murder* v
cinsiyet jeen-see-*yet* *sex (gender)*
— **ayrımı** ai-ruh-*muh* *sexism*
cip jeep *jeep*
Cuma joo-*ma* *Friday*
Cumartesi joo-mar-te-*see* *Saturday*
cumhuriyet joom-hoo-ree-*yet* *republic*
cüzdan jewz-*dan* *purse*

Ç

çabuk cha-*book* *quick* a
çadır cha-*duhr* *tent*
— **kazığı** ka-zuh-*uh* *tent peg*
çağırmak cha-uhr-*mak* *call (shout)* v
çakı cha-*kuh* *pocketknife*
çakmak chak-*mak* *cigarette lighter*
çalar saat cha-*lar* sa-*at* *alarm clock*
çalıntı cha-luhn-*tuh* *stolen*
çalışan cha-luh-*shan* *employee*
çalışma izni cha-luhsh-*ma* eez-*nee*
work permit
çalışmak cha-luhsh-*mak* *work* v
çalmak chal-*mak* *play (an instrument)* v •
ring (phone) v • *steal* v
çamaşır cha-ma-*shuhr* *laundry (clothes)*
— **ipi** ee-*pee* *clothesline*
— **makinesi** ma-kee-ne-*see*
washing machine
çamaşırhane cha-ma-shuhr-ha-*ne*
launderette
çamaşırlık cha-ma-shuhr-*luhk*
laundry (room)
çamur cha-*moor* *mud*
çanta chan-*ta* *bag*
çarpışma char-puhsh-*ma* *crash* n
çarşaf char-*shaf* *sheet (bed)*
Çarşamba char-sham-*ba* *Wednesday*

çatal cha-*tal fork* n
— **bıçak takımı** buh-*chak* ta-kuh-*muh cutlery*
çay chai *tea*
— **bahçesi** bah-che-*see tea garden*
— **bardağı** chai bar-da-*uh tea glass*
— **kaşığı** ka-shuh-*uh teaspoon*
çaydanlık chai-dan-*luhk teapot*
çek bozdurmak chek boz-door-*mak cash a cheque*
çekici che-kee-*jee charming*
çekiç che-*keech hammer* n
çekmek chek-*mek pull* v
çene che-*ne jaw*
çerez che-*rez nut*
çeşit che-*sheet type* n
çeşme suyu chesh-me soo-*yoo tap water*
çevirmek che-veer-*mek translate • turn* v
çevir sesi che-veer se-*see dial tone*
çevre chev-*re environment*
çeyrek chay-*rek quarter* n
çıkıkçı chuh-kuhk-*chuh chiropractor*
çıkıntı chuh-kuhn-*tuh ledge*
çıkış chuh-*kuhsh exit* n
çıkmak chuhk-*mak date (a person)* v
çiçek chee-*chek flower* n
çiçekçi chee-chek-*chee florist*
çift cheeft *double* a • *pair* a
— **yatak** ya-*tak twin beds*
çiftçi cheeft-*chee farmer* n
çiftlik cheeft-*leek farm* n
çiğ chee *raw*
çim cheem *grass (lawn)* n
Çin cheen *China*
Çince cheen-*jee Mandarin (language)*
çit cheet *fence* n
çizim chee-*zeem drawing*
çocuk cho-*jook child*
— **aldırma** al-duhr-*ma abortion*
— **bakımı** ba-kuh-*muh childminding*
— **koltuğu** kol-too-*oo child seat*
çocuklar cho-jook-*lar children*
çok chok *a lot • many • too • very*
çorap cho-*rap stockings*
çoraplar cho-rap-*lar socks*
çöl cherl *desert* n
çömlekçilik cherm-lek-chee-*leek pottery*
çöp cherp *garbage • rubbish*
— **tenekesi** te-ne-ke-*see garbage can*
çünkü chewn-*kew because*
çürük chew-*rewk bruise* n

D

dadı da-*duh babysitter*
dağ da *mountain*
— **bisikleti** bee-seek-le-*tee mountain bike*
— **yolu** yo-*loo mountain path*
dağcılık da-juh-*luhk mountaineering*
daha az da-*ha az less*
daha büyük da-ha bew-*yewk bigger*
daha fazla da-ha faz-*la more*
daha iyi da-ha ee-*yee better*
daha küçük da-ha kew-*chewk smaller*
dahil da-*heel included*
dakika da-kee-*ka minute*
dalga dal-*ga tide • wave (sea)*
dalış da-*luhsh dive* n • *diving*
— **kursu** koor-*soo diving course*
— **malzemeleri** mal-ze-me-le-*ree diving equipment*
— **ortağı** or-ta-*uh dive buddy*
— **teknesi** tek-ne-*see diving boat*
dalmak dal-*mak dive* v
damar da-*mar vein*
dantel dan-*tel lace*
davet etmek da-*vet* et-*mek invite* v
davul da-*vool drum (music)* n
debriyaj deb-ree-*yazh clutch (car)*
değer de-*er value* n
değerli de-er-*le valuable* a
değil de-*eel not*
değişiklik de-ee-sheek-*leek change* n
değiştirmek de-eesh-teer-*mek exchange* v
değiş-tokuş de-eesh-to-*koosh exchange* n
deli de-*lee crazy*
denemek de-ne-*mek try on* v
deneyim de-ne-*yeem experience • work experience*
deniz de-*neez sea*
— **gözlüğü** gerz-lew-*ew swimming goggles*
— **kenarı** ke-na-*ruh seaside* n
— **otobüsü** o-to-bew-*sew hydrofoil*
— **tutmuş** toot-*moosh seasick*
— **yoluyla gönderi** yo-*looy-*la gern-de-*ree surface mail (sea)*
deprem dep-*rem earthquake*
derece de-re-*je degrees • temperature (weather)*
dergi der-*gee magazine*
deri de-*ree leather*
derin de-*reen deep*
devlet dev-*let government*
dışarıda duh-sha-ruh-*da outside*

dışarıya çıkmak duh-sha-ruh-*ya chuhk-mak go out*
diğer dee-*er another • other*
dikiş dikmek dee-*keesh deek-mek sew*
dikiş iğnesi dee-*keesh ee-ne-see needle (sewing)*
dilekçe dee-lek-*che petition* n
dilemek dee-*le-mek wish* v
dilenci dee-len-*jee beggar*
dilim dee-*leem slice* n
dilsiz deel-*seez mute (person)*
din deen *religion*
dini dee-*nee religious*
dinlemek deen-le-*mek listen to*
dinlenmek deen-len-*mek relax* v • *rest* v
dipte deep-*te bottom (position)*
direk dee-*rek direct* a
diş deesh *tooth*
    — **ağrısı** a-ruh-*suh toothache*
    — **fırçası** fuhr-cha-*suh toothbrush*
    — **ipi** ee-*pee dental floss*
    — **macunu** ma-joo-*noo toothpaste*
dişçi deesh-*chee dentist*
dişi dee-*shee female (animal)* a
diz deez *knee*
    — **üstü bilgisayar** ews-*tew beel-gee-sa-yar laptop*
doğa do-*a nature*
doğal gaz do-*al gaz gas (for cooking)*
doğru do-*roo right (correct)* a
    — **yön** yern *right (direction)* a
doğu do-*oo east*
doğum belgesi do-oom bel-ge-*see birth certificate*
doğum günü do-oom gew-*new birthday*
doğum kontrol hapı do-oom kon-*trol ha-puh contraceptives • the pill*
doğum tarihi do-oom ta-ree-*hee date of birth*
doğum yeri do-oom ye-*ree place of birth*
dokunma do-koon-*ma feeling (physical)*
dokunmak do-koon-*mak touch* v
dolap do-*lap cupboard*
doldurmak dol-door-*mak fill* v
dolu do-*loo full • booked out*
domuz do-*mooz pig*
don don *frost* n
dondurmacı don-door-ma-*juh ice-cream parlour*
donmuş don-*moosh frozen*
doymuş doy-*moosh full (not hungry)*
döviz kuru der-veez koo-*roo currency exchange • exchange rate*

dua doo-*a prayer*
    — **kitabı** kee-ta-*buh prayer book*
dudaklar doo-dak-*lar lips*
durak doo-*rak stop (bus etc)* n
durdurmak door-door-*mak stop (prevent)* v
durgun su door-*goon soo still water*
durmak door-*mak stay (in one place)* v • *stop (cease)* v
duş doosh *shower* n
duvar doo-*var wall*
duygular dooy-goo-*lar feelings*
duygusal dooy-goo-*sal emotional*
duymak dooy-*mak hear*
düğme dew-*me button*
düğün dew-*ewn wedding*
    — **hediyesi** he-dee-ye-*see wedding present*
    — **pastası** pas-ta-*suh wedding cake*
dükkan dewk-*kan shop* n
dün dewn *yesterday*
dünya dewn-*ya world*
dürbün dewr-*bewn binoculars*
düşmek dewsh-*mek fall* v
düşük dew-*shewk miscarriage*
düşünmek dew-shewn-*mek think* v
düz dewz *flat a • straight*
düzine dew-zee-*ne dozen*

E

eczacı ej-za-*juh pharmacist*
eczane ej-za-*ne pharmacy*
Ege Denizi e-ge de-nee-*zee Aegean Sea*
egzoz eg-*zoz exhaust (car)*
eğer e-*er if*
eğitim e-ee-*teem education*
eğlence e-len-*je fun a • gig* n
    — **rehberi** reh-be-*ree entertainment guide*
eğlenmek e-len-*mek enjoy (oneself) • have fun*
ehliyet eh-lee-*yet drivers licence • licence*
Ekim e-*keem October*
ekmek ek-*mek bread*
    — **ve şarap ayini** ve sha-*rap a-yee-nee mass (Catholic)*
eksiklik ek-seek-*leek shortage*
el el *hand (body)*
    — **bileği** bee-le-*ee wrist*
    — **çantası** chan-ta-*suh handbag*
    — **feneri** fe-ne-*ree torch* n
    — **işi** ee-*shee handmade*
    — **sanatları** sa-nat-la-*ruh handicrafts*

elbise el·bee·*se dress* n
elçilik el·chee·*leek embassy*
eldivenler el·dee·ven·*ler gloves (warm)*
emanet e·ma·*net left luggage*
— **bürosu** bew·ro·soo *left-luggage office*
emekli e·mek·*lee pensioner* n • *retired* a
emlakçı em·lak·*chuh*
estate agency • *real estate agent*
emniyet kemeri em·nee·yet ke·me·*ree*
seatbelt
emniyetli em·nee·yet·*lee safe* a
emzik em·*zeek dummy* • *pacifier*
en en *most*
— **büyük** bew·*yewk biggest*
— **iyi** ee·*yee best*
— **küçük** kew·*chewk smallest*
— **yakın** ya·*kuhn nearest*
endişeli en·dee·she·*lee worried*
erkek er·*kek male* a
— **arkadaş** ar·ka·*dash boyfriend*
erkekler bölümü er·kek·*ler* ber·lew·*mew*
men's quarters
erken er·*ken early*
erzak er·*zak food supplies* • *provisions*
esas e·*sas main* a
eski es·*kee old (object)*
— **eser** e·*ser relic*
eskici es·kee·*jee second-hand shop*
eskrim es·*kreem fencing (sport)*
esrar es·*rar hash (drug)*
eşcinsel esh·jeen·*sel gay (homosexual)*
eşitlik e·sheet·*leek equality*
et et *meat*
ET (enformasyon teknolojisi)
e·te (en·for·mas·*yon* tek·no·lo·jee·*see) IT*
etek e·*tek skirt*
etrafında et·ra·fuhn·*da about*
ev ev — **house**
— **işi** ee·*shee housework*
— **hanımı** ha·nuh·*muh homemaker*
evlenmek ev·len·*mek marry* v
evli ev·*lee married*
evlilik ev·lee·*leek marriage*
evrak çantası ev·rak chan·ta·*suh briefcase*
evsiz ev·*seez homeless*
eyer e·*yer saddle* n
Eylül ay·*lewl September*

F

fabrika fab·ree·*ka factory*
— **işçisi** eesh·chee·*see factory worker*
fahişe fa·hee·*she prostitute* n

fakir fa·*keer poor*
falcı fal·*juh fortune teller*
fare fa·*re mouse (animal)*
farklı fark·*luh different*
farlar far·*lar headlights*
fatura fa·too·ra *bill* n • *check n (restaurant)*
faul fa·ool *foul (football)* n
fazla yük faz·la yewk *excess baggage*
felçli felch·*lee*
paraplegic n • *stroke (health)* n
fermuar fer·moo·ar *zip* • *zipper*
fikir fee·*keer opinion*
fiks ücret feeks *ewj·ret cover charge*
film hızı feelm huh·*zuh film speed*
filtre edilmiş feelt·re e·deel·*meesh filtered*
fincan feen·*jan cup (drinking)*
fırça fuhr·*cha brush* n
fırın fuh·*ruhn bakery* • *oven*
fırsat eşitliği fuhr·sat e·sheet·lee·*ee*
equal opportunity
fırtına fuhr·tuh·*na storm* • *thunderstorm*
fıskiye fuhs·kee·*ye fountain (decorative)*
fiş feesh *plug (electricity)* n
fiyat fee·*yat price* n
fotoğraf fo·to·*raf photo*
— **çekmek** chek·*mek take a photo*
fotoğrafçı fo·to·raf·*chuh*
camera shop • *photographer*
fotoğrafçılık fo·to·raf·chuh·*luhk*
photography
fren fren *brakes*

G

galip ga·*leep winner*
Galler gal·*ler Wales*
garantili ga·ran·tee·*lee guaranteed*
gardırop gar·duh·*rop wardrobe*
gazete ga·ze·*te newspaper*
— **bayii** ba·yee·*ee newsagency*
gazeteci ga·ze·te·*jee journalist*
gazlı bez gaz·luh bez *gauze*
gaz tüpü gaz tew·pew *gas cartridge*
gebelik test çubuğu ge·be·*leek* test
choo·boo·oo *pregnancy test kit*
gece ge·*je night*
— **kulübü** koo·lew·*bew nightclub*
— **yarısı** ya·ruh·*suh midnight*
gecikme ge·jeek·*me delay* n
geç gech *late*
geçen a ge·*chen last*
geçici iş ge·chee·*jee* eesh *casual work*
geçmek gech·*mek pass* v

geçmiş gech·meesh past n
gelecek ge·le·jek future n · next
gelenek ge·le·nek custom
gelen yolcu ge·len yol·joo arrivals
gelir vergisi ge·leer ver·gee·see income tax
gelmek gel·mek come
gemi ge·mee ship n
genç gench young
gençlik hosteli gench·leek hos·te·lee
   youth hostel
geniş ge·neesh wide
gerçekçi ger·chek·chee realistic
gerekli ge·rek·lee necessary
geri ge·ree rear (location)
   — dönmek dern·mek return v
getirmek ge·teer·mek bring
gezegen ge·ze·gen planet
gezi ge·zee trip (journey)
gidilecek yer gee·dee·le·jek yer
   destination
gidiş gee·deesh departure
   — bileti bee·le·tee one-way a
   — kapısı ka·puh·suh departure gate
gidiş-dönüş gee·deesh·der·newsh return a
giriş ge·reesh
   admission price · check-in desk · entry
girmek geer·mek enter
gitmek geet·mek go
giyim gee·yeem clothing
   — mağazası ma·a·za·suh clothing store
giymek geey·mek wear v
glandüler ateş glan·dew·ler a·tesh
   glandular fever
golf sahası golf sa·ha·suh golf course
golf topu golf to·poo golf ball
göç gerch immigration
göğüs ger·ews breast · chest
gökyüzü gerk·yew·zew sky
göl gerl lake
gölge gerl·ge shade · shadow
   — oyunu o·yoo·noo
   shadow-puppet theatre
gömlek germ·lek shirt
göndermek gern·der·mek send
görmek ger·mek see
görüşme ger·rewsh·me small conference
gösterge gers·ter·ge indicator
gösteri gers·te·ree demonstration
   (protest) · performance · show n
göstermek gers·ter·mek point v · show v
göz damlası gerz dam·la·suh eye drops
gözlem yeri gerz·lem ye·ree lookout

gözler gerz·ler eyes
gözlük gerz·lewk glasses (spectacles)
gözlükçü gerz·lewk·chew optometrist
grev grev strike (stop work) n
gri gree grey
grip greep influenza
gulet goo·let traditional Turkish yacht
güçlü gewch·lew strong
gülmek gewl·mek laugh v
gülümsemek gew·lewm·se·mek smile v
gümrük gewm·rewk customs
gümüş gew·mewsh silver n
gün gewn day
   — batımı ba·tuh·muh sunset
   — doğumu do·oo·moo sunrise
   — ortası or·ta·suh midday
günah çıkarma gew·nah chuh·kar·ma
   confession (religious)
gündem gewn·dem current affairs
güneş gew·nesh sun
   — çarpması charp·ma·suh sunstroke
   — gözlüğü gerz·lew·ew sunglasses
   — yağı ya·uh tanning lotion
   — yanığı ya·nuh·uh sunburn
güneşli gew·nesh·lee sunny
güneşten koruma kremi gew·nesh·ten
   ko·roo·ma kre·mee sunblock
güney gew·nay south
günlük gewn·lewk daily · diary n
Gürcistan gewr·jees·tan Georgia
gürültülü gew·rewl·tew·lew noisy
güvenli seks gew·ven·lee seks safe sex
güvenmek gew·ven·mek trust v
güzel gew·zel beautiful
güzellik salonu gew·zel·leek sa·lo·noo
   beauty salon

haberler ha·ber·ler news
haç hach cross (religious) n
hafif ha·feef light (weight) a
   — yemek ye·mek snack n
hafta haf·ta week
   — sonu so·noo weekend
hakem ha·kem referee
haksız hak·suhz unfair
hala ha·la aunt (paternal)
halkla ilişkiler halk·la ee·leesh·kee·ler
   communications (job) · public relations
halüsinasyon ha·lew·see·nas·yon
   hallucination

hamak ha·*mak* hammock
hamam ha·*mam* Turkish bath
hamile ha·mee·*le* pregnant
hangi han·gee which
hap hap pill
hapishane ha·pees·*ha*·ne jail n
harabeler ha·ra·be·*ler* ruins
hariç ha·*reech* excluded
harika ha·ree·*ka* great (fantastic)
hasta has·*ta* ill • sick
hastalık has·ta·*luhk* disease
hastane has·ta·ne hospital
haşhaş hash·*hash* dope (drugs)
hata ha·*ta* someone's fault • mistake
hava ha·*va* air • weather
— **yolları** yol·la·*ruh* airline
— **yoluyla** yo·*looy*·la airmail
havaalanı ha·va·a·la·nuh airport
havlu hav·*loo* towel
havra hav·ra synagogue
hayat ha·*yat* life n
hayvan hai·*van* animal
hayvanat bahçesi
hai·va·*nat* bah·che·*see* zoo
hazımsızlık ha·zuhm·suhz·*luhk* indigestion
hazır ha·*zuhr* ready
hazırlamak ha·zuhr·la·*mak* prepare
Haziran ha·zee·ran June
hediye he·dee·*ye* gift • present
hediyelik eşya he·dee·ye·*leek* esh·ya
souvenir
— **dükkanı** dewk·ka·*nuh* souvenir shop
hemen hemen he·*men* he·*men* almost
hemşire hem·shee·re nurse
hentbol hent·bol handball
henüz (değil) he·*newz* (de·*eel*) (not) yet
hepsi hep·see all
her her every
— **bir** beer each
— **iki kolu ve bacağı felçli** ee·*kee* ko·loo
ve ba·ja·uh felch·lee quadriplegic a
— **ikisi** ee·kee·*see* both
— **zaman** za·*man* always
herhangi bir her·*han*·gee beer any
herkes her·kes everyone
herşey her·shay everything
hesap he·*sap* account (bank) • bill
— **bakiyesi** ba·kee·ye·*see* balance (bank)
— **makinesi** ma·kee·ne·*see* calculator
heykel hay·*kel* sculpture • statue
hırdavatçı dükkanı huhr·da·vat·*chuh*
dewk·ka·nuh hardware store
Hıristiyan huh·rees·tee·*yan* Christian n

hırsız huhr·*suhz* thief
hız huhz speed n
— **göstergesi** gers·ter·ge·*see*
speedometer
— **sınırı** suh·nuh·*ruh* speed limit
hızlı huhz·*luh* fast a
hiç birşey heech beer·*shay* nothing
hiçbiri heech·bee·ree neither • none
hijyenik kadın bağı heezh·ye·*neek*
ka·*duhn* ba·uh sanitary napkin
hikaye hee·ka·ye story
Hindistan heen·dees·*tan* India
hissetmek hees·set·*mek* feel (touch) v
hizmet ücreti heez·*met* ewj·re·*tee*
service charge
hoş hosh cool (exciting) • nice • pretty
— **geldiniz** gel·dee·neez welcome v
hukuk hoo·*kook* law (study, profession)

I

ılık uh·*luhk* warm a
ırkçılık uhrk·chuh·*luhk* racism
ısı uh·*suh* heat n
ısıtıcı uh·suh·tuh·*juh* heater
ısıtılmış uh·suh·tuhl·*muhsh* heated
ısıtma uh·suht·*ma* heating
ıslak uhs·*lak* wet a
ışık uh·*shuhk* light n
— **ölçer** erl·cher light meter

İ

ibadet etmek ee·ba·det et·*mek* worship v
iç çamaşırı eech cha·ma·shuh·*ruh*
underwear
içecek ee·che·*jek* drink n
içeride ee·che·ree·de inside
— **yapılan** ya·puh·lan indoor
içinde ee·cheen·de in • within
iç lastik eech las·*teek* inner tube
içmek eech·*mek* drink v
idrar yolları enfeksiyonu eed·*rar* yol·la·ruh
en·fek·see·yo·noo urinary infection
iğne ee·ne injection
— **yapmak** yap·*mak* inject
ihtiyacı olmak eeh·tee·ya·*juh* ol·*mak* need v
iki ee·*kee* two
— **hafta** haf·ta fortnight
— **kez** kez twice
— **kişilik oda** kee·shee·*leek* o·da
double room
— **kişilik yatak** kee·shee·*leek* ya·tak
double bed

243

ikinci ee-keen-jee second a
— el el second-hand a
— sınıf suh-nuhf second class n
ikiz ee-keez twins
ikram eek-ram complimentary (free)
ilaç ee-lach medication
ilan ee-lan advertisement
ile ee-le with
— çıkmak chuhk-mak go out with
— paylaşmak pai-lash-mak share with v
ileride ee-le-ree-de ahead
ilginç eel-geench interesting
ilişki ee-leesh-kee relationship (general)
ilk eelk first a
— yardım çantası yar-duhm chan-ta-suh
first-aid kit
ilkbahar eelk-ba-har spring (season)
iltihap eel-tee-hap inflammation
imkansız eem-kan-suhz impossible
imza eem-za signature
imzalamak eem-za-la-mak sign v
inatçı ee-nat-chuh stubborn
ince een-je thin a
incil een-jeel bible
indirim een-dee-reem discount n
indirimli satış een-dee-reem-lee sa-tuhsh
sale n
inek ee-nek cow
inmek een-mek get off
insan hakları een-san hak-la-ruh
human rights
inşa etmek een-sha et-mek build v
inşaatçı een-sha-at-chuh builder
ip eep rope • string
ipek ee-pek silk
iplik eep-leek thread
iptal etmek eep-tal et-mek cancel
İranlı ee-ran-luh Farsi (language)
iri ee-ree large
ishal ees-hal diarrhoea
isilik ee-see-leek rash
istemek ees-te-mek
ask for something • want v
İsveç ees-vech Sweden
İsviçre ees-veech-re Switzerland
iş eesh business • work n
— adamı a-da-muh businessman
— arkadaşı ar-ka-da-shuh colleague
— gezisi ge-zee-see business trip
— kadını ka-duh-nuh businesswoman
işaret ee-sha-ret sign n
işçi eesh-chee labourer

işitme cihazı ee-sheet-me jee-ha-zuh
hearing aid
işsiz eesh-seez unemployed
işveren eesh-ve-ren employer
itmek eet-mek push v
iyi ee-yee fine • good • well
izin ee-zeen permission
izlemek eez-le-mek watch v

jambon zham-bon ham
jandarma zhan-dar-ma gendarme
jilet jee-let razor blade
jinekolog zhee-ne-ko-log gynaecologist

kabakulak ka-ba-koo-lak mumps
kabarcık ka-bar-juhk blister
kabızlık ka-buhz-luhk constipation
kabul etmek ka-bool et-mek admit
kaburga ka-boor-ga rib
kadar ka-dar until
kadın ka-duhn woman
— bağı ba-uh panty liners
kadınlar bölümü ka-duhn-lar ber-lew-mew
women's quarters
kafa derisi ka-fa de-ree-see scalp n
kafatası ka-fa-ta-suh skull
kağıt ka-uht paper
— işlemleri eesh-lem-le-ree paperwork
— mendil men-deel tissues
— oynamak oy-na-mak play cards v
— para pa-ra banknote
kahvaltı kah-val-tuh breakfast
kahverengi kah-ve-ren-gee brown
kainat ka-ee-nat universe
kalabalık ka-la-ba-luhk crowded
kalacak yer ka-la-jak yer accommodation
kale ka-le castle • fortress
— içi ee-chee citadel
kaleci ka-le-jee goalkeeper
kalın ka-luhn thick
kalmak kal-mak stay (at a hotel) v
kalp kalp heart (body)
— krizi kree-zee
cardiac arrest • heart attack
— pili pee-lee pacemaker
— rahatsızlığı ra-hat-suhz-luh-uh
heart condition
kamp alanı kamp a-la-nuh camping ground

kamp malzemeleri dükkanı kamp mal·ze·me·le·ree dewk·ka·nuh *camping store*
kamp yapmak kamp yap·mak *camp* v
kamp yeri kamp ye·ree *camp site*
kamyon kam·yon *truck*
kan kan *blood*
— **gurubu** goo·roo·boo *blood group*
— **tahlili** tah·lee·lee *blood test*
kansızlık kan·suhz·luhk *anaemia*
kanun ka·noon *law*
kapalı ka·pa·luh *closed • shut*
kapatmak ka·pat·mak *close* v
kapı ka·puh *door • gate (airport)*
kaplıca kap·luh·ja *thermal spring*
— **hamamı** ha·ma·muh *thermal bath*
kar kar *profit* n • *snow* n
kara yoluyla gönderi ka·ra yo·looy·la gern·de·ree *surface mail (land)*
karaciğer ka·ra·jee·er *liver*
Karadeniz ka·ra·de·neez *Black Sea*
karanlık ka·ran·luhk *dark (night)*
karar vermek ka·rar ver·mek *decide*
kardeş kar·desh *brother/sister*
karı ka·ruh *wife*
karınca ka·ruhn·ja *ant*
karıştırmak ka·ruhsh·tuhr·mak *mix* v
karmak kar·mak *deal (cards)* v
karşısında kar·shuh·suhn·da *across • opposite*
kas kas *muscle*
kasa ka·sa *safe* n
kasaba haritası ka·sa·ba ha·ree·ta·suh *town map*
kasap ka·sap *butcher*
kase ka·se *bowl* n
Kasım ka·suhm *November*
kasiyer ka·see·yer *cashier*
kask kask *helmet*
kaşık ka·shuhk *spoon* n
kaşıntı ka·shuhn·tuh *itch* n
kat kat *floor (storey)*
kavanoz ka·va·noz *jar* n
kavga kav·ga *fight* n
kaya ka·ya *rock* n
kaya tırmanışı ka·ya tuhr·ma·nuh·shuh *rock climbing*
kayak ka·yak *skiing*
— **gözlüğü** gerz·lew·ew *skiing goggles*
— **yapmak** yap·mak *ski* v
kaybetmek kai·bet·mek *lose*
kaydetmek kai·det·mek *record* v
kayınpeder ka·yuhn·pe·der *father-in-law*

kayınvalide ka·yuhn·va·lee·de *mother-in-law*
kayıp ka·yuhp *lost*
— **eşya bürosu** esh·ya bew·ro·soo *lost-property office*
kayış ka·yuhsh *fanbelt*
kayıt ka·yuht *recording*
kay-kay kai·kai *skateboarding*
kaza ka·za *accident*
kazak ka·zak *jumper • sweater*
kazanmak ka·zan·mak *earn • win* v
kazıklama ka·zuhk·la·ma *rip-off* n
KDV (Katma Değer Vergisi) ka·de·ve (kat·ma de·er ver·gee·see) *KDV (Value Added Tax)*
keçi ke·chee *goat*
kedi ke·dee *cat*
kelebek ke·le·bek *butterfly*
kelime ke·lee·me *word* n
kemik ke·meek *bone*
kenar ke·nar *side* n
kertenkele ker·ten·ke·le *lizard*
kesme tahtası kes·me tah·ta·suh *chopping board*
kesmek kes·mek *cut* v
keşiş ke·sheesh *monk*
Kıbrıs kuhb·ruhs *Cyprus*
kırda uzun yürüyüş kuhr·da oo·zoon yew·rew·yewsh *hiking*
kırık kuh·ruhk *broken*
kırılabilir kuh·ruh·la·bee·leer *fragile*
kırmak kuhr·mak *break* v
kırmızı kuhr·muh·zuh *red*
kırtasiyeci kuhr·ta·see·ye·jee *stationer's*
kısa kuh·sa *short (height)*
kıskanç kuhs·kanch *jealous*
kış kuhsh *winter*
kız kuhz *daughter • girl*
— **arkadaş** ar·ka·dash *girlfriend*
— **kardeş** kar·desh *sister*
kızamık kuh·za·muhk *measles*
kızamıkçık kuh·za·muhk·chuhk *rubella*
kızartmak kuh·zart·mak *fry* v
kızartma tavası kuh·zart·ma ta·va·suh *frying pan*
kızgın kuhz·guhn *angry*
kibar kee·bar *kind (nice)*
kibrit keeb·reet *matches (for lighting)*
kilim kee·leem *rug*
kilise kee·lee·se *church*
kilit kee·leet *lock* n
kilitlemek kee·leet·le·mek *lock* v

kilitli kee-leet-*lee locked*
  — eşya dolabı esh-*ya* do-la-*buh luggage locker*
kim keem *who*
kimlik keem-*leek identification*
  — kartı kar-*tuh identification card (ID)*
kiralamak kee-ra-la-*mak hire* v • *rent* v
kirli keer-*lee dirty* a
kirlilik keer-lee-*leek pollution*
kişi kee-*shee person* • *people*
kitap kee-*tap book* n
kitapçı kee-tap-*chuh book shop*
klavye klav-*ye keyboard*
klima klee-*ma air conditioning*
klimalı klee-ma-*luh air-conditioned*
koca ko-*ja husband*
kocaman ko-ja-*man huge*
koku ko-*koo smell* n
kol kol *arm (body)*
kolay ko-*lai easy*
kolye kol-*ye necklace*
konak ko-*nak mansion*
konjonktivit iltihabı kon-jonk-tee-*veet* eel-tee-ha-*buh conjunctivitis*
konserve açacağı kon-ser-ve a-cha-ja-*uh can opener* • *tin opener*
konsolosluk kon-so-los-*look consulate*
kontrol etmek kon-*trol* et-*mek check* v
kontrol noktası kon-*trol* nok-ta-*suh checkpoint*
konuşmak ko-noosh-*mak speak* • *talk*
korkunç kor-*koonch awful* • *terrible*
koruma altına alınmış ko-roo-ma al-tuh-*na* a-luhn-*muhsh protected species*
korumak ko-roo-*mak protect*
koşmak kosh-*mak run* v
koşu ko-*shoo running*
kot pantolon kot pan-to-*lon jeans*
kova ko-*va bucket*
koymak koy-*mak put*
koyu ko-*yoo dark (colour)*
koyun ko-*yoon sheep*
köpek ker-*pek dog*
  — ısırması uh-suhr-ma-*suh dog bite* n
köprü kerp-*rew bridge (structure)*
kör ker *blind* a
köşe ker-*she corner* n
kötü ker-*tew bad*
köy kay *village*
kral kral *king*
kraliçe kra-lee-*che queen*
krem krem *cream (lotion)*

krema kre-*ma cream (food)*
kuaför koo-a-*fer hairdresser*
kubbe koob-*be dome*
kulak koo-*lak ear*
  — temizleme çubuğu te-meez-le-*me* choo-boo-*oo cotton buds*
  — tıkacı tuh-ka-*juh earplugs*
kule koo-*le tower* n
kulp koolp *handlebars*
kum koom *sand* n
kumaş koo-*mash fabric*
kurabiye koo-ra-bee-*ye cookie*
kural koo-*ral rule* n
kurşun kalem koor-*shoon* ka-*lem pencil*
kurşunsuz koor-shoon-*sooz unleaded*
kuru koo-*roo dried* • *dry* a
kurulamak koo-roo-la-*mak dry (general)* v
kurutmak koo-root-*mak dry (clothes)* v
kuş koosh *bird*
kutlama koot-la-*ma celebration*
kutu koo-*too box* n
kuyruk kooy-*rook tail* n
kuzey koo-*zay north*
Kuzey Kıbrıs Türk Cumhuriyeti (KKTC) koo-*zay* kuhb-*ruhs* tewrk joom-hoo-ree-ye-*tee* (ka-ka-te-je) *Turkish Republic of Northern Cyprus (TRNC)*
küçücük kew-chew-*jewk tiny*
küçük kew-*chewk little* • *small*
külotlu çorap kew-lot-*loo* cho-*rap pantyhose*
kül tablası kewl tab-la-*suh ashtray*
küpe kew-*pe earrings*
kürdan kewr-*dan toothpick*
kürek çekme kew-*rek* chek-*me rowing*
kütüphane kew-tewp-ha-ne *library*

L

lakap la-*kap nickname* n
lastik las-*teek tire* • *tyre*
lateks eldiven la-*teks* el-dee-*ven gloves (medical)*
Lefkoşa lef-ko-*sha Lefkosia (Nikosia)*
lezzetli lez-zet-*lee tasty*
libre leeb-*re pound (weight)*
liman lee-*man harbour* • *port*
lisan lee-*san language*
lise lee-*se high school*
lokum lo-*koom Turkish delight*
Lübnan lewb-*nan Lebanon*
lüks lewks *luxury* a

M

maaş ma-*ash* salary • wage
maden suyu ma-*den* soo-*yoo* mineral water
madeni para ma-de-*nee* pa-*ra* coins
mağara ma-a-*ra* cave n
mahalle ma-hal-*le* neighbourhood
mahcup mah-*joop* embarrassed
mahkeme mah-ke-*me* court (legal)
mahkum mah-*koom* prisoner
makas ma-*kas* scissors
makbuz mak-*booz* receipt
makul ma-*kool* sensible
makyaj mak-*yazh* make-up
mal olmak mal ol-*mak* cost v
malzeme mal-ze-*me* ingredient
mama sandalyesi ma-*ma* san-dal-ye-*see* highchair
manastır ma-nas-*tuhr* convent • monastery
manav ma-*nav* greengrocer
manzara man-za-*ra* view n
Mart mart March
masa ma-*sa* table n
masum ma-*soom* innocent
mavi ma-*vee* blue
Mayıs ma-*yuhs* May
mayo ma-*yo* bathing suit • swimsuit
medeni haklar me-de-*nee* hak-*lar* civil rights
medeni hal me-de-*nee* hal marital status
mektup mek-*toop* letter • mail
meme röntgeni me-*me* rernt-ge-*nee* mammogram
memur me-*moor* office worker
mendil men-*deel* handkerchief
merkez mer-*kez* centre n
mesane me-sa-*ne* bladder
meslek mes-*lek* job
meşgul mesh-*gool* busy • engaged (phone)
meşrubat mesh-roo-*bat* soft drink
mevsim mev-*seem* season
meydan may-*dan* town square
meyhane may-ha-*ne* winehall
meyve toplama may-ve top-la-*ma* fruit picking
mezar me-*zar* grave • tomb
mezarlık me-zar-*luhk* cemetery
mide mee-*de* stomach
— **ağrısı** a-ruh-*suh* stomachache
— **ve bağırsak enfeksiyonu** ve ba-uhr-*sak* en-fek-see-yo-*noo* gastroenteritis
milli park meel-lee-*lee* park national park
milliyet meel-lee-*yet* nationality

mimar mee-*mar* architect
mimarlık mee-mar-*luhk* architecture (profession)
mimari yapı mee-ma-ree ya-*puh* architecture (art)
misafirhane mee-sa-feer-ha-*ne* guesthouse
misafirperverlik mee-*sa*-feer-per-ver-*leek* hospitality
mobilya mo-*beel*-ya furniture
mor mor purple
muhtemel mooh-te-*mel* possible
mum moom candle
musluk moos-*look* faucet • tap
mutfak moot-*fak* kitchen
mutlu moot-*loo* happy
mücevherler mew-jev-her-*ler* jewellery
müdür mew-*dewr* manager (business)
mühendis mew-hen-*dees* engineer n
mühendislik mew-hen-dees-*leek* engineering
mükemmel mew-kem-*mel* excellent • perfect
mülakat mew-*la*-kat interview n
mülk sahibi mewlk sa-hee-*bee* landlady • landlord
mülteci mewl-te-*jee* refugee
müsil ilacı mew-*seel* ee-la-*juh* laxative
Müslüman din adamı mews-lew-*man* deen a-da-*muh* Muslim cleric
müşteri mewsh-te-*ree* client
müteşekkir mew-te-shek-*keer* grateful

N

nargile nar-gee-*le* water-pipe
nakit na-*keet* cash n
nasıl na-*suhl* how
ne ne what
neden ne-*den* why
nefes almak ne-*fes* al-*mak* breathe
nehir ne-*heer* river
nemlendirici nem-len-dee-ree-*jee* moisturiser
— **ruj** roozh lip balm
nerede ne-re-*de* where
nesli tükenmekte olan hayvanlar nes-*lee* tew-ken-mek-*te* o-*lan* hai-van-*lar* endangered species
ne zaman ne za-*man* when
Nisan nee-*san* April
nişan nee-*shan* engagement (to marry)
nişanlı nee-shan-*luh* engaged (to marry) • fiancé • fiancée

nitelikler nee·te·leek·*ler* qualifications
Noel no·*el* Christmas
　— **yortusu** yor·too·*soo* Christmas Day
　— **yortusu arifesi** yor·too·*soo*
　a·ree·fe·*see* Christmas Eve
nokta nok·*ta* point (decimal/dot) n
not defteri not def·te·*ree* notebook
nükleer atık newk·le·*er* a·*tuhk*
　nuclear waste
nükleer deneme newk·le·*er* de·ne·*me*
　nuclear testing

O

o o *he · she · it · that*
Ocak o·*jak* January
ocak o·*jak* stove
oda o·*da* room n
　— **numarası** noo·ma·ra·*suh*
　room number
odun o·*doon* wood
oğlan o·*lan* boy
oğul o·*ool* son
okul o·*kool* school
okuma o·koo·*ma* reading
okumak o·koo·*mak* read v
okutman o·koot·*man* lecturer
okyanus ok·ya·*noos* ocean
Olimpiyat Oyunları o·leem·pee·*yat*
　o·yoon·la·*ruh* Olympic Games
olmak ol·*mak* be
olumlu o·loom·*loo* positive a
olumsuz o·loom·*sooz* negative a
omuz o·*mooz* shoulder
onlar on·*lar* they
onların on·la·*ruhn* their
onu o·*noo* that (one)
onun o·*noon* her · his
opera binası o·pe·*ra* bee·na·*suh*
　opera house
orada o·ra·*da* there
oral seks kondomu o·*ral* seks
　kon·do·*moo* dental dam
orman or·*man* forest
otobüs o·to·*bews* bus · coach
　— **durağı** doo·ra·*uh* bus stop
　— **terminali** ter·mee·na·*lee* bus station
oto ön camı o·*to* ern ja·*muh* windscreen
otoyol o·to·*yol* highway
oturma odası o·toor·*ma* o·da·*suh*
　family room (home)
oturmak o·toor·*mak* live (somewhere) · sit

oyun o·*yoon* game (sport) · play (theatre)
　— **kağıdı** ka·uh·*duh* playing cards
oyuncak bebek o·yoon·*jak* be·*bek* doll
oyuncakçı o·yoon·jak·*chuh* toy shop
oyuncu o·yoon·*joo* actor · player
oy vermek oy ver·*mek* vote v
ozon tabakası o·*zon* ta·ba·ka·*suh*
　ozone layer

Ö

öbür gün er·*bewr* gewn day after tomorrow
ödeme er·de·*me* payment
ödemek er·de·*mek* pay v
ödemeli telefon er·de·me·*lee* te·le·*fon*
　collect call
ödünç almak er·*dewnch* al·*mak* borrow
öğle er·*le* noon
　— **yemeği** ye·me·*ee* lunch
öğleden sonra er·le·*den* son·*ra* afternoon
öğrenci er·ren·*jee* student n
öğrenmek er·ren·*mek* learn
öğretmen er·ret·*men* instructor · teacher
öksürmek erk·sewr·*mek* cough v
öksürük ilacı erk·sew·*rewk* ee·la·*juh*
　cough medicine
ölmek erl·*mek* die
ölü er·*lew* dead
önce ern·*je* ago · before
önceki ern·je·*kee* last (previous)
　— **gün** gewn day before yesterday
önemli er·nem·*lee* important
önünde er·newn·*de* in front of
öpmek erp·*mek* kiss v
öpücük er·pew·*jewk* kiss n
ördek er·*dek* duck
örnek er·*nek* example
örümcek er·rewm·*jek* spider
özel er·*zel* private · special
özgeçmiş erz·gech·*meesh* CV · résumé
özlemek erz·le·*mek* miss (feel absence of)
özürlü er·zewr·*lew* disabled

P

pahalı pa·ha·*luh* expensive
palto pal·*to* coat · overcoat
pamuk pa·*mook* cotton
　— **yumağı** yoo·ma·*uh* cotton balls
pamukçuk pa·mook·*chook* thrush (medical)
pantolon pan·to·*lon* pants · trousers
papaz pa·*paz* priest

para pa·*ra* money
— **bozdurmak** boz·door·*mak* exchange (money) v
— **cezası** je·za·*suh* fine n
— **iadesi** ee·a·de·*see* refund n
paralı yol pa·ra·*luh* yol motorway (tollway)
parça par·*cha* component • part • piece
park etmek park et·*mek* park (a car) v
parmak par·*mak* finger
parti par·*tee* party (night out/politics)
Paskalya pas·*kal*·ya Easter
paspas pas·*pas* mat
pastane pas·*ta*·ne cake shop
paten pa·*ten* rollerblading n
patenle kaymak pa·ten·le kai·*mak* skate v
patika pa·*tee*·ka footpath • path • track • trail
patlak pat·*lak* puncture n
paylaşmak pai·lash·*mak* share v
pazar pa·*zar* bazaar • market
— **yeri** ye·ree·*see* agora (market place)
Pazar pa·*zar* Sunday
Pazartesi pa·zar·te·*see* Monday
peçete pe·che·*te* napkin • serviette
pembe pem·*be* pink
— **dizi** dee·*zee* soap opera
pencere pen·je·*re* window
peron pe·*ron* platform (train)
Perşembe per·shem·*be* Thursday
peynirci pay·neer·*jee* cheese shop
pınar puh·*nar* spring (fountain)
pil peel battery (dry)
pire pee·*re* flea
pişik pee·*sheek* nappy rash
pişirmek pee·sheer·*mek* cook v
plaj plazh beach
— **voleybolu** vo·lay·bo·*loo* beach volleyball
plaka pla·*ka* car registration • license plate number • numberplate
polis karakolu po·lees ka·ra·ko·*loo* police station
polis memuru po·lees me·moo·*roo* police officer
politika po·lee·tee·*ka* policy • politics
politikacı po·lee·tee·ka·*juh* politician
pompa pom·*pa* pump n
popo po·*po* bottom (body)
posta pos·*ta* mail (postal system)
— **kutusu** koo·too·*soo* mailbox
— **ücreti** ewj·re·*tee* postage
postane pos·*ta*·ne post office

pratik konuşma kılavuzu pra·*teek* ko·noosh·*ma* kuh·la·voo·*zoo* phrasebook
prezervatif pre·zer·va·*teef* condom
puan poo·*an* point n • score n
— **tahtası** tah·ta·*suh* scoreboard
pul pool stamp (postage) n
puro poo·*ro* cigar
puset poo·*set* pram • stroller
pusula poo·soo·la compass

R

raf raf shelf
rahat ra·*hat* comfortable
rahatlatıcı ra·hat·la·tuh·*juh* inhaler
rahatsız ra·hat·*suhz* uncomfortable
rahibe ra·hee·*be* nun
rahim ağzı kanser tarama testi ra·*heem* a·zuh kan·*ser* ta·ra·*ma* tes·*tee* pap smear
rahim içi araç ra·*heem* ee·*chee* a·*rach* IUD
Ramazan ra·ma·*zan* Ramadan
reçete re·che·*te* prescription
reddetmek red·det·*mek* refuse v
refah re·*fah* welfare
rehber reh·*ber* guide (person) n
— **kitap** kee·*tap* guidebook
— **köpek** ker·*pek* guide dog
rehberli tur reh·ber·*lee* toor guided tour
rehidrasyon tuzu re·heed·ras·*yon* too·*zoo* rehydration salts
renk renk colour n
ressam res·*sam* painter (artist)
ressamlık res·sam·*luhk* painting (the art)
rıhtım ruh·*tuhm* quay
rota ro·*ta* route n
ruhsat rooh·*sat* permit n
ruj roozh lipstick
Rusça roos·*cha* Russian (language)
rüşvet rewsh·*vet* bribe n
rüya rew·*ya* dream n
rüzgar rewz·*gar* wind n
— **sörfü** ser·*few* windsurfing

S

saat sa·*at* clock • hour • watch n
sabah sa·*bah* morning
— **bulantıları** boo·lan·tuh·la·*ruh* morning sickness
sabun sa·*boon* soap
sabunluk sa·boon·*look* wash cloth (flannel)
saç sach hair
— **fırçası** fuhr·cha·*suh* hairbrush
— **kestirme** kes·teer·*me* haircut

sadaka sa·da·ka *dole*
sadece sa·de·je *only*
saf saf *pure*
sağ-kanat sa·ka·nat *right-wing*
sağır sa·uhr *deaf*
sağlık sa·luhk *health*
sahip sa·heep *owner*
 — olmak ol·mak *have*
sakız sa·kuhz *chewing gum*
sakin sa·keen *quiet* a
Salı sa·luh *Tuesday*
saman nezlesi sa·man nez·le·se *hay fever*
sanat sa·nat *art • crafts*
 — galerisi ga·le·ree·se *art gallery*
sanatçı sa·nat·chuh *artist*
sandalet san·da·let *sandal*
sandalye san·dal·ye *chair*
saniye sa·nee·ye *second (time)* n
sara sa·ra *epilepsy*
saray sa·rai *palace*
sarhoş sar·hosh *drunk* a
sarı sa·ruh *yellow*
sarılık sa·ruh·luhk *hepatitis*
sarılmak sa·ruhl·mak *hug* v
sarp sarp *steep*
satın almak sa·tuhn al·mak *buy* v
satış kulübesi sa·tuhsh koo·lew·be·se *kiosk*
satış vergisi sa·tuhsh ver·gee·se
 sales tax
satmak sat·mak *sell*
satranç sat·ranch *chess*
 — tahtası tah·ta·suh *chess board*
savaş sa·vash *war* n
sayfa sai·fa *page* n
sayı sa·yuh *number*
saymak sai·mak *count* v
sebep se·bep *reason* n
sebze seb·ze *vegetable* n
seçim se·cheem *election*
 — bürosu bew·ro·soo *electrical store*
seçmek sech·mek *choose*
sel sel *flood* n
semaver se·ma·ver *tea urn*
semt pazarı semt pa·za·ruh *street market*
sen sen *you* sg inf
senin se·neen *your*
sepet se·pet *basket*
serbest ser·best *free (not bound) • loose*
 — çalışan cha·luh·shan *self-employed*
sergi ser·gee *exhibition*
serin se·reen *cool (temperature)* a
sert sert *hard (not soft)*
ses ses *voice • volume*

sevgili sev·gee·lee *lover*
sevmek sev·mek *like* v
seyahat se·ya·hat *travel* v
 — acentesi a·jen·te·see *travel agency*
 — çeki che·kee *travellers cheque*
sıcak suh·jak *hot*
 — su soo *hot water*
sıçan suh·chan *rat*
sıkı suh·kuh *tight*
sıkıcı suh·kuh·juh *boring*
sık sık suhk suhk *often*
sınır suh·nuhr *border*
sıra suh·ra *queue* n
 — dağlar da·lar *mountain range*
sıradan suh·ra·dan *ordinary*
sırt suhrt *back (body)*
 — çantası chan·ta·suh *backpack*
sigara see·ga·ra *cigarette*
 — içilmeyen ee·cheel·me·yen
 nonsmoking
 — içmek eech·mek *smoke* v
sigorta see·gor·ta *insurance*
silah see·lah *gun*
sipariş see·pa·reesh *order (food/goods)* n
 — vermek ver·mek *order (food/goods)* v
sisli sees·lee *foggy*
sistit sees·teet *cystitis*
sivrisinek seev·ree·see·nek *mosquito*
siyah see·yah *black*
 — beyaz film be·yaz feelm *B&W film*
siz seez *you* sg pol & pl inf/pol
slayt slait *slide (film)*
soğan so·an *onion*
soğuk so·ook *cold* n & a
sohbet etmek soh·bet et·mek *chat up* v
sokak so·kak *street*
 — çalgıcısı chal·guh·juh·suh *busker*
sol sol *left (direction)*
sol-kanat sol·ka·nat *left-wing*
solucanlar so·loo·jan·lar *worms*
son son *end* n
 — kullanma tarihi kool·lan·ma
 ta·ree·hee *expiry date*
sonbahar son·ba·har *autumn • fall*
sonra son·ra *after • later*
sonsuza dek son·soo·za dek *forever*
sormak sor·mak *ask (a question)* v
soru so·roo *question* n
sos tenceresi sos ten·je·re·see *saucepan*
soy soy *descendent*
soyad soy·ad *family name • surname*
soymak soy·mak *rob*

soyunma kabini so·yoon·*ma* ka·bee·*nee* changing room
sömürü ser·mew·*rew* exploitation
sörf serf surfing
— **tahtası** tah·ta·*suh* surfboard
— **yapmak** yap·*mak* surf v
söylemek say·le·*mek* say v
söz vermek serz ver·*mek* promise v
sözlük serz·*lewk* dictionary
spiral sinek kovar spee·*ral* see·*nek* ko·*var* mosquito coil
spor malzemeleri mağazası spor mal·ze·me·le·*ree* ma·a·za·*suh* sports store
sporcu spor·*joo* sportsperson
sterlin ster·*leen* pound (money)
su soo water n
— **çiçeği** chee·che·*ee* chicken pox
— **geçirmez** ge·cheer·*mez* waterproof
— **kayağı** ka·ya·*uh* waterskiing
— **şişesi** shee·she·*see* water bottle
suçlu sooch·*loo* guilty
sunak soo·*nak* altar
Suriye soo·ree·*ye* Syria
susamış soo·sa·*muhsh* thirsty
suyu soo·*yoo* juice n
sürmek sewr·*mek* drive v
süt sewt milk
sütyen sewt·*yen* bra

Ş

şafak sha·*fak* dawn n
şahane sha·ha·*ne* wonderful
şaka sha·*ka* joke n
şampiyona sham·pee·yo·*na* championships
şampuan sham·poo·*an* shampoo
şans shans chance • luck
şanslı shans·*luh* lucky
şapka *shap*·ka hat
şarap sha·*rap* wine
— **dükkanı** dewk·ka·*nuh* wine shop
şarkı shar·*kuh* song
— **söylemek** say·le·*mek* sing
şarkıcı shar·kuh·*juh* singer
şarküteri shar·kew·te·*ree* delicatessen
şehir she·*heer* city
— **dışı** duh·*shuh* countryside
— **merkezi** mer·ke·*zee* city centre
— **otobüsü** o·to·bew·*sew* city bus
şehirlerarası otobüs she·heer·*ler*·a·ra·*suh* o·to·*bews* intercity bus

şeker she·*ker* candy • lollies • sugar • sweets
— **hastalığı** has·ta·luh·*uh* diabetes
şelale she·la·*le* waterfall
şemsiye shem·see·*ye* umbrella
şımarık shuh·ma·*ruhk* spoilt (person)
şiddet yanlısı sheed·*det* yan·luh·*suh* activist
şiir shee·*eer* poetry
şikayet shee·ka·*yet* complaint
— **etmek** et·*mek* complain
şilte sheel·*te* mattress
şimdi sheem·*dee* now
şimdiki zaman sheem·dee·*kee* za·*man* present (time)
şirket sheer·*ket* company (firm)
şişe shee·*she* bottle n
— **açacağı** a·cha·ja·*uh* bottle opener
şişlik sheesh·*leek* swelling
şişman sheesh·*man* fat a
şort short shorts
Şubat shoo·*bat* February
şunu shoo·*noo* that (one)

T

taahhütlü posta ta·ah·hewt·*lew* pos·*ta* registered mail/post
tablo tab·*lo* painting (a work)
taciz ta·*jeez* harassment
tahmin etmek tah·*meen* et·*mek* guess v
takım ta·*kuhm* team n
takip etmek ta·*keep* et·*mek* follow
taksi durağı tak·*see* doo·ra·*uh* taxi rank
takvim tak·*veem* calendar
tam mesai tam me·sa·*ee* full-time
tam olarak tam o·la·*rak* exactly
tamir etmek ta·*meer* et·*mek* repair v
tanışmak ta·nuhsh·*mak* meet (first time) v
tanrı tan·*ruh* god (general)
tansiyon tan·see·*yon* blood pressure
tapa ta·*pa* plug (bath) n
tapınak ta·puh·*nak* shrine • temple
taraftar ta·raf·*tar* fan • supporter
tarak ta·*rak* comb n
tarım ta·*ruhm* agriculture
tarife ta·ree·*fe* timetable
tarih ta·*reeh* date (day) • history
tarihi ta·ree·*hee* ancient • historical
tartışmak tar·tuhsh·*mak* argue
tartmak tart·*mak* weigh
tarz tarz style n
taş tash stone n
taşımak ta·shuh·*mak* carry

tatil ta·teel holiday(s) • vacation
tatlı tat·luh dessert n • sweet a
tava ta·va pan
tavla tav·la backgammon
tavsiye tav·see·ye advice
  — **etmek** et·mek recommend
tavşan tav·shan rabbit
taze ta·ze fresh
tebrikler teb·reek·ler congratulations
tecavüz te·ja·vewz rape n
  — **etmek** et·mek rape v
teçhizat tech·hee·zat equipment
tehlikeli teh·lee·ke·lee dangerous • unsafe
tekel bayii te·kel ba·yee·ee liquor store
tekerlek te·ker·lek wheel
  — **parmaklığı** par·mak·luh·uh spoke n
tekerlekli sandalye te·ker·lek·lee
  san·dal·ye wheelchair
tek kişilik oda tek kee·shee·leek o·da
  single room
tekmelemek tek·me·le·mek kick v
tekrar tek·rar again
tel tel wire n
teleferik te·le·fe·reek cable car
telefon te·le·fon telephone n
  — **etmek** et·mek telephone v
  — **konuşması** ko·noosh·ma·suh
  phone call n
  — **kulübesi** koo·lew·be·see phone box
  — **rehberi** reh·be·ree phone book
  — **santralı** san·tra·luh telephone centre
telesiyej te·le·see·yezh chairlift (skiing)
telgraf tel·graf telegram n
tembel tem·bel lazy
temiz te·meez clean a
temizlemek te·meez·le·mek clean v
temizlik te·meez·leek cleaning
Temmuz tem·mooz July
teneke kutu te·ne·ke koo·too can • tin
tepe te·pe hill
tercih etmek ter·jeeh et·mek prefer
tercüman ter·jew·man interpreter
termofor ter·mo·for hot water bottle
terzi ter·zee tailor
teslim etmek tes·leem et·mek deliver
teşebbüs etmek te·sheb·bews et·mek
  try (attempt) v
teşekkür etmek te·shek·kewr et·mek
  thank v
teyit etmek te·yeet et·mek
  confirm (a booking) v
teyze tay·ze aunt
ticaret tee·ja·ret trade n

tıkalı tuh·ka·luh blocked
tıp tuhp medicine (study, profession)
tıraş kremi tuh·rash kre·mee
  shaving cream
tıraş olmak tuh·rash ol·mak shave v
tırmanmak tuhr·man·mak climb v
tirbüşon teer·bew·shon corkscrew
top top ball (sport) n
toplantı yeri top·lan·tuh ye·ree venue
toplum refahı top·loom re·fa·huh
  social welfare
toprak bastı top·rak bas·tuh airport tax
toprak kap top·rak kap pot (ceramics)
toprak parçası top·rak par·cha·suh land n
torun to·roon grandchild
trafik adası tra·feek a·da·suh roundabout
trafik ışığı tra·feek uh·shuh·uh traffic light
transit yolcu salonu tran·seet yol·joo
  sa·lo·noo transit lounge
traş losyonu trash los·yo·noo aftershave
traş makinesi trash ma·kee·ne·see razor
turuncu too·roon·joo orange (colour)
tutkal toot·kal glue n
tutucu too·too·joo conservative n
tutuklamak too·took·la·mak arrest v
tutulmuş too·tool·moosh booked out
tuvalet too·va·let toilet
  — **kağıdı** ka·uh·duh toilet paper
tuz tooz salt
tüccar tewj·jar tradesperson
tükenmez kalem tew·ken·mez ka·lem
  ballpoint pen
tütün tew·tewn tobacco
tütüncü tew·tewn·jew tobacconist

U

ucuz oo·jooz cheap
uçak oo·chak airplane
uçmak ooch·mak fly v
uçurum oo·choo·room cliff
uçuş oo·choosh flight
ulaşım oo·la·shuhm transport n
ultrason ool·tra·son ultrasound
uluslararası oo·loos·lar·a·ra·suh
  international a
umumi telefon oo·moo·mee te·le·fon
  public telephone
umumi tuvalet oo·moo·mee too·va·let
  public toilet
unutmak oo·noot·mak forget
utangaç oo·tan·gach shy
uyandırmak oo·yan·duhr·mak wake up v

uyarmak oo·yar·mak warn
uygarlık tarihi ooy·gar·luhk ta·ree·hee
  humanities
uyku hapı ooy·koo ha·puh sleeping pills
uyku tulumu ooy·koo too·loo·moo
  sleeping bag
uykulu ooy·koo·loo sleepy
uyumak oo·yoo·mak sleep v
uyuşturucu oo·yoosh·too·roo·joo
  drug (illegal) n
  — alış-verişi a·luhsh·ve·ree·shee
  drug trafficking
  — bağımlılığı ba·uhm·luh·luh·uh
  drug addiction
  — bağımlısı ba·uhm·luh·suh drug user
  — etkisi altında et·kee·see al·tuhn·da
  stoned (drugged)
  — satıcısı sa·tuh·juh·suh drug dealer
uzak oo·zak far • remote
uzaktan kumanda oo·zak·tan
  koo·man·da remote control
uzanmak oo·zan·mak lie (not stand) v
uzatma oo·zat·ma extension (visa)
uzay oo·zai space (universe)
uzman ooz·man specialist (medical) n
uzun oo·zoon long a
  — boylu boy·loo tall (person)
  — yürüyüşe çıkmak yew·rew·yew·she
  chuhk·mak hike v

Ü

ücretsiz ewj·ret·seez free (gratis)
üçüncü ew·chewn·jew third a
ülke ewl·ke country
  — haritası ha·ree·ta·suh country map
ünlü ewn·lew famous
üretmek ew·ret·mek produce v
ürün ew·rewn crop (food) n
üşütmek ew·shewt·mek have a cold
ütü ew·tew iron (clothes) n
üye ew·ye member
üzgün ewz·gewn sad

V

vadi va·dee valley
vaftiz vaf·teez baptism
vapur va·poor boat
varmak var·mak arrive
vatandaşlık va·tan·dash·luhk citizenship
ve ve and
vergi ver·gee tax n
vermek ver·mek give

vestiyer ves·tee·yer cloakroom
veya ve·ya or
video kayıt cihazı vee·de·o ka·yuht
  jee·ha·zuh video recorder
vites kutusu vee·tes koo·too·soo gearbox
vücut vew·joot body

Y

yabancı ya·ban·juh foreign a • stranger n
yağ ya oil n
yağlayıcı madde ya·la·yuh·juh mad·de
  lubricant
yağmur ya·moor rain n
yağmurluk ya·moor·look raincoat
Yahudi ya·hoo·dee Jewish
yakacak odun ya·ka·jak o·doon firewood
yakın ya·kuhn close adv • nearby adj
  — zamanda za·man·da recently
yakında ya·kuhn·da near • soon
yakışıklı ya·kuh·shuhk·luh handsome
yalan söylemek ya·lan say·le·mek
  lie (not tell the truth) v
yalancı ya·lan·juh liar
yalnız yal·nuhz alone
yangın yan·guhn fire (out of control)
yanık ya·nuhk burnt
yanında ya·nuhn·da beside • next to
yanlış yan·luhsh wrong
yanma yan·ma burn n
yapmak yap·mak do • make
yaprak yap·rak leaf n
yara ya·ra injury
  — bandı ban·duh Band-Aid
yaralı ya·ra·luh injured
yararlı ya·rar·luh useful
yardım yar·duhm help n
  — etmek et·mek help v
yargıç yar·guhch judge n
yarım ya·ruhm half
  — gün gewn part-time a
yarın ya·ruhn tomorrow
  — akşam ak·sham tomorrow evening
  — öğleden sonra er·le·den son·ra
  tomorrow afternoon
  — sabah sa·bah tomorrow morning
yarış ya·ruhsh race (sport) n
  — bisikleti bee·seek·le·tee racing bike
  — pisti pees·tee racetrack • track (sport)
yasal ya·sal legal
yasama ya·sa·ma legislation
yastık yas·tuhk pillow
  — kılıfı kuh·luh·fuh pillowcase

yaşlı yash·*luh* old (person)
yaş yash age n
yatak ya·*tak* bed • sleeping berth
— **odası** o·da·*suh* bedroom
— **takımı** ta·kuh·*muh* bedding
yavaş ya·*vash* slow a
— **koşu** ko·*shoo* jogging
yavaşça ya·vash·*cha* slowly
yay yai spring (coil) n
yaya ya·*ya* pedestrian
— **geçidi** ge·chee·*dee* pedestrian crossing
yaz yaz summer
yazar ya·*zar* writer
— **kasa** ka·*sa* cash register
yazı yazmak ya·zuh yaz·*mak* write
yemek ye·*mek* dish • meal
— **listesi** lees·te·*see* menu
— **pişirme** pee·sheer·*me* cooking
— **yemek** ye·*mek* eat
yeni ye·*nee* new
Yeni Yıl ye·*nee* yuhl New Year's Day
— **arifesi** a·ree·fe·*see* New Year's Eve
yeniden gözden geçirme ye·nee·*den* gerz·*den* ge·cheer·*me* review n
yeniden kazanılabilir ye·nee·*den* ka·za·nuh·*la*·bee·leer recyclable
yeniden kazanmak ye·nee·*den* ka·zan·*mak* recycle
yer yer floor • place • seat • space • vacancy
yerel ye·*rel* local a
yönetmen yer·net·*men* director
yeryüzü yer·yew·*zew* Earth
yeşil ye·*sheel* green
yeterli ye·ter·*lee* enough
yetişkin ye·teesh·*keen* adult n
yıkamak yuh·ka·*mak* wash something v
yıkanmak yuh·kan·*mak* wash oneself v
yıl yuhl year
yılan yuh·*lan* snake
yıldız yuhl·*duhz* star
— **falı** fa·*luh* horoscope
(dört) yıldızlı (dert) yuhl·duhz·*luh* (four-) star
yiyecek yee·ye·*jek* food
yoksulluk yok·sool·*look* poverty
yokuş aşağı yo·*koosh* a·sha·*uh* downhill
yokuş yukarı yo·*koosh* yo·ka·*ruh* uphill
yol yol road • way
— **haritası** ha·ree·ta·*suh* road map
— **parası** pa·ra·*suh* fare
— **yorgunluğu** yor·goon·*loo*·oo jet lag
yolcu yol·*joo* passenger

yolculuk yol·joo·*look* journey n
yolculukta izlenecek yol yol·joo·look·*ta* eez·le·ne·*jek* yol itinerary
yorgun yor·*goon* tired
yön yern direction
yönetim yer·ne·*teem* administration
yukarı yoo·ka·*ruh* up
yukarısında yoo·ka·ruh·suhn·*da* above
yumru yoom·*roo* lump
yumurta yoo·moor·*ta* egg
yumurtalık yoo·moor·ta·*luhk* ovary
— **tümörü** tew·mer·*rew* ovarian cyst
Yunanistan yoo·na·nees·*tan* Greece
yurt dışı yoort duh·*shuh* abroad • overseas
yuvarlak yoo·var·*lak* round a
yüksek yewk·*sek* high a
— **ses** ses loud
yükseklik yewk·sek·*leek* altitude
yün yewn wool n
yürümek yew·rew·*mek* walk v
yürüyen merdiven yew·rew·*yen* mer·dee·*ven* escalator
yürüyüş ayakkabısı yew·rew·*yewsh* a·yak·ka·buh·*suh* hiking boots
yürüyüş güzergahı yew·rew·*yewsh* gew·zer·ga·*huh* hiking route
yüz yewz face • hundred
— **havlusu** hav·loo·*soo* face cloth
yüzde yewz·*de* per cent
yüzme yewz·*me* swimming (sport)
— **havuzu** ha·voo·*zoo* swimming pool
yüzmek yewz·*mek* swim v
yüzük yew·*zewk* ring (on finger)

Z

zaman za·*man* time n
— **farkı** far·*kuh* time difference
zamanında za·ma·nuhn·*da* on time
zar zar dice n
zararlı atık za·rar·*luh* a·*tuhk* toxic waste
zarf zarf envelope n
zaten za·*ten* already
zayıf za·*yuhf* weak
zehirli ze·heer·*lee* poisonous
zengin zen·*geen* rich • wealthy
zincir zeen·*jeer* chain n
zirve zeer·*ve* peak (mountain)
ziyaret etmek zee·ya·*ret* et·*mek* visit v
zona zo·*na* shingles (illness)
zor zor difficult • hard
zührevi hastalık zewh·re·*vee* has·ta·*luhk* venereal disease

KEY PATTERNS

When's (the next bus)?	(Sonraki otobüs) ne zaman?	(son·ra·*kee* o·to·*bews*) ne za·*man*
Where's (the market)?	(Pazar yeri) nerede?	(pa·*zar* ye·*ree*) ne·re·de
Where do I (buy a ticket)?	Nereden (bilet alabilirim)?	ne·re·den (bee·*let* a·*la*·bee·lee·reem)
How much is it (per night)?	(Geceliği) ne kadar?	(ge·je·lee·*ee*) ne ka·*dar*
I have (a reservation).	(Rezervasyonum) var.	(re·zer·vas·yo·*noom*) var
Do you have (a map)?	(Haritanız) var mı?	(ha·ree·ta·*nuhz*) var muh
Is there (a toilet)?	(Tuvalet) var mı?	(too·va·*let*) var muh
I'd like (the menu).	(Menüyü) istiyorum.	(me·new·*yew*) ees·*tee*·yo·room
I want (to make a call).	(Bir görüşme yapmak) istiyorum.	(beer ger·rewsh·*me* yap·*mak*) ees·*tee*·yo·room
Could you please (write it down)?	Lütfen (yazar) mısınız?	*lewt*·fen (ya·*zar*) muh·suh·*nuhz*
Do I have to (declare this)?	(Bunu beyan etmem) gerekli mi?	(boo·*noo* be·*yan* et·*mem*) ge·rek·*lee* mee
I need (assistance).	(Yardıma) ihtiyacım var.	(yar·duh·*ma*) eeh·tee·ya·*juhm* var